Controversial Issues in Social Work Practice

Edited by

Bruce A. Thyer
University of Georgia

Series Editors

Eileen Gambrill

Robert Pruger

University of California, Berkeley

ALLYN AND BACON
Boston • London • Toronto • Sydney • Tokyo • Singapore

Series Editor, Social Work: Judy Fifer
Editor-in-chief, Social Sciences: Karen Hanson
Editorial Assistant: Mary Visco
Marketing Manager: Quinn Perkson
Sr. Editorial Production Administrator: Susan McIntyre
Editorial Production Service: Ruttle, Shaw & Wetherill, Inc.
Composition Buyer: Linda Cox
Manufacturing Buyer: Suzanne Lareau
Cover Administrator: Suzanne Harbison

Copyright © 1997 by Allyn & Bacon
A Viacom Company
160 Gould Street
Needham Heights, MA 02194
Internet: www.abacon.com
America Online: Keyword: College Online

Library of Congress Cataloging-in-Publication Data
Controversial issues in social work practice / edited by Bruce A.
   Thyer.
       p.   cm.
   Includes bibliographical references.
   ISBN 0-205-18705-6
   1. Social service—Miscellanea.   2. Social service—Methodology.
3. Social workers—Professional ethics.   I. Thyer, Bruce A.
HV40.C665   1997
361.3'2—dc20   96-18534
                                                             CIP

Printed in the United States of America
10   9   8   7   6   5   4   3   2   1   01   00   99   98   97   96

Contents

I   Controversial Interventions

II Controversial Professional Issues

Preface

Where there is much desire to learn, there of necessity will be much arguing, much writing, many opinions; for opinion in good men is but knowledge in the making.

—John Milton

One of the most difficult aspects of preparing *Controversial Issues in Social Work Practice* was in selecting from among the infinity of topics that could be included. Those appearing in this volume are best seen as representative of the many important issues facing the field, and the omission of others should not be taken as reflective of minimizing their significance. The selection of the included topics was a function not only of the salience of the issues themselves, but also of the availability of qualified social workers. Apart from my personally recruiting potential authors because of their recognized expertise in selected areas of controversial social work practice, I also issued a call for chapter proposals over several social work Internet bulletin boards. This was quite fruitful in generating topics and authors, and clearly there remain many unaddressed topics.

One theme that runs through a number of the debates is that of "data versus practice wisdom." In chapter after chapter, one author cites empirical data or notes the virtual absence of scientifically credible data in relation to a particular social work intervention or assessment method, to justify his or her position. The opposing author often relies on clinical experience or practice wisdom to justify the opposing point of view. Thus these debates reflect larger tensions at work within the field. As certain forms of psychosocial interventions develop a sound empirical basis, the heretofore virtually unbridled latitude enjoyed by practitioners becomes circumscribed. Is it sound practice to provide clients with Rogerian (e.g., client-centered) counseling to treat obsessive–compulsive disorder? What if (as is the case) client-centered counseling has no credible evidence of efficacy in treating clients with OCD? What if (as is the case) the psychosocial treatments of exposure therapy and response prevention *do* have a strong foundation of empirical support? Should social workers provide Rogerian counseling for clients meeting DSM-IV criteria for OCD, before trying the behavioral approaches and seeing if they are efficacious? If the clients do not get better with Rogerian counseling, should they sue the social worker for malpractice?

The NASW's National Committee on Lesbian and Gay Issues (NCOLGI), back in 1992, issued a position paper that condemns as *unethical* treatments that attempt to alter a homosexual orientation to a heterosexual one. Here is what was actually said:

> Proponents of reparative therapies claim—without documentation—many successes. They assert that their processes are supported by conclusive scientific data which are in fact *little more than anecdotal.* NCOLGI protests these efforts to 'convert' people through irresponsible therapies...empirical research does not demonstrate that...sexual orientation (heterosexual or homosexual) can be changed through these so-called reparative therapies (NCOGLI, 1991, p. 1, italics added).

This has the potential to be a remarkable precedent for *all* of social work practice. How many of our practices/therapies are supported by little more than anecdotal data? How many lack empirical evidence of success? If reparative therapies are unethical in part because of their lack of credible empirical support, what does this say for the balance of social work treatments? How long will it be before the NASW's *Code of Ethics* contains a statement along the lines of:

> Clients should be offered as a first choice treatment, psychosocial interventions with some significant degree of empirical support, where such knowledge exists, and only provided with other treatments after such first choice treatments have been given a legitimate trial and shown not to be helpful with a given client.

Personally, I (Thyer, 1995, in press) think that this principle would be a good idea, and similar developments are occurring within psychology and psychiatry (e.g., Goldner & Bilsker, 1995). As these debates make clear, there does seem to be a movement toward what could be called "evidence-based social work practice." This is being driven internally, from professional organizations and through a gradual evolution of progressive ethical thinking, and externally through contingencies being established by managed care corporations and other funding sources (e.g., state and local governments).

I would like to make one thing perfectly clear to readers: In no case should it be automatically assumed that the argued case represents the author's *personal views.* The authors were asked to do their very best, as scholars and as practitioners, in arguing their respective positions. This is necessary to ensure a thorough airing of controversial points of view. But in no instance should extreme views be attributed to the chapter authors themselves. Each was committed to researching his or her topic and to organizing the arguments using data, logic, and practice expertise. In this task they succeeded admirably. To the extent that this volume is a success, credit belongs to the talented authors, social workers and scholars all, who contributed to the fine debates contained herein. Perhaps this volume will have accomplished what Oscar Wilde noted in *The Importance of Being Earnest:* "Arguments are to be avoided; they are always vulgar and often convincing." Finally, I would like to dedicate this volume to my sons, John and William, and to their mother, Laura, whose patience and support have made it possible to undertake this work.

Bruce A. Thyer
Athens, Georgia

REFERENCES

Goldner, E. M., & Bilsker, D. (1995). Evidence-based psychiatry. *Canadian Journal of Psychiatry, 40,* 97–101.

National Committee on Lesbian and Gay Issues. (1992). *Position statement on "Reparative" or "conversion" therapies for lesbians and gay men.* Washington, DC: National Association of Social Workers.

Thyer, B. A. (1995). Promoting an empiricist agenda within the human services: An ethical and humanistic imperative. *Journal of Behavior Therapy and Experimental Psychiatry, 26,* 93–98.

Thyer, B. A. (in press). Guidelines for applying the empirical clinical practice model to social work. *Journal of Applied Behavioral Sciences.*

Foreword

This book addresses eighteen of the current controversies in the field of social work. When I began to study social work in 1955, there were fewer fields employing social workers, and there were certainly fewer controversial issues in the profession. In that era, for instance, social workers were neatly divided between the two schools of thought labeled "diagnostic" and "functional," with the Freudian diagnostics outnumbering the Rankian functionalists. Graduate students in functional schools frequently were required to write an autobiographical essay comparing their entry into graduate school with the trauma of their birth.

Historically, social work was centered on work with the client in the social environment, but by the time I entered the field, the profession had changed to an emphasis on the individual. Because the profession has not yet reclaimed its heritage of focusing on the person in the environment, social workers of the time were aptly termed "junior analysts" or "psychoanalysts for the poor." Social work actively competed within the intrapsychic emphasis of psychiatry and psychology.

Fortunately, the late 1950s saw the reinstatement of the "social back into social work." This was excellent timing because national mental health legislation in the early 1960s funded massive public mental health programs that were needed to address the communities and families of the clients. Employment opportunities for social workers were greatly expanded, and the numbers of graduate programs increased to keep pace with the demand. Social work was positioned to become the predominant profession in public mental health in our society during the past twenty-five years.

With the growth of the profession has come more divergent views and controversial issues; hence the need for this book. Some of the topics are products of the last decade of the twentieth century, for example, eye movement desensitization and reprocessing, and others have been argued about by social workers for twenty-five years, such as the advantages and disadvantages of professional social work licensing and the arguable thesis that a therapist can perform more effectively if he or she has been the recipient of psychotherapy.

Some mental health professionals do maintain that being the recipient of personal treatment does strengthen the therapists' (workers') ability to provide treatment. This is in marked contrast to a prevailing controversy in the 1950s, when members of the National Council on Family Relations vigorously differed with members of the American Association of Marriage Counselors, maintaining that having been divorced negated a worker's effectiveness in offering marital counseling.

Early in my social work graduate student orientation, I was taught that social work had no single unique attribute, but that the constellation of knowledge, values, and skills did make our profession unique. It is my conviction that the profession is strengthened by the increased diversity and range demonstrated in treatments during the last thirty years. Certainly, this book, with its breadth of topics, enables the readers to become more familiar about specific knowledge, values, and skills extant in the social work profession during the last four years of the twentieth century.

Charles A. Stewart, Ph.D.
Former Dean (1964–1995)
The University of Georgia School of Social Work

Should Social Workers Support the Use of "Hypnosis"?

William R. Nugent, Ph.D., is an Associate Professor in the College of Social Work at the University of Tennessee, Knoxville. He has conducted several clinical studies of the effects of hypnotic interventions. He has also conducted research on measurement and assessment problems and on interventions for adult and adolescent problems with anger.

Barry Cournoyer, D.S.W., is Associate Dean for Quality Improvement at Indiana University School of Social Work. Currently engaged in several projects intended to assess and enhance quality in all three of the School's educational programs (B.S.W., M.S.W., and Ph.D.), he is the author of the recently published second edition of *The Social Work Skills Workbook* (Brooks/Cole).

YES

WILLIAM R. NUGENT

"Should social workers support the use of 'hypnosis' as therapy for mental disorders?" This question is like the old issue, "Does 'psychotherapy' work?" I want to recast this question into, "For what problems should social workers support the use of hypnosis as an intervention?" This question, in my opinion, leads to more useful answers.

There is evidence that hypnotic interventions can have a positive impact for several types of problems (see Wodden & Anderton, 1982, Bowers & LeBaron, 1986, for reviews). Considerable evidence suggests that hypnosis can be effective for the control of pain associated with numerous medical conditions (Hilgard & Hilgard, 1975). For example, hypnosis has been found to be an effective pain control intervention with burn patients (Schafer, 1975; Wakeman & Kaplan, 1978). Laboratory studies have confirmed clinical findings, with one study indicating that the effects of hypnotic suggestions on persons of high hypnotic ability exceeded the analgesic effects of morphine (Bowers & LeBaron, 1986). The exact mechanisms of pain reduction through hypnosis are unclear, but evidence suggests that it does not depend on either endorphins (Speigal & Albert, 1983) or the inhibition of cholinergic mechanisms (Sternbach, 1982).

There is also evidence that hypnosis can be an effective treatment for asthma, psychosomatic disorders (DePiano & Salzberg, 1979), and anxiety disorders (Bowers & LeBaron, 1986). I have conducted clinical research on the effects of hypnosis in the treatment of anxiety disorders. For example, I used an Ericksonian hypnotic intervention with two clients suffering from agoraphobia with panic attacks. A multiple-baseline design across clients was used to evaluate the effects of the intervention, and the dependent variable was scores on the Clinical Anxiety Scale (CAS; Corcoran & Fischer, 1987). The results of this evaluation are shown in Figure 1.1. Both clients appeared to have experienced a reduction in the severity of their anxiety concomitant with the implementation of the intervention. The woman's CAS scores dropped below clinically significant levels, a change corroborated by scores on other measures (Nugent, 1993).

I also conducted an experimental investigation of the effects of an Ericksonian hypnotic intervention on problematic interactions that a client was having with her daughter and husband. One outcome measure in this study was an individualized rating scale (IRS; Bloom, Fischer, & Orme, 1995) that measured the woman's emotional and behavioral reaction to what the woman called "provocative verbal and/or nonverbal behavior." Scores on this scale ranged from −10 to +10. A −10 indicated the most reactive type of response, characterized by totally uncontrolled cursing, yelling, and feelings of rage. A +10 indicated the most positive response possible, characterized by a total lack of angry feelings, yelling, or cursing, and by the client both listening to the person behaving provocatively and expressing her feelings and desires in a nonattacking manner. A 0 indicated a point halfway between these two extremes. The arithmetic average for a given week with each family member was used as an overall index of the interactional problem she was having with that family member for that week. The results of this multiple baseline investigation are shown in Figure 1.2 on page 4. As can be seen in this graph, there is evidence suggestive of an effect associated with the intervention. A follow-up eight weeks after the termination of my work with this woman showed a continuation of the gains apparently made from use of this intervention. Results from measures on Hudson's Index of Parental Attitudes and Index of Marital Satisfaction (Corcoran & Fischer, 1987) were consistent with these IRS results (see Nugent, 1990, p. 59).

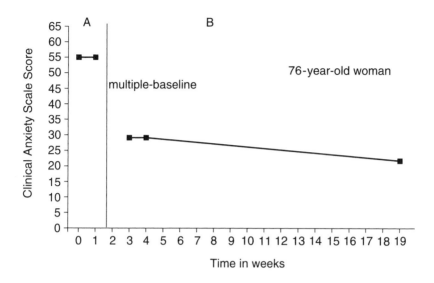

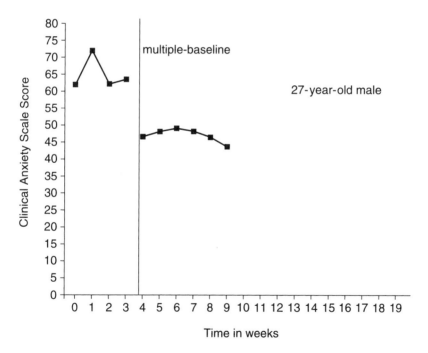

Figure 1.1　*Multiple baseline data on the Clinical Anxiety Scale for seventy-six-year-old female and twenty-seven-year-old male agoraphobia clients.*

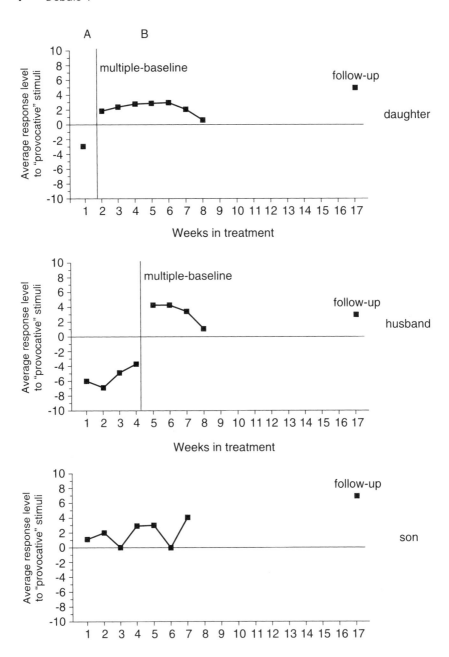

FIGURE 1.2 *Multiple baseline data for interactional problems. Reprinted from Nugent (1990) by permission.*

Research has also suggested that hypnotizability may play an important role in who benefits most from hypnosis (Wodden & Anderton, 1982; Bowers & LeBaron, 1986), though this issue is somewhat controversial. Some argue that all persons are hypnotizable and that hypnotizability as measured by standardized scales is not an important predictor of success (Erickson & Rossi, 1979). There is also evidence that children may be more amenable to hypnotic interventions than adults (Bowers & LeBaron, 1986). Research has also suggested, however, that hypnosis should *not* be used as a memory aid (Smith, 1983) or as an intervention for such problems as smoking, weight loss, or addictions because it is ineffective (Wodden & Anderton, 1982).

Although evidence suggests that hypnosis can be an effective intervention with certain problems, the exact nature of hypnosis is still controversial (Wodden & Anderton, 1982). Some theorists speculate that hypnotic procedures initiate mental processes of an involuntary, unconscious nature that can be focused on problem alleviation (Erickson & Rossi, 1979). Research evidence suggests that humans do, in fact, receive and process information by unconscious processes (Foa & Kozak, 1991; MacLeod, Mathews, & Tata, 1986). Clinical evidence exists to support the claim that hypnotic interventions access and initiate unconscious processes (Erickson & Rossi, 1979). There is also research evidence that indirectly supports this claim (e.g., Zimbardo, Marshall, White, & Maslach, 1973).

In conclusion, there is good evidence that hypnosis can be an effective intervention for certain clients with certain problems, as outlined above. Although the exact mechanisms of the empirical successes associated with use of hypnosis are not yet clearly understood, social workers in settings working with clients having problems like those discussed above might reasonably consider hypnosis as a treatment option, comparing the likely changes from use of hypnosis with those anticipated from alternative treatments with an empirical basis of effectiveness. Social workers also might reasonably consider the addition of hypnosis to other intervention procedures (Nugent, 1993).

References

Bloom, M., Fischer, J., & Orme, J. (1995). *Evaluating practice: Guidelines for the accountable professional* (2nd ed.). Englewood Cliffs, NJ: Prentice-Hall.

Bowers, K., & LeBaron, S. (1986). Hypnosis and hypnotizability: Implications for clinical intervention. *Hospital & Community Psychiatry, 37,* 457–467.

Corcoran, K., & Fischer, J. (1987). *Measures for clinical practice.* New York: The Free Press.

DePiano, F., & Salzberg, H. (1979). Clinical applications of hypnosis to three psychosomatic conditions. *Psychological Bulletin, 86,* 1223–1235.

Erickson, M., & Rossi, E. (1979). *Hypnotherapy: An exploratory casebook.* New York: Irvington Publishers.

Foa, E., & Kozak, M. (1991). Emotional processing: Theory, research, and clinical implications for anxiety disorders. In J. Safran and L. Greenberg (Eds.), *Emotion, psychotherapy, and change* (pp. 21–49). New York: Guilford.

Hilgard, E., & Hilgard, J. (1975). *Hypnosis in the relief of pain.* Los Altos, CA: Kaufmann.

MacLeod, C., Mathews, A., & Tata, P. (1986). Attentional bias in emotional disorders. *Journal of Abnormal Psychology, 95,* 15–20.

Nugent, W. (1990). An experimental and qualitative evaluation of an Ericksonian hypnotic intervention for family relationship problems. *Ericksonian Monographs, 7,* 51–68.

Nugent, W. (1993). A series of single case design clinical evaluations of an Ericksonian hypnotic intervention used with clinical anxiety. *Journal of Social Service Research, 17,* 41–69.

Schafer, D. (1975). Hypnosis use on a burn unit. *International Journal of Clinical and Experimental Hypnosis, 23,* 1–14.

Smith, M. (1983). Hypnotic memory enhancement of witnesses: Does it work? *Psychological Bulletin, 94,* 387–407.

Speigal, D., & Albert, L. (1983). Naloxone fails to reverse hypnotic alleviation of chronic pain. *Psychopharmacology, 81,* 140–143.

Sternbach, R. (1982). On strategies for identifying neurochemical correlates of hypnotic analgesia. *International Journal of Clinical and Experimental Hypnosis, 30,* 251–256.

Wakeman, R., & Kaplan, J. (1978). An experimental study of hypnosis in painful burns. *American Journal of Clinical Hypnosis, 21,* 3–11.

Wodden, T., & Anderton, C. (1982). The clinical use of hypnosis. *Psychological Bulletin, 91,* 215–243.

Zimbardo, P., Marshall, G., White, G., & Maslach, C. (1973). Objective assessment of hypnotically induced time distortion. *Science, 181,* 282–284.

Rejoinder to Dr. Nugent
BARRY COURNOYER

Dr. Nugent, whose scholarly work I have long admired, presents substantial evidence that hypnosis can be effective for pain management, asthma, psychosomatic conditions, and anxiety disorders. He cites favorable single-subject findings from his own Ericksonian-based hypnotic interventions with two clients who met diagnostic criteria for agoraphobia with panic attacks and a third client who experienced strain in relationships with her spouse and daughter. Studies of this kind are essential for establishing a track record of research in the application of hypnosis to social work practice. Unfortunately, there are far too few such studies in the social work literature.

In arguing the affirmative position, Dr. Nugent does not directly address the elusive questions concerning the definition and identification of hypnosis. Can he be certain, even in his own practice, that his three clients were in fact "hypnotized" and that the "hypnotic" condition was the primary factor accounting for the positive changes? Might the therapeutic "suggestions" and Ericksonian interventions been just as effective had they been provided outside the presumed hypnotic state?

Dr. Nugent acknowledges that the nature of hypnosis remains unclear and controversial. He implies that hypnotizability, which appears to vary widely among the adult population, could be a major factor determining which individuals find hypnosis beneficial. In fact, in citing one laboratory study of the efficacy of hypnotic suggestion in managing pain, he reports that "persons of high hypnotic ability exceeded the analgesic effects of morphine." Presumably, then, persons of lesser hypnotic ability would experience fewer beneficial effects.

Dr. Nugent would probably agree that hypnosis is extremely difficult to define and nearly impossible to identify reliably. Nonetheless, Dr. Nugent's overall response to the question "Should social workers support the use of hypnosis?" seems to be one of general advocacy. To his credit, he recommends against the use of hypnosis for problems such as smoking, weight loss, and addictions because of insufficient empirical support. Also, he wisely cautions against the use of hypnosis for memory enhancement with witnesses. Furthermore, he urges social workers interested in hypnosis to consider alternative interventions that have empirical support of effectiveness. However, in advocating for the use of hypnosis, Dr. Nugent's fails to discuss other important considerations. For example, he does not describe the credentials, qualifications, or training needed before social workers could ethically "consider hypnosis as a treatment option." Would he conclude that bachelor's-level social workers educated as generalist practitioners or M.S.W.s who concentrated in social policy are adequately prepared to use hypnosis? Perhaps Dr. Nugent believes that only well-experienced masters- or doctoral-level clinical social workers would be interested in hypnosis. Perhaps he presumes that social workers would, of course, secure high-quality education and training in clinical hypnosis before considering its use with clients. Perhaps he anticipates that social workers would, of course, secure competent supervision as they begin to apply hypnosis in their social work practice. Perhaps Dr. Nugent believes that social workers who learn to induce a hypnotic trance would, of course, carefully consider its appropriateness for each unique client; and would, of course, understand and fully inform each client about the potential risks as well as benefits of the use of hypnosis; and would, of course, understand and accept the "additional burden of responsibility" that the use of hypnosis involves. Unfortunately, I cannot find such discussion in Dr. Nugent's argument. Personally, I believe that Dr. Nugent possesses all of these qualifications. However, I am extremely doubtful that all persons who graduate with a B.S.W., M.S.W., or a doctoral degree in social work are adequately prepared to use hypnosis safely and ethically with clients.

Before social workers support the use of hypnosis, I would strongly urge the following: First, many more research studies such as Dr. Nugent himself has conducted should be undertaken. The appropriateness as well as the effectiveness of hypnosis in social work practice should be empirically researched. Second, clear guidelines concerning the qualifications, education, training, and supervision necessary before social workers consider the use of hypnosis in their professional practices should be promulgated. Third, specific criteria concerning when, how, with whom, and under what circumstances social workers might appropriately and ethically consider the use of interventive procedures generally, and hypnosis particularly, should be generated. Once developed, they should be tested, proven valid and reliable, and disseminated.

When these relatively modest expectations are met, we can revisit this issue. Until that time, however, social workers should not support the use of hypnosis.

NO

BARRY COURNOYER

Hypnosis has been endorsed by numerous professional associations throughout the United States and indeed the world. The American Medical Association, the American Psychiatric Association, the American Psychological Association, the British Medical Association, and various dental associations have officially supported hypnosis as a legitimate therapeutic modality. Social work, however, would do well to depart from its sister professions on this issue. Social workers should not support or endorse the use of hypnosis.

What Is Hypnosis?

The Scottish surgeon James Braid is reported to have coined the term *hypnosis* in the 1840s, deriving it from the Greek word for sleep. Hypnotic phenomena, however, have a much longer human history than that, perhaps going back to the origins of our species. Throughout the centuries, hypnotic experiences have been an important part of ceremonial, religious, and healing processes throughout the world. Shamans from many cultures have commonly used trance-inducing procedures in making connections between a visible physical world and an invisible spirit world as they provide healing services, offer divine interpretations, and attempt to exert control over natural occurrences such as droughts or floods. In contemporary North American society, a vast array of lay "helpers" promote themselves and their services—sometimes at incredibly high fees—to people in distress. Many claim rapid relief for physical pain and emotional discomfort through "quick fix" measures, including hypnosis. Sometimes associated with psychic and various "new age" processes, hypnotic services are widely advertised through televised promotions and, as might be expected, on the Internet as well. A brief search of the World Wide Web yielded dozens of hypnosis sites, several of which also advertised psychic, Tarot, and astrological readings.

Throughout its lengthy human history, controversy has accompanied hypnosis. The phenomenon has also been extremely difficult to define:

> It has been variously theorized to be an altered state of consciousness, a disso-ciated state, an access to the unconscious, a form of conditioning, or merely a compliant response to suggestion or social cues. The professional literature teems with a variety of metaphors and descriptive phrases intended to capture its theoretical essence, including the concepts of fantasy absorption, believed-in imaginings, role enactment, focused attention, loss of generalized reality orientation, goal-directed fantasy, regression in the service of the ego, archaic involvement, and altered brain function. Although of theoretical interest, such hypothetical constructs have proved to be extremely difficult to operationalize empirically. Consequently, determining the essence of hypnosis by attempting to distinguish experimentally among these descriptors has been fraught with ambiguity. (Orne & Dinges, 1989, p. 1502)

Indeed, the ambiguity is so extreme that some authors have argued that there is no such thing as hypnosis. Others have strongly advocated for hypnosis, praising its health-enhancing properties. Clinical hypnosis has been used during childbirth; as an aid in the treatment of gastrointestinal disorders; in attempts to strengthen the immune system, control cigarette smoking, and manage over-weight; as part of the treatment of anxiety and phobic disorders; in the treatment of sexual dysfunction; and during dental procedures (Hammond, 1994). Adver-tised as helpful for a wide range of purposes, hypnosis has been used in attempts to advertise commercial products, win political campaigns, and, incredibly, to pro-mote breast enlargement!

After a comprehensive review of the various definitions of hypnosis, Ham-mond et al. (1995, p. 2) concluded that "a large number of the definitions refer to three concurrent, overlapping components... 1) dissociation; 2) absorption, and 3) suggestibility." Dissociation has been described as a "segregation of any group of mental processes from the rest of the psychic apparatus" (Hinsie & Campbell, 1970, p. 221). To dissociate, then, is to split off some part of one's mental life in such a way that it is disconnected from other aspects. In regard to hypnosis, this splitting-off experience has been described as involuntariness, unconscious re-sponse, and altered consciousness. Absorption is a heightened state of mental concentration. It has been described as imaginative involvement, focused concen-tration, and imagery vividness. Suggestibility involves the suspension of critical judgment and may be viewed as a state, quality, or ability to be influenced by the statements (i.e., suggestions) of oneself or others.

Hammond et al. (1995) note that these three dimensions are mentioned in most descriptions of hypnosis. Unfortunately, hypnosis continues to be virtually impossible to identify accurately or reliably. Hypnotized persons cannot reliably be distinguished from nonhypnotized persons; and hypnotic capacity, or hypnotizability, varies significantly among the general population. Some people find it impossible to enter a trance state, whereas others are hypnotically gifted, accessing a deep and profound state quickly and easily.

Application of Hypnosis in Clinical Social Work

Perhaps because of the aura of mystery and controversy that surrounds it, hypnosis can be an extremely appealing, even seductive, experience. Its potential for application in counseling or psychotherapy is apparent. Clinical social work, "the professional application of social work theory and methods to the treatment and prevention of psychosocial dysfunction, disability, or impairment, including emotional and mental disorders" (Barker, 1991, p. 39), would seem a reasonable context for the use of hypnosis. Of course, hypnosis has long been used by psychiatrists, psychologists, and some social workers as an adjunctive process in the treatment of selected mental and emotional disorders. However, because hypnotized clients often manifest aspects of dissociation, absorption, and especially heightened suggestibility, the use of hypnosis "places an additional burden of responsibility" on the clinician, who "should never be any more interested . . . in using hypnosis" than the client (Spiegel & Spiegel, 1985, p. 1395). In fact, most medical and psychological authorities state emphatically that "hypnosis should never be used in the treatment of a condition that the therapist is unprepared to treat without it" (Orne & Dinges, 1989, p. 1502).

In spite of its appeal, several factors mitigate against social work support for the use of hypnosis. First, the profession of social work is not sufficiently well regarded by the general public or by other professionals to withstand close association with controversial therapeutic procedures. Until social workers are more widely viewed as competent, effective, and efficient in accomplishing their primary missions and purposes, it would be wise to avoid endorsement of practices commonly viewed with skepticism. Although several well-designed studies do, in fact, support the use of hypnosis as an adjunctive procedure for selected psychological and emotional problems, social workers should be extremely cautious about aligning themselves too closely with hypnotic procedures that focus primarily on "intrapsychic" phenomena to the exclusion of social and environmental factors.

Although the American Medical Association (AMA) endorsed hypnosis decades ago, it has had to modify and qualify its position. So has psychology.

Both professions have necessarily become considerably more cautious in their support of hypnosis, particularly with regard to its use in forensic circumstances and for memory enhancement. "Controlled studies on hypnotic age regression have shown that memories evoked under hypnosis can be erroneous" (Robbins, 1995, p. 673). In part because of the increased suggestibility and the vivid quality of images often experienced during hypnosis, recollections that have been hypnotically refreshed must be considered suspect. The controversy surrounding the recovery of repressed memories has been fueled, in part, because hypnotic procedures such as age regression and guided imagery have been commonly used to retrieve childhood memories. It is now clear that substantial risks are associated with these processes, for clients and clinicians alike. Recognizing this, the AMA has taken the position that recovered memories of childhood sexual abuse should be considered to be of "uncertain authenticity, which should be subject to external verification. The use of recovered memories is fraught with problems of potential misapplication" (AMA, 1994, p. 4). This is consistent with the conclusion "that memory (particularly for details) is imperfect, whether or not formal hypnosis is used. People have been shown to be capable of filling in gaps of memory with confabulated information, of distorting information, and of being influenced in what is 'remembered' by leading questions or suggestions" (Hammond et al., 1995, p. 11). Because the experience of hypnosis commonly involves dissociation, absorption, and suggestibility, some people will become better able to accurately recall memories of events previously forgotten. Others, however, will experience extremely vivid but false "memories" of events that never actually occurred.

Second, the number of social workers who have conducted scientific studies of hypnosis appears to be negligible, perhaps nonexistent. Before social workers can reasonably consider support for the use of hypnosis, at least a modest track record of research into the topic and its application to social work practice would seem necessary. An electronic search of social work journals included in *Social Work Abstracts* yielded only two articles that directly addressed the topic of hypnosis. Neither report is research based. Rather, they are advocacy pieces that encourage social workers to use hypnosis in social work practice (Knight, 1991; Winsor, 1993). Reference to empirical research concerning hypnosis, its use by social workers, and its efficacy or efficiency in treating psychosocial problems in social functioning are absent. Neither author discusses social workers' ethical obligation (NASW, 1993) to be qualified and competent in the performance of professional social work functions. Presumably, appropriate training, qualifications, and competence in the use of hypnosis would be considered legally and ethically necessary before its use with clients. Knight (1991) makes no reference whatsoever to this ethical principle, whereas Winsor (1993) states that hypnosis "is not difficult to learn, and weekend workshops—the only source of training for most social workers—are increasingly available.... Practice with friends and colleagues and with self-hypnosis, as well as supervision when undertaking work with clients, is important" (p. 606). Contrast Winsor's suggestions about how social workers may learn to use hypnosis with the standards of the American Society of Clinical Hypnosis (ASCH), the preeminent association of helping professionals qualified in the use of hypnosis. Full membership in ASCH requires an earned doctoral degree in one of the traditional helping professions (e.g., medicine, dentistry, psychology, social work) and a minimum of forty hours of approved training in clinical or experimental hypnosis (M.S.W.-level social workers may be eligible for associate membership). Also, consider the eligibility requirements for the Diplomate in Clinical Hypnosis awarded by the American Hypnosis Board for Clinical Social Work (AHBCSW), an affiliate organization of the ASCH. The Diplomate in Clinical Hypnosis is limited to masters- or doctoral-level social workers who have Diplomate status in clinical social work (NASW or ABECSW), a state license to practice clinical social work, five years of supervised experience with hypnosis, three reference letters, a transcript of a therapeutic session in which hypnosis played a significant role, reprints of relevant scholarly publications, and successful passage of an oral examination conducted by three examiners.

If, for example, NASW were to support or endorse the use of hypnosis by its members, specific standards for training and credentials, and guidelines for the professional application and ethical use of hypnosis within the context of social work practice would need to be formulated and disseminated. One would hope rigorous standards and guidelines would be adopted. Currently, however, very few social workers could meet even modest standards of competency in the clinical use of hypnosis.

Rather than endorsing the use of hypnosis, social workers would be better advised to develop criteria for the ethical selection and use of intervention procedures generally. Specific techniques, such as hypnosis, could then be considered within the framework of these overarching clinical practice guidelines. Suppose social workers were to adopt, among others, these four guidelines for the selection and use of intervention procedures: (1) The technique under consideration must help to maximize a client's participation, self-direction, and empowerment; (2) the use of the technique must be congruent with social work's ethical prohibition against dishonesty, fraud, deceit, and misrepresentation; (3) the technique and the rationale for its consideration must be clearly explained to clients so they truly understand the procedure as well as its potential positive and negative effects on them and their social world; and (4) the social worker should be knowledgeable, qualified, and skillful enough in the use of the technique to ethically consider its use with other human beings.

Hypnosis, a subjective experience that is virtually impossible to validly and reliably identify, might or might not meet these and other guidelines for the selection of safe, ethical, and effective intervention procedures for social work practice. Until or unless it does, social workers should not support the use of hypnosis.

REFERENCES

American Medical Association. (1994). *Report of the Council on Scientific Affairs* (CSA Report 5-A-04). Chicago: Author.

Barker, R. (1991). *The social work dictionary* (2nd ed.). Silver Spring, MD: NASW Press.

Hammond, D. C. (1994). *Medical & psychological hypnosis: How it benefits patients.* Des Plaines, IL: American Society of Clinical Hypnosis Press.

Hammond, D. C., & Elkins, G. R. (1994). *Standards of training in clinical hypnosis.* Des Plaines, IL: American Society of Clinical Hypnosis Press.

Hammond, D. C., Garver, R. B., Mutter, C. B., Crasilneck, H. B., Frischholz, E., Gravitz, M. A., Hibler, N. S., Olson, J., Scheflin, A., Spiegel, H., & Wester, W. (1995). *Clinical hypnosis and memory: Guidelines for clinicians and for forensic hypnosis.* Des Plaines, IL: American Society of Clinical Hypnosis Press.

Hinsie, L. E., & Campbell, R. J. (1970). *Psychiatric dictionary* (4th ed.). New York: Oxford University Press.

Knight, B. M. (1991). Using hypnosis in private social work practice. *Journal of Independent Social Work, 5,* 43–52.

Mason, M. A. (1991). The McMartin case revisited: The conflict between social work and criminal justice. *Social Work, 36,* 391–399.

National Association of Social Workers. (1994). *Code of ethics.* Washington, DC: Author.

Orne, M. T., & Dinges, D. F. (1989). Hypnosis. In H. I Kaplan & B. J. Sadock (Eds.), *Comprehensive textbook of psychiatry* (5th ed., pp. 1501–1516). Baltimore, MD: Williams & Wilkins.

Spiegel, D., & Spiegel, H. (1985). Hypnosis. In H. I Kaplan & B. J. Sadock (Eds.), *Comprehensive textbook of psychiatry* (4th ed., pp. 1389–1403). Baltimore, MD: Williams & Wilkins.

Robbins, S. (1995). Cults. In National Association of Social Workers, *Encyclopedia of Social Work* (19th ed.) (pp. 667–677). Washington, DC: National Association of Social Workers.

Winsor, R. M. (1993). Hypnosis: A neglected tool for client empowerment. *Social Work, 38,* 603–608.

Yapko, M. (1993). The seductions of memory. *Family Therapy Networker, 17,* 31–37.

Rejoinder to Dr. Cournoyer   WILLIAM R. NUGENT

Barry Cournoyer gives several reasons that social workers should not use hypnosis. It is noteworthy that none of his reasons concerns its potential effectiveness.

Indeed, he acknowledges that it can be an effective intervention, stating that "... several well-designed studies do, in fact, support the use of hypnosis. ..." In fact, quite a few empirical studies have been conducted that support its potential effectiveness with a variety of problems, as I have noted in my earlier response.

Controversy has indeed surrounded hypnosis, and its acceptability to various professional communities has waxed and waned across time. This history should not prevent hypnosis from being used by adequately trained social workers to treat specific problems for which hypnosis has been shown to be an effective intervention. The use of leeches for various physical problems also has a long and not-so-positive history. Yet, today leeches are used as part of a medical procedure to help in the reattachment of fingers and other severed body parts. The history of a particular intervention procedure should be less important than its demonstrated effectiveness as an intervention for specific human problems.

The statement that hypnotic procedures focus exclusively on intrapsychic processes is not accurate. A reading of many of the case studies discussed, for example, in Volume IV of *The Collected Papers of Milton H. Erickson* (Rossi, 1980), shows that it can be used as a part of a complex intervention process that focuses on multiple system levels. To say that hypnosis focuses exclusively on intrapsychic processes is a very limited, misleading, and misinformed view.

Dr. Cournoyers states that *no* empirical research on hypnosis has been conducted by social workers. This is not true. I have conducted several studies, two of which have been referenced in my earlier response. It is true, however, that relatively few studies of hypnosis have been conducted by social workers. The paucity of research by social workers on hypnosis is not, however, a reason to advocate that it not be used. Social workers work with a great diversity of clients and problem types, and relatively little research in general has been conducted by social workers on intervention procedures. Hypnosis is not unique in that respect. Interventions that have been researched by other professional disciplines and shown to be effective should be options for adequately trained social workers.

Dr. Cournoyers correctly points out that social workers should be adequately trained to conduct hypnotic interventions. This need for training, however, is certainly no reason to say that hypnosis should not be used by social workers. If the need for training were an adequate reason for a profession to avoid use of a particular intervention, then we would need to avoid use of *any* intervention procedure that requires professional training, such as systematic desensitization or the cognitive–behavioral package developed by Beck for treating depression. Social workers need to be trained to competently conduct these two intervention procedures, but that need for training is most certainly not a reason to advocate that social workers not use them at all.

As Dr. Cournoyer correctly points out, for some things hypnosis should *not* be used. One example is memory revivification. Numerous studies have suggested that hypnotic procedures can distort memory or actually create false memories (see Smith, 1983, in my earlier reference list, and Yapko, 1993, in Dr. Cournoyer's references). Hypnosis, like any other potentially useful procedure, should be used as an intervention, or as part of an intervention, only for problems for which there is evidence that it produces positive outcomes.

As I prepared to write my response to Dr. Cournoyer's position, I read a front-page article in the *Knoxville News-Sentinel* (October 19, 1995) stating that an independent panel of the National Institutes of Health recently endorsed hypnosis as an alternative treatment for several problems, including chronic pain associated with cancer. Furthermore, this panel recommended that hypnosis be used by social workers as a means of providing this intervention to clients at lower costs than if physicians administered it. Hypnosis can be an effective intervention for certain problems, and there are no compelling reasons why social workers should avoid providing hypnotic procedures for their clients.

REFERENCE

Rossi, E. (1980). *Innovative hypnotherapy: The collected papers of Milton H. Erickson on hypnosis (Vol. IV.)* New York: Irvington.

Does Constructivist Therapy Offer Anything New to Social Work Practice?

Cynthia Franklin, Ph.D., is an Associate Professor of Social Work at the University of Texas at Austin, where she teaches courses in clinical practice and research. She is the author of numerous publications on clinical assessment, the effectiveness of school social work practice, and teen pregnancy prevention. Dr. Franklin also maintains a part-time private practice.

Catheleen Jordan, Ph.D., received her doctorate from the University of California at Berkeley in 1986. She is Professor of Social Work and Director of the Office of Equal Opportunity and Affirmative Action at the University of Texas at Arlington. Her teaching and research interests include clinical assessment, child and family treatment, and clinical treatment efficacy research.

YES

CYNTHIA FRANKLIN

Constructivism is an umbrella term that covers a group of diverse theories and models of therapy. Learning about the constructivist therapies is like recycling old products to produce something new. The constructivist therapies are filled with the familiar but also new understandings concerning human cognition and behavior. The new, however, is important and, I believe, worth consideration by social work practitioners. In this chapter, I first describe the major views held by constructivist psychotherapies. Second, I briefly discuss three reasons why constructivism offers something new to social work practice. Finally, I point to empirical research being completed that is important to both process and outcomes in constructivist therapy.

Constructivist Therapy

The term *constructivism* is sometimes used synonymously with a distinct theoretical perspective, social constructionism. Constructivism and social constructionism, however, represent related but diverse perspectives. See Franklin (1995) for a discussion of the differences. Constructivism and social constructionism may be thought of as related because they share some commonalties (i.e., they both emphasize how humans participate in their own cognitive and social constructions of reality). To use a metaphor, both are related because they are types of fruit, but constructivism is apples and social constructionism is oranges.

It is important to define the type of constructivism that you are discussing. This chapter discusses cognitive constructivist therapies, a group of therapies that have evolved out of psychological science and complex systems theories. Constructivist models of therapy have evolved out of practice orientations such as Kelly's personal construct theory (Neimeyer & Neimeyer, 1990), cognitive–behavioral practice models (Mahoney & Lyddon, 1988), constructivist family therapies that were influenced by cybernetic systems theories (Keeney, 1983) and structural–developmental cognitive theories (Ivey & Gonçalves, 1988). A diversity of perspectives in constructivist therapy have influenced authors to develop schemes that define the differing approaches (cf. Gonçalves, 1995; Lyddon, 1995).

Because of the diversity of theoretical models used in constructivist therapy, the term *constructivism* cannot be defined by a singular definition. In general, however, constructivist therapies have the following metatheoretical beliefs (DiGiuseppe & Linscott, 1993; Mahoney, 1988; Neimeyer, 1993):

1. Humans actively participate in the construction of the reality in which they respond. They are proactive beings with higher cortical structures, who are capable of using generative, feedforward mechanisms in storing sensory perceptions and memories, and using anticipation, goals, and expectations to motivate and self-regulate their own behavior.
2. Humans cannot absolutely objectively know (perceive) reality without the constructions inherent in their cognitive and emotional schema (matrix of meanings that prompt attention, memory, and interpretations of environmental stimuli). In this sense humans create their own realities. This view, however, differs from solipsism (belief that the self is the only reality), because most constructivist therapies do not deny the existence of an objective, ontologically based reality beyond the self. Constructiv-

ists have a range of views concerning the degree of direct perception and influence that the objective reality has on human cognitive perceptions, structures, and behaviors.

3. Human cognition, affect, and behavior are believed to exist in an interactive system and cannot be clearly separated from one another.

4. Life span development and the changes in organisms over time are important.

5. Behavior is best understood by an analysis of systemic, complex, and reciprocal aspects of causality.

6. Internal cognitive (including affective) structures such as core ordering processes, deep structures, meaning systems, and narratives (life stories) are important in maintaining and changing behavior.

Constructivist Therapies Offer Something New?

As stated by Patton (1988), the favorite ideas found in constructivism may be traced to earlier psychologists such as "Brentano (1955), Bruner, (1973), Freud (1972), Piaget (1952), Erickson (1963), Adler (1959), Rogers (1951), Kelly (1955), Kohut (1977) and many other theorists" (p. 258). Although the views held by constructivist therapies may be traced to these traditions in psychology, the current wave of constructivist theories and therapies also provide new models from research in cognitive and neuroscience and developmental psychology. This brings me to my three main points as to why constructivist therapies are new and worth consideration by social work practitioners:

1. *Constructivist therapies have an empirical basis in cognitive science.* There is an ongoing cognitive revolution within psychology. In addition, new systems theories (chaos theory and nonlinear dynamics) have ushered in waves of new information on complex human systems and cognition (Mahoney, 1995). Developments within cognitive science and complex systems theories have pushed the concept of constructivism to the forefront of working models. An interesting futuristic idea proposed by Mahoney is that the term *constructivism* likely will not survive. But the research that undergirds complex systems and the knowledge concerning the constructivist processes involved in human cognitive functioning will continue to evolve.

2. *Constructivism offers new knowledge for understanding internal, cognitive, and emotional structures.* Historically, social workers have relied on psychoanalytical theory and other nonempirical alternatives for explaining the internal structures of human functioning. These theories served as foundations for the so-called person functioning in our person–environment perspectives. Constructivist therapies are rooted in cognitive science and other empirical research and provide

new formulations for consideration. Research into cognitive and social structures and processes such as (1) memory (Brower & Nurius, 1993), (2) social cognition (Fiske & Taylor, 1984), (3) evolutionary epistemology [how humans construct knowledge] (Mahoney, 1991), (4) ecological psychology (Greenberg & Pascual-Leone, 1995), (5) narrative psychology (van den Broek & Thurlow 1991), and (6) new social cognitive and learning theories (Bandura, 1989; Prawat, 1993) provide support for the ideas found in constructivism.

Brower and Nurius (1993), for example, review empirical research from cognitive, personality, and social psychology, as well as ecological psychology, and describe the importance of the constructivist perspectives. Selective perceptions, life stories, and the processes of memory are found to play a significant role in social realities. To understand a client's problem, it is necessary to comprehend their cognitive construction of reality or how an individual makes sense or meaning out of the world.

Van den Broek & Thurlow (1991) review empirically supported research that supports the importance of narratives in cognitive representations and the effects of mental representations on behavior. These authors further use the empirical data from this research to describe ways to understand the level of developmental competence of a particular narrative, as well as systematic ways to intervene to change that narrative. Borrowing from cognitive science, Mahoney (1991) further proposed the concept of core ordering processes, powerful, nonlinguistic processes of human organization that order human experiences. Core ordering processes operate according to dimensions such as good–bad, right–wrong, self–other, and so forth. Personal construct psychology has produced thousands of empirical research studies that support the dichotomous nature of these core ordering processes, as well as methods of validly and reliably measuring these constructs (See Neimeyer & Neimeyer, 1990, for reviews).

3. *Constructivism provides new models that explain person–environment interactions and the complexity of human behavior.* Greenberg & Pascual-Leone (1995), for example, propose a model known as "dialectical constructivism" that helps practitioners explain the complexities between persons and their environments. This model is rooted in research on cognitive mediational processes and experiential change in psychotherapy. The model goes further than other models of constructivism in its abilities to account for the restraints of the environment on one's constructions, as well as the novelties found in human experience.

Finally, I want to mention that empirical research being accomplished by therapists and researchers is important to supporting the process and outcomes of constructivist therapy. Research is focusing on such areas as mapping clients' self-theories and cognitive processes, explaining how therapy works, and investigating the importance of metaphors in psychotherapeutic change. Most of this research is taking place and being published within and counseling and clinical psychology, and is following both paradigmatic (traditional, experimental) and narrative (qualitative) process outcome studies. Hoshmand & Martin (1995) provide an edited volume that delineates and summarizes several of these studies.

Conclusion

Constructivist therapy may seem old because it explains in new ways many of the complexities of human behavior that have been of interest to social work practitioners. Constructivism represents new eras of research and theorizing in psychological practice. Constructivist therapy is in its infancy. It remains to be seen if the constructivist therapies (the applied counterparts of psychological research) will be as effective as the cognitive–behavioral therapies derived from similar traditions.

REFERENCES

Bandura, A. (1989). Human agency in social cognitive theory. *American Psychologist, 44,* 1175–1184.

Brower, A. M., & Nurius, P. S. (1993). *Social cognition and individual change: Current theory and counseling guidelines.* Newbury Park, CA: Sage.

DiGiuseppe, R., & Linscott, J. (1993). Philosophical differences among cognitive–behavioral therapists: Rationalism, constructivism, or both? *Journal of Cognitive Psychotherapy, 7,* 117–130.

Fiske, S. T. & Taylor, S. T. (1984). *Social cognition.* New York: Random House.

Franklin, C. F. (1995). Expanding the vision of social constructionist debates: Creating relevance for practitioners. *Families in Society, 76,* 395–407.

Gonçalves, Ó. F. (1995). Hermeneutics, constructivism, and cognitive-behavioral therapies: From the object to the project. In R. A. Neimeyer & M. J. Mahoney, (Eds.), *Constructivism in psychotherapy* (pp. 195–230). Washington, DC: American Psychological Association.

Greenberg, L., & Pascual-Leone, J. (1995). A dialectical constructivist approach to experiential change. In R. A. Neimeyer & M. J. Mahoney, (Eds.), *Constructivism in psychotherapy* (pp. 169–191). Washington, DC: American Psychological Association.

Hoshmand, L. T., & Martin, J. (1995). *Research as praxis: Lessons from programmatic research in therapeutic psychology.* New York: Teacher's College Press.

Ivey, A. E., & Gonçalves, Ó. F. (1988). Developmental therapy: Integrating developmental processes into clinical practice. *Journal of Counseling and Development, 66,* 406–412.

Keeney, B. P. (1983). *Aesthetics of change.* New York: Guilford.

Lyddon, W. J. (1995). Forms and facets of constructivist psychology. In R. A. Neimeyer & M. J. Mahoney (Eds), *Constructivism in psychotherapy* (pp. 69–92). Washington, DC: American Psychological Association.

Mahoney, M. J. (1988). Constructive meta-theory: Basic features and historical foundations. *International Journal of Personal Construct Psychology, 1,* 1–35.

Mahoney, M. J. (1991). *Human change processes.* New York: Basic Books.

Mahoney, M. J. (1995). Continuing evolution of the cognitive sciences and psychotherapies. In R. A. Neimeyer & M. J. Mahoney (Eds.), *Constructivism in psychotherapy* (pp. 39–68). Washington, DC: American Psychological Association.

Mahoney, M. J., & Lyddon, W. J. (1988). Recent development in cognitive approaches to counseling and psychotherapy. *The Counseling Psychologist, 16,* 190–234.

Neimeyer, R. A. (1993). An appraisal of the constructivist psychotherapies. *Journal of Consulting and Clinical Psychology, 61,* 221–234.

Neimeyer, G. J., & Neimeyer, R. A. (1990). *Advances in personal construct psychology.* Greenwich, CT: JAI Press.

Patton, M. J. (1988). Mind as metaphor in the construction of cognitive theories of counseling. *The Counseling Psychologist, 16,* 257–260.

Prawat, R. S. (1993). The value of ideas: Problems versus possibilities in learning. *Educational Researcher, 22*(6), 5–16.

van den Broek, P., & Thurlow, R. (1991). The role and structures of personal narratives. *Journal of Cognitive Psychotherapy, 5,* 257–274.

Rejoinder to Dr. Franklin

CATHELEEN JORDAN

Dr. Franklin, in her argument in support of the contribution of constructivist therapies to social work, presents three major points: (1) major views of constructivist psychotherapies; (2) reasons why constructivism offers something new to social work practice; and (3) the empirical research supporting constructivist therapies.

Franklin is remiss in largely limiting her discussion to the *cognitive* constructivists. Theoretically, the cognitive constructivists are on the fringes of constructivist thinking because of their origins in learning theory. Additionally, I doubt that most constructivist social workers would identify with this approach or would label themselves in the cognitive tradition. However, this criticism aside, Franklin goes on to aptly delineate the philosophical commonalties between the various constructivists groups for focusing on the importance of self-perception of reality and so forth.

Then Franklin argues that what is new in constructivism is its empirical basis in cognitive science and new knowledge for understanding interpersonal and intrapersonal processes. I found it interesting that the authors cited in this section include Mahoney and Bandura, noted learning theorists. Though Franklin cites literature reporting research in the processes described by cognitive constructivists, she fails to show the link to social work practice.

Finally, Franklin concludes by mentioning constructivist outcome research done in counseling and clinical psychology. However, she summarizes by noting that the constructivist contribution to therapy remains to be seen. My point exactly!

NO

Catheleen Jordan

When a client is sitting in your office seeking help for her depression, the latest debate on the philosophy of science is probably not the first idea that will come into your head as you try to plan a realistic course of treatment. However, this chapter addresses the philosophical debate between proponents of social constructivism versus empiricism, the current theoretical debate in social work, and relates the argument to social work practice.

Proponents of social constructivism purport that objective reality does not exist, that the only truth is the subjective perceptions of the individual. This is contrasted with logical empiricism, or the view that objective reality exists, can be perceived through the senses, and therefore can be measured and agreed on collectively. Social work methods advocated by constructivists include qualitative techniques, including narrative approaches, solution-focused therapy and so forth, in which clients are responsible for telling their stories or identifying their own solutions. Empirically based social work practice recommends a systematic approach to practice, including problem specification, measurement, data analysis, and follow-up.

Though the empirical approach in social work evolved to counteract the constructivist philosophy of pre–twentieth century thought, constructivist advocates now claim they bring something new to the social work profession. This treatise offers four arguments to persuade the reader that constructivism offers nothing new to social work practice.

Grandiose Theoretical Claims

Constructivists seek to justify and promote their theory by claiming to offer a new epistemology, though the literature suggests that constructivism is anything but new. Thyer (1995), in "Constructivism and Solipsism: Old Wine in New Bottles," notes the similarities between the two theoretical perspectives. As does constructivism, solipsism assumes that nothing exists outside the self and that experience is all-important, as is the individual's unique perception of that experience. Solipsism is a philosophical paradigm promoted by A. Schopenhauer (1788–1860). Wakefield (1993) addresses constructivist claims that the theory is the first to completely avoid cultural and racial bias: "Declaring that one's own theory 'completely' lacks biases while attributing biases to every theory that came before seems naive, at best" (p. 676).

Other criticisms of constructivist beliefs center around assumptions of how knowledge can be acquired. Gambrill (1995) notes problems with constructivist thinking: ". . . many qualitative researchers claim there is no "truth" but still want their particular account to be believed without providing any evidence that it is accurate" (Phillips, cf. Gambrill, 1995, p. 39); and "Calling a study qualitative does not magically remove potential sources of bias that may gravely limit the accuracy of claims" (Gambrill, 1995, p. 40).

Constructivists Misrepresent Empiricism

Proponents claim that constructivism contributes uniquely to social work practice by filling a void left by the empiricists. Four constructivist criticisms, which misrepresent the empirical approach, follow.

First, empiricism leads to oversimplification. Atherton suggests that the current debate began with papers written by Heineman-Pieper (Heineman, and Pieper, cf. Atherton, 1993), who suggested that the empiricists' reliance on measurement leads to a limited and oversimplified picture of clients and their functioning. Attempts to reduce clients' problems to measurable entities were believed to trivialize the problems, with a resulting loss of the context in which the problem occurs. Gambrill (1983) addressed this issue and identified methods and techniques for assessing the complexities of life, as did Jordan & Franklin more recently (1995). The authors identify global and rapid assessment tools for obtaining a holistic picture of the client.

Second, everything cannot be measured. Empiricism implies that objective reality exists and may be measured through the senses. Rephrasing some prior axioms developed by Hudson and cited by Atherton (1993), empiricism contends that "if a client's problem really exists, then it is potentially measureable," and that "if clients' problems are measured in a reliable and valid manner, you are in a better position to provide effective treatment."

Empirically based practice is based on the assumption that it is a violation of the contract between practitioner and client to approach treatment from an anything-goes perspective. Ethical practice requires that practitioners monitor client progress and evaluate whether their treatment makes a difference in the client's life. Problem conceptualization includes the client's attitudes, beliefs, and feelings as well as overt behaviors. For example, modification of a client's irrational beliefs (e.g., that she has to be perfect to be loved) is a typical treatment goal.

Third, objective and value-free science is impossible to achieve. Empiricism identifies the process whereby objective truth may be ascertained. Constructivist assumptions are antithetical to meaningful intellectual inquiry and have absurd consequences. If truth is consensus and if there are no objectively true facts about cause and effect, then, for example, the question of whether the Nazis caused the deaths of millions of Jews has no objective answer. Consequently, the constructivist view makes all claims of professional competence meaningless. Even simple causal questions, such as whether lack of food causes people to die or whether a given child's bruises were caused by walking into a door or by parental abuse, would have no objective answer. Yet we know that such questions have answers (cf. Wakefield, 1995, p. 16).

The constructivist claim that empiricism is value free is also mistaken. Atherton (1993) reviews the history of logical empiricism and points out that empiricism is not value free; early empirical scientists, by adopting a view that nothing exists outside of that which can be experienced by the senses, "embraced a statement of belief that one either accepts or rejects, similar to the premises of religion or idealistic philosophies" (p. 622). Relatedly, empiricists do not believe in "absolute, unchanging truth. Truth is always subject to further review, as are methods. Good contemporary scientists do not believe in absolute truth" (Atherton, 1993, p. 622).

Fourth, clients are treated as objects. Witkin and Gottschalk (cf. Atherton, 1993) argued that empiricism leads to "research aimed at technical control of behavior in which clients (subjects) are conceived of as objects.... This, they said, was at variance with social work's mission of liberation, empowerment, and self-actualization of people" (p. 619). In actuality, empirically based practice seeks to empower clients by practitioners and clients contracting together for the goals of treatment, by practitioners giving clients the success rates of various treatment options, and by practitioners emphasizing treatment in the client's world as a way of encouraging generalization and maintenance of positive client changes.

Social Work Practice Was Already Eclectic

Constructivists claim to have developed qualitative assessment and intervention methods. In fact, they have evolved not only from constructivist theory, but also from several disciplines within the social sciences, including ethnography/ethnomethodology, symbolic interactionism, psychoanalytic theory, cybernetic systems theory, and ecological psychology (Franklin & Jordan, 1995).

Lancy (1993) reviewed qualitative methodologies across several disciplines, including anthropology, sociology, psychology, and human ethology, and drew many comparisons in philosophical orientations and methodologies. Historically, social work practice has been influenced by the qualitative/naturalistic research traditions. Borrowing from the sociological traditions, in particular, early social workers made use of interviews, participant observations, and field methods in their work. Diverse approaches to practice, such as psychoanalytically based casework and the settlement house movement, used case studies and other qualitative methods to study and diagnose human problems (Franklin & Jordan, 1995, p. 282).

Efficacy of Constructivist Methods Is Not Established

Harrison, Hudson, and Thyer (cf. Atherton, 1993) highlighted the paucity of research studies establishing the superiority of constructivist methods. Also, qualitative methods may be too time consuming and process intensive, particularly in agency-based or private practice settings and in managed care environments (Franklin & Jordan, 1995). Fraser (1995) worries that qualitative methods "involve extensive sensitization; immersion; copious recording (often done on the spot); and hours of coding, analysis, and writing" (p. 26).

Conclusion

Let us return to the depressed client who is still sitting in your office waiting for your treatment recommendation. Though we have ascertained that constructivism is not a new contribution to social work practice, constructivists have reminded us of our historical commitment to viewing our client in the context of her environment in a warm, empathic, and humane manner. You will start where the client is, and you will be interested in her view of her current reality. But you will venture beyond a warm, supportive client–practitioner relationship, to assessing and measuring the degree and extent of her depression and the environmental context in which it occurs. You will recommend a treatment based on the latest state-of-the-art methodology known, through empirical research, to alleviate depression. You will monitor, through measurement, her progress during treatment, and you will follow-up after treatment to ensure maintenance of the positive changes made in treatment. You will provide ethical social work treatment based on traditional social work methods of joining with your client, plus cutting-edge empirically based methods.

REFERENCES

Atherton, C. (1993). Empiricists versus social constructivists: Time for a cease-fire. *Families in Society, 74,* 617–624.

Franklin, C., & Jordan, C. (1995). Qualitative assessment: A methodological review. *Families in Society, 76,* 281–295.

Fraser, M. (1995). Rich, relevant, and rigorous: Do qualitative methods measure up? *Social Work Research, 19,* 25–27.

Gambrill, E. (1983). *Casework: A competency-based approach.* Englewood Cliffs, NJ: Prentice-Hall.

Gambrill, E. (1995). Less marketing and more scholarship. *Social Work Research, 19,* 38–46.

Jordan, C., & Franklin, C. (1995). *Clinical assessment for social workers: Quantitative and qualitative methods.* Chicago, IL: Lyceum.

Lancy, D. (1993). *Qualitative research in education: An introduction to the major traditions.* New York: Longman.

Thyer, B. (1995). Constructivism and solipsism: Old wine in new bottles? *Social Work in Education, 17,* 63–64.

Wakefield, J. (1993). Following the Piepers: Replies to Tyson, Steinberg, and Miller. *Social Service Review, 67,* 673–681.

Wakefield, J. (1995). When an irresistible epistemology meets an immovable ontology. *Social Work Research, 19,* 9–17.

Rejoinder to Dr. Jordan   CYNTHIA FRANKLIN

After reading Dr. Jordan's arguments against the constructivist therapy, I am wondering if we are experiencing the same reality. Dr. Jordan argues that what she calls "social constructivism" is anti-empirical, anti-intellectual, nonsystematic in method, and unethical. She further constructs a false dichotomy, contrasting constructivism with the Empirical Practice Model. The Empirical Practice Model emphasizes the importance of grounding social work practice in science, and conducting research to verify the effectiveness of practice methods. In this viewpoint, Dr. Jordan and I do not disagree concerning the importance of empirical research for developing effective practice methods.

I have argued for the empirical basis of constructivist approaches to therapy, suggesting that constructivism is rooted in the cognitive sciences. This approach to therapy is increasing in importance and currently being integrated into well-researched systems of psychotherapy. To quote the renowned behavior therapist, Marvin Goldfried:

> Many of our cognitive–behavioral theoretical assumptions have also been undergoing a redefinition by a group of therapist referred to as "constructivists" (e.g., Guidano, Guidano & Liotti, 1983; Mahoney, 1991). Central to this redefinition is the belief in the individual's active participation in knowing and learning, the role of tacit processes in the perception of self and others, and the importance of emotional and interpersonal relationships throughout one's development (p. 176).... Given the fact that different approaches to therapy acknowledge that patients' perceptions of self and reality contribute to their problems, we may anticipate that there will be an increasing incorporation of concepts and findings from the cognitive sciences in helping us understand the process of therapeutic change. As more therapists receive undergraduate and graduate education that allows them to appreciate advances in the cognitive sciences, a greater number of professionals will be able to identify the potential applications of such research findings to the clinical setting. (Goldfried, 1995, p. 243)

My first impression of Dr. Jordan's arguments against the constructivist therapy is that her objections have little to do with the actual practice methods of constructivist therapy, and more to do with her perceptions concerning what philosophical and research views that constructivists hold. Most of her arguments are based on an erroneous idea that constructivists do not believe in an objective reality. As I discussed in my former remarks, this is not the case for most constructivists. Mahoney (1988) pointed out that "critical realism" is the philosophical viewpoint of most cognitive constructivists. This viewpoint assumes that there is an ontologically based reality in which humans seek to develop an accurate anticipatory match between the environment and their own subjective cognitive constructions. Critical realism also assumes that there are certain universal laws or "restraints" in the universe that make up the basis of reality. So, for Dr. Jordan to suggest that constructivists do not believe in physical laws (i.e., lack of food causes people to die) is both inaccurate and absurd.

Constructivists, however, do not believe that humans can make an exact replica of the environment through their senses (known as the correspondence theory) because all perceptions are filtered through one's past learning experiences, cognitive schema, and values. Contemporary scientists accept postpositivist philosophies of science that do not propagate a value-free science or that scientist can gain knowledge of the absolute truth. Constructivists have similar views. I agree with Dr. Jordan that, in all good science, "the truth is always subject to further review, as are methods."

Dr. Jordan compares constructivism with qualitative research and infers that constructivist therapies are against the concept of measurement. She further states that approaches to constructivist therapy such as the solution-focused methods are based on qualitative techniques. Dr. Jordan's obvious biases toward qualitative research are apparent in these accusations, but her views are inconsistent with constructivist practice and research. G. J. Neimeyer (1993) has summarized a number of constructivist assessment methods including measurement approaches. Constructivists apply diverse approaches to research, using both quantitative and qualitative methods (R. A. Neimeyer, 1993). Jack Martin and colleagues, for example, performed studies on constructivist theory in counseling practice using both hypothesis testing and exploratory approaches to research (Martin, Cummings & Hallberg, 1992; Martin, Pavio, & Labadie, 1990). Besa (1994) recently published a single-case experiment on the effectiveness of narrative methods. One of the major techniques used in the solution-focused therapy is known as the "scaling technique." This technique produces quantitative measurements of presenting problems that therapists use to prescribe meaningful changes in behavior.

It appears that Dr. Jordan may be equating the constructivist psychotherapy with the extreme subjectivism propagated by those who subscribe to a particular type of social constructionism and further gathers her information from debates in the literature about the philosophy of science and the suitability of qualitative research methods for social work. I base this view on the fact that most of Dr. Jordan's citations are about research debates in social work and not about constructivist therapy. Despite the contributions of the articles she cites toward ongoing discussions concerning research methods and philosophy of science in social work, these articles do not specifically address constructivist therapies or their practice methods. As I have discussed in more detail elsewhere, social constructionism and constructivism are not the same, and even among these divergent theories there is a range of theoretical and philosophical views (Franklin, 1995). Perhaps, Dr. Jordan's reliance on research squabbles and allegiance to particular dogmas may partly account for our divergent views concerning this subject matter. I encourage practitioners to read the practice literature on constructivist therapy and to draw their own conclusions concerning both the newness and the research basis for these theories.

REFERENCES

Besa, D. (1994). Evaluating narrative family therapy using single system research designs. *Research on Social Work Practice, 4* 309–325.

Franklin, C. (1995). Expanding the vision of the social constructionist debates: Creating relevance for practitioners. *Families in Society, 76,* 395–407.

Goldfried, M. R. (1995). *From cognitive-behavior therapy to psychotherapy Integration.* New York: Springer.

Mahoney, M. J. (1988). Constructive meta-theory: Basic features and historical foundations. *International Journal of Personal Construct Psychology, 1,* 1–35.

Martin, J., Cummings, A. L., & Hallberg, E. T. (1992). Therapists' intentional use of metaphor: Memorability, clinical impact, and epistemic/motivational functions. *Journal of Consulting and Clinical Psychology, 60,* 143–145.

Martin, J., Pavio, S., & Labadie, D. (1990). Memory-enhancing characteristics of client-recalled important events in cognitive and experiential therapy: Integrating cognitive experimental and therapeutic psychology. *Counseling Psychology Quarterly, 3,* 67–83.

Neimeyer, G. J. (1993). *Constructivist assessment: A casebook.* Newbury Park, CA: Sage.

Neimeyer, R. A. (1993). An appraisal of the constructivist psychotherapies. *Journal of Consulting and Clinical Psychology, 61,* 221–234.

Should Social Workers Support Facilitated Communication for Persons with Developmental Disabilities?

Edwin Risler, M.S.W., is a licensed clinical social worker in Georgia, having earned his M.S.W. in 1982 from the University of Georgia, where he is currently a doctoral student in social work. **Susan S. Risler, M.Ed.,** is licensed by the state of Georgia and certified by the American Speech and Hearing Association as a Speech and Language Pathologist. She has practiced in the public elementary school system for more than ten years, after receiving her M.Ed. in 1983 from the University of Georgia. Ms. Risler is trained in the use of facilitated communication.

John Gerdtz, Ph.D., received his M.S.W. in 1979 from Washington University in St. Louis and his Ph.D. in special education from the University of Wisconsin–Madison in 1986. At the time this chapter was prepared, Dr. Gerdtz was an Assistant Professor with the Department of Psychiatry and Behavioral Sciences at Emory University School of Medicine, and Director of Family and Adult Services at the Emory Autism Resource Center. He is currently an educational consultant with the Spectrum Center in Berkeley, California.

YES

EDWIN A. RISLER
SUSAN S. RISLER

Facilitated communication (FC) is a teaching technique involving a trained facilitator who provides physical and emotional support to an individual while that individual communicates through pointing to letters or pictures or by typing (Biklen, 1990). The goal of FC is for an individual to gain full independence of communication by the gradual withdrawal of the support provided. The method has been described as relevant for those individuals with developmental disabilities and language impairments. FC originated in Australia (Crossley & McDonald, 1980) and gained popularity in the United States through the work of Douglas Biklen and his colleagues. Recently, the methodology of FC has fostered enormous controversy because the technique appears to enable some individuals who were noncommunicative and diagnosed as autistic and intellectually impaired to communicate far above expected levels. A central theme in the debate concerns the authorship of the communication and whether the manifestations of FC can be attributed reliably to the individual being facilitated (Cardinal, 1994; Rimland, 1993; Vazquez, 1994; Wheeler, Jacobson, Paglieri, Schwartz, 1993).

In addressing the question posed by the editor, whether social work as a profession should support FC as a therapy for persons with developmental disabilities, we are pleased to respond positively. Indeed, not to support FC would be unethical and violate the canons of the social work profession. A social worker should make every effort to foster the maximum self-determination of the client and should not discriminate on the basis of, among other things, a mental or physical handicap or any other personal characteristic, condition, or status (NASW, 1990). We concede that this may be viewed as zealous and acknowledge that the issues pertaining to self-determination are confounding. We recognize that FC is controversial and make no definitive claim as to its effectiveness. The basis of our argument in support of FC is twofold: First, in our opinion, the research on the validity of FC has been misguided and inconclusive, and the benefits gained through the use of FC outweigh any presumed harm a client may receive. Second, social workers should not blindly support premature prohibitive moratoriums to withhold treatment from anyone without clear and convincing evidence of potential harm to clients.

The Specter of Validity

The manner in which the controversy over FC has grown is as perplexing as the issues themselves. What was developed more than a decade ago as a simple tool to improve the quality of life for some quickly became the focus of a national debate in the United States. Like many past controversies, FC was seemingly spawned from a theory. Biklen (1990) theorized that autistic people suffer from developmental dyspraxia, a neuromotor condition that is characterized by an ability to perform automatic tasks but not deliberate ones. An individual with dyspraxia may spontaneously complete a behavior but have difficulty repeating that same behavior if requested. Biklen further theorizes that for those with dyspraxia communication difficulties are problems of expression rather than of thinking. For them, FC is seen as a method of augmentive communication. The foundation for Biklen's theory is based partly on the earlier works on autism by Dr. Margaret Bauman. She suggested that the differences in the abnormal brains of autistic individuals were not in the cerebral cortex, which controls higher thinking, but were located in the cerebellum, the locus of behavior (Biklen, 1993). Biklen's idea had far-reaching implications, and the storm clouds of conflict began to gather.

What did this suggest? That autistic people previously labeled profoundly retarded and unable to communicate could express thoughts and ideas and that FC was a master key that unlocked some hidden intelligence? That previously theoretical views of autism, communication, and intelligence were suddenly suspect? Autobiographical accounts and qualitative reports of dramatic behavioral and intellectual advances began to surface in some individuals thought to be profoundly retarded. The storm erupted, and the validity of FC was questioned when individuals began to communicate allegations of physical and sexual abuse. The heated debate over FC began, and a plethora of studies were initiated that produced negative results. Fanning the flames of hysteria, the television media has presented FC unfavorably (Palfreman, 1993). The American Psychological Association (1994) and other professional groups have passed judgment and developed official resolutions in opposition to FC. Learned scholars expounding the presumed risks have called for a ban on FC while disclaiming any significant virtues it may possess for individuals (Levine, Shane, & Wharton, 1994). Fueled with emotion, the controversy has become polarized, and the epistemological debate ensued.

Thus far, the scientific evidence on FC is clearly contradictory. Skeptics continue to argue with much vituperation that FC is totally without empirical merit, liken it to a Ouija board, and cite published studies that seem to support the claim that all FC is influenced by the facilitator (e.g., Wheeler et al., 1993). Proponents of FC have countered with criticism of the methodology used in the negative reports, suggesting that traditional protocols of inquiry are inappropriate, and have presented equally compelling reports of controlled studies that appear to support the validity of FC (Vazquez, 1994; Cardinal, 1994). Similarly, a report of a number of controlled studies by Rimland (1993) showed that FC was supported in nine studies and failed in thirty-four.

In an attempt to maintain an unbiased position, our aim is not to emotionally critique the merits of either position, but to suggest that the results of the current methods of inquiry neither conclusively support nor refute the validity of FC. We simply question the motivating factors that subject FC to such scrutiny and sanctions when other instructional methods have not been. Seemingly, at this point the endeavors for "proof" have been misguided by focusing primarily on the aspects of authorship without considering the behavioral benefits associated with FC. Likewise, one could establish similarities between the debate over FC and the recent controversy concerning the use of hypnosis and reported allegations of sexual abuse from an individual's repressed memories. Hypnosis as a form of treatment for certain conditions that have affected behavioral improvements for individuals has not suddenly been deemed invalid.

Most treatments or interventions are evaluated on the basis of behavioral changes in determining their effectiveness. Further studies to ascertain the behavioral changes affecting the quality of life for an individual using FC would be a simple undertaking with much greater implications. The most significant and meaningful behavioral evidence are those individuals that have progressed from FC to independent communication. Other reports, perhaps less dramatic, are from parents and teachers who facilitate with children and describe numerous small but significant improvements in daily behavior. Could it be that underlying the current controversy is a debate about the validity of Biklen's (1990) theory and the ramifications for well-established constructs and ideas about communication and intelligence?

Who Is Really at Risk?

Like all tools, techniques, and treatments, valid or otherwise, FC has its limitations. It may be misinterpreted and could be a source of potential misuse. The greatest risk seems to be from those who wish to discount FC as a hoax because it appears to contraindicate the prevailing theories, and argue why it should not work rather than developing an understanding of why some have benefited from its use and some have not. Others, like medical historian and father of an autistic son Stuart Galishoff, suggest that FC represents a paradigm shift in our view of autism, and like most change, it is being met with tenacious resistance. They contend that the biggest detractors of FC tend to be those with the most invested in the established theories. Biklen asserts that we have very strong cultural notions about behavior, speaking, and competence. It seems that the real dangers are related to the assumptions one makes about an individual whose intellect cannot truly be measured reliably by current methods. Let us remember that intelligence is, after all, a social construct that is not directly observable. The fallout from the debate has been widespread. Reportedly, FC has been unilaterally removed from educational programs supported by parents who have experienced behavioral improvements in their children.

Social work practice has historically endeavored to improve the quality of life for all individuals, and FC should be supported for what it is, a tool that may be effective for some as a medium of expression and not a magical cure for autism or mental retardation.

References

American Psychological Association. (1994). *Resolution on facilitated communication.* Adopted in council, August 14th, Los Angeles, CA.

Biklen, D. (1990). Communication unbound: Autism and praxis. *Harvard Educational Review, 60,* 291–314.

Biklen, D. (1993). *Questions and answers about facilitated communication.* Unpublished manuscript available from the author at the Facilitated Communication Institute, Syracuse University, Syracuse, NY.

Cardinal, D. (1994, May). *Presentation of preliminary results of a validation study regarding facilitated communication.* Paper presented at the Facilitated Communication Institute, Syracuse University, Syracuse, NY.

Crossley, R., & McDonald, A. (1980). *Annie's coming out.* New York: Penguin Press.

Levine, K., Shane, H. C., & Wharton, R. H. (1994). What if . . . : A plea to professionals to consider the risk benefit ratio of facilitated communication. *Mental Retardation, 32,* 300–304.

National Association of Social Workers. (1990). *Code of ethics.* Washington, DC: Author.

Palfreman, J. (1993, October 19) *Prisoners of silence.* (J. Palfreman, Director). In J. Palfreman (Producer), Frontline. Boston: Corporation for Public Broadcasting.

Rimland, B. (1993). Facilitated communication under siege. *Autism Research Review International, 7*(2), 7.

Vazquez, C. (1994). Brief report: A multitask controlled evaluation of facilitated communication. *Journal of Autism and Developmental Disorders, 24,* 369–379.

Wheeler, D. L., Jacobson, J. W., Paglieri, R. A., & Schwartz, A. A. (1993). An experimental assessment of facilitated communication. *Mental Retardation, 31,* 49–60.

Rejoinder to Mr. and Ms. Risler
JOHN GERDTZ

A book critic in the *New York Times* once noted that a certain book contained information that was new and information that was true. Unfortunately, the true information was not always new, and the new information was not always true! Proponents of facilitated communication provide information that is true but not necessarily new. It is true that we are still in the beginning phase of research on interventions to help people with severe handicaps communicate effectively and efficiently. There has been considerable progress in this area in terms of research and clinical intervention, but much more progress is needed before we can confidently claim to be able to assist every person with a severe handicap. Also, our understanding of autism and related handicaps has improved considerably over recent years, but we are still far from a complete understanding of even the basic neurology and biology of these handicaps. I agree with Risler and Risler that we must never give up our attempts to help children and adults with disabilities grow and learn.

There were also many statements in Risler and Risler that were new but not necessarily true. Risler and Risler referred to the theories of Biklen (1990), who proposed that persons with autism suffered not from certain cognitive deficits but from an impairment in motor behavior. Biklen (1990) claimed a scientific breakthrough in the understanding of autism and related handicaps. As Risler and Risler noted, Biklen's theories were based on the autopsy studies of Margaret Bauman, and on the studies of postencephalitic Parkinsonism by Oliver Sacks (Biklen, 1992, p. 250). Margaret Bauman (see personal communication, p. 12, Shane, 1994a) is not convinced that her research has any relevance to Biklen's claims. Oliver Sacks (1994, p. 108) also rejected the concept of autism as a motor disorder and expressed doubts about the validity of facilitated communication. Researchers have found a pattern of cognitive deficits associated with autism (see Gillberg, 1993, for an overview of this research) that contradicts Biklen's claims. When Biklen's claims were challenged, he first responded (Biklen, 1992) that he was conducting scientific research within the generally accepted paradigm but that he was using qualitative rather than quantitative research methodologies. As the negative research findings on facilitated communication accumulated, proponents began to discuss alternative paradigms of research. Some of the new facilitated communication research paradigms were truly bizarre, as proponents (e.g., Haskew & Donnellan, 1992, pp. 11–13) included such factors as telepathic communication and demonic possession!

Contrary to Risler and Risler, facilitated communication has faced the same scientific scrutiny as virtually every other intervention used in the field of developmental disabilities. Those who make dramatic claims of scientific breakthrough need dramatic evidence to back up these claims! So far, the proponents of facilitated communication have not provided such evidence. Risler and Risler stated that the scientific evidence on the validity of facilitated communication is "contradictory." The overwhelming evidence in the refereed publications is negative as to the validity of facilitated communication (Green, 1994), and the more recent published studies (Montee, Miltenberger, & Wittrock, 1995) confirm this trend.

Risler and Risler made two extraordinary statements: "not to support FC would be unethical" but "We recognize that FC is controversial and make no definitive claim as to its effectiveness." One could imagine the response to a physician making such a claim about a medication! My position is that unqualified support for facilitated communication, given the research evidence available on facilitator influence on communication, could be a violation of the NASW Code of Ethics regarding the primacy of client self-determination. There needs to be a determination of the validity of important communications produced through facilitated communication, for every client (see Shane, 1994b, for validation techniques).

Raising questions about the validity of facilitated communication does not imply that a social worker should attempt to stop families or individuals from using the technique, or to necessarily prevent the use of facilitated communication in various programs. Social workers, as professionals, do have the responsibility to ask the hard questions and to provide accurate information, even when others are caught up in a whirlwind of enthusiasm and do not welcome such questions or information.

REFERENCES

Biklen, D. (1990). Communication unbound: Autism and praxis. *Harvard Educational Review, 60,* 291–314.

Biklen, D. (1992). Autism orthodoxy versus free speech: A reply to Cummins and Prior. *Harvard Educational Review, 62,* 242–256.

Gillberg, C. (1993). Autism and related behaviours. *Journal of Intellectual Disability Research, 37,* 343–372.

Green, G. (1994). The quality of the evidence. In H. C. Shane (Ed.), *Facilitated Communication: The clinical and social phenomenon* (pp. 157–225). San Diego, CA: Singular Publishing.

Haskew, P., & Donnellan, A. M. (1992). *Emotional maturity and well-being: Psychological lessons of facilitated communication.* Danbury, CT: DRI Press.

Montee, B. B., Miltenberger, R. G., & Wittrock, D. (1995). An experimental analysis of facilitated communication. *Journal of Applied Behavior Analysis, 28,* 189–200.

Sacks, O. (1994, January 3). A neurologist's notebook. An anthropologist on Mars. *The New Yorker,* pp. 106–125.

Shane, H. C. (1994a). Facilitated communication: Factual, fictional, or factitious? In H. C. Shane (Ed.), *Facilitated Communication: The clinical and social phenomenon* (pp. 1–31). San Diego, CA: Singular Publishing.

Shane, H. C. (1994b). Establishing the source of the communication. In H. C. Shane (Ed.), *Facilitated communication: The clinical and social phenomenon* (pp. 259–298). San Diego, CA: Singular Publishing.

NO

JOHN GERDTZ

There are three important reasons why social workers should not support facilitated communication for their clients with developmental disabilities. First, there is no evidence that facilitated communication is an effective method of communication. There is now good evidence from a number of studies that the source of much of the "facilitated" communication is the facilitator! Second, accepting facilitated communications as valid communications may have potentially serious consequences for the person with disabilities, his or her family, and the staff members working with that person. Third, the resources of time and money devoted to facilitated communication reduce the resources available for other, more effective, methods of teaching communication skills.

Does facilitated communication work? Proponents of facilitated communication such as Crossley (Palfreman, 1994) and Biklen (1990) argued that this form of communication is not only valid for the vast majority of persons with significant impairment in communication skills, but that it also reveals previously unknown cognitive and language abilities in this population. How real are these claims? The results of the research are not encouraging.

More than twenty controlled studies of the validity of facilitated communication have been published in the professional literature. The results of most of these studies (see reviews by Cummins & Prior, 1992; Green, 1994: & Jacobson et al., 1994) clearly indicate that the facilitator (usually unknowingly) was the source of most of the communication. There was no evidence from these studies that persons with severe disabilities had advanced or unexpected literacy, language, or cognitive skills. The outcomes of virtually all of the controlled studies are strikingly similar: studies by different researchers, using various methodologies, sometimes from different countries, found that in most cases facilitators controlled the output of facilitated communication.

These research results were immediately dismissed by proponents of facilitated communication. The major objections to the research were summarized by Shane (1994a). Readers who want a more detailed discussion of these issues should consult Green (1994), Jacobson et al. (1994), and Shane (1994a).

Even proponents of facilitated communication acknowledge that facilitators often influence the communications of the person being facilitated. Supporters of facilitated communication have conceded that facilitators, at times, control not only the form, but also the content of the communications obtained through facilitated communication (for example, Sabin & Donnellan, 1993, p. 208).

Facilitated communication also has potentially serious negative consequences for persons with disabilities, their families, and the staff who work in programs serving persons with disabilities. The basic danger comes from the dubious validity of facilitated communication, as discussed above. Facilitators, with the best of intentions, and without meaning to do so, may actually be substituting their communications for the communications of the person with disabilities. There are reports of significant decisions being made for persons with disabilities in such areas as educational placements, living arrangements, and even medications and other medical procedures based on facilitation (see, for example, Shane, 1994c). To act on information or requests received through facilitation without attempting to independently validate the communication seems to be a clear violation of a social worker's ethical responsibility to "foster the maximum self-determination on the part of clients" (National Association of Social Workers, 1990). It is possible to accurately and efficiently validate facilitated communication for a particular client (Shane, 1994b), but these validation methods have been rejected by supporters of facilitated communication (see examples in Jacobson et al., 1994).

The most publicized danger of facilitated communication is the accusations of sexual and other abuse made against family members of persons with disabilities, and staff members of programs serving disabled populations (Margolin, 1994). The only evidence for many of these accusations appears to be information obtained through facilitated communication. Well-designed validation studies (see for example, Bligh & Kupperman, 1993; Hostler, Allaire, & Christoph, 1993; Hudson, Melita, & Arnold, 1993) have been used in courts to determine the truth of the allegations. Accusations of abuse, including accusations made through facilitated communication, have to be taken seriously and investigated according to the law and agency policy. An essential part of this investigation, as recommended by Heckler (1994a, 1994b), is to determine whether the person making the allegations is actually communicating through facilitated communication.

Several professional organizations have expressed concern about the potential dangers posed by facilitated communication. The American Association on Mental Retardation, the American Academy of Child and Adolescent Psychiatry (the statement was also endorsed by the American Academy of Pediatrics), the American Psychological Association, the Association for Behavior Analysis, and the American Speech-Language-Hearing Association, have all issued position statements rejecting facilitated communication as a scientifically valid intervention for persons with disabilities.

Other problems with facilitated communication include the possibility that the procedures used during facilitation may prevent a person with disabilities from developing potentially more functional communication skills (see Prizant, Wetherby, & Rydell, 1994, for more information). There is the problem of the diversion of scarce resources from empirically validated interventions to unproven techniques such as facilitated communication. Money for services is always scarce and seems to be getting scarcer by the day, yet some sources have estimated that expenditures on facilitated communication in the United States have so far exceeded $100 million (Shane, 1994c, p. 311).

The developers and proponents of facilitated communication are correct in their claims that children and adults with severe disabilities have talents and abilities that remain untapped and unknown to us. This is a great tragedy, because these talents and abilities could enrich the lives of the people with disabilities, their families and friends, the professionals and paraprofessionals who serve them, and our society in general. We have interventions available with good research evidence of effectiveness that develop and improve the communication skills of people with severe disabilities, for example, interventions to develop and shape functional verbal communication (Kaiser, Alpert, & Warren, 1994), augmentative communication systems (Miller & Allaire, 1994), and the use of communication skills to address problem behaviors (Carr et al., 1994).

Social workers have a clear moral, ethical, and legal obligation to provide persons with disabilities and their families with accurate information about the options and interventions available to them. There are no other interventions commonly used in programs for persons with developmental disabilities that have so many published research reports with such consistently negative results as facilitated communication. Why would any social worker recommend or support facilitated communication?

REFERENCES

Biklen, D. (1990). Communication unbound: Autism and praxis. *Harvard Educational Review, 60,* 291–314.

Bligh, S., & Kupperman, P. (1993). Brief report: Facilitated communication evaluation procedure accepted in a court case. *Journal of Autism and Developmental Disorders, 23,* 553–557.

Carr, E. G., Levin, L., McConnachie, G., Carlson, J. I., Kemp, D. C., & Smith, C. E. (1994). *Communication-based intervention for problem behavior: A user's guide for producing positive change.* Baltimore, MD: Paul Brookes Publishers.

Cummins, R. A., & Prior, M. P. (1992). Autism and assisted communication: A response to Biklen. *Harvard Educational Review, 62,* 228–241.

Green, G. (1994). The quality of the evidence. In H. C. Shane (Ed.), *Facilitated communication: The clinical and social phenomenon* (pp. 157–225). San Diego, CA: Singular Publishing.

Heckler, S. (1994a). Facilitated communication: A response by child protection. *Child Abuse and Neglect, 18,* 495–503.

Heckler, S. (1994b). Letter to the editor. *Child Abuse and Neglect, 18,* 539–540.

Hostler, S. L., Allaire, J. H., & Christoph, R. A. (1993). Childhood sexual abuse reported by facilitated communication. *Pediatrics, 91,* 1190–1192.

Hudson, A., Melita, B., & Arnold, N. (1993). A case study assessing the validity of facilitated communication. *Journal of Autism and Developmental Disorders, 23,* 165–173.

Jacobson, J. W., Eberlin, M., Mulick, J. A., Schwartz, A. A., Szempruch, J., Wheeler, D. L. (1994). Autism, facilitated communication, and future directions. In J. L. Matson (Ed.) *Autism in children and adults: Etiology, assessment and intervention* (pp. 59–83). Pacific Grove, CA: Brooks/Cole.

Kaiser, A. P., Alpert, C. A., Warren, S. F. (1987). Teaching functional language: Strategies for language intervention. In M. E. Snell (Ed.), *Systematic instruction of persons with severe handicaps* (3rd ed., pp. 247–272). Columbus, OH: Merrill.

Margolin, K. N. (1994). How shall facilitated communication be judged? Facilitated communication and the legal system. In H. C. Shane (Ed.), *Facilitated communication. The clinical and social phenomenon* (pp. 227–257). San Diego, CA: Singular Publishing.

Miller, J., & Allaire, J. (1994). Augmentative communication. In M. E. Snell (Ed.), *Systematic instruction of persons with severe handicaps* (3rd ed., pp. 273–297). Columbus, OH: Merrill.

National Association of Social Workers (1990). *Code of Ethics.* Washington, DC: Author.

Palfreman, J. (1994). The Australian origins of facilitated communication. In H. C. Shane (Ed.), *Facilitated communication: The clinical and social phenomenon* (pp. 33–56). San Diego, CA: Singular Publishing.

Prizant, B. M., Wetherby, A. M., & Rydell, P. J. (1994). Implications of facilitated communication for education and communication enhancement practices for persons with autism. In H. C. Shane (Ed.), *Facilitated communication: The clinical and social phenomenon* (pp. 123–155). San Diego, CA: Singular Publishing.

Sabin, L. A., & Donnellan, A. M. (1993). A qualitative study of the process of facilitated communication. *The Journal of the Association for Persons with Severe Handicaps, 18,* 200–211.

Shane, H. C. (1994a). Facilitated communication: Factual, fictional, or factitious? In H. C. Shane (Ed.), *Facilitated communication: The clinical and social phenomenon* (pp. 1–31). San Diego, CA: Singular Publishing.

Shane, H. C. (1994b). Establishing the source of communication. In H. C. Shane (Ed.), *Facilitated communication: The clinical and social phenomenon* (pp. 259–298). San Diego, CA: Singular Publishing.

Shane, H. C. (1994c). The facilitated nightmare: The dark side of the phenomenon. In H. C. Shane (Ed.), *Facilitated communication: The clinical and social phenomenon* (pp. 299–319). San Diego, CA: Singular Publishing.

Rejoinder to Dr. Gerdtz

Edwin A. Risler
Susan S. Risler

Summarily, the positions enumerated by Dr. Gerdtz pertain to the effectiveness of facilitated communication (FC) as a valid form of communication, the presumed potential harmful consequences from its use, and the limited resources that could effectively be used elsewhere rather than for FC. Although Dr. Gerdtz articulates well the popular views currently held by many of those in opposition to FC, he has not established an equal position that the profession of social work should assume. Likewise, we acknowledge the importance of the premise of the points presented by him, but our response consists of conclusions of a different sort.

He raises the issue of the validity of the communication and cites several of the controlled studies that pertain to FC: "there is now good evidence from a number of studies that the source of much of the 'facilitated' communication is the facilitator!" However, most proponents of FC do concede facilitator influence, because a goal of the method is for the individual to eventually progress and communicate independently, as some have. Similarly, proponents of FC recognize and support the need for further empirical examinations that will contribute to the validity of the technique.

Clearly the most controversial aspect of FC and the validity of the author-ship of the communication relates to allegations of abuse made by individuals. Proponents and opponents of FC alike agree that individuals with disabilities who are unable to communicate are perhaps the most vulnerable of all populations to abuse and that such claims may have serious ramifications. Arguably, it seems that, regardless of whether facilitated communications regarding allegations of abuse are validated, this issue will continue to stir controversy. For the sake of ar-gument, let us assume that FC has been "officially" deemed a valid form of com-munication. Would one presume then that all allegations of abuse made by an individual through FC would be true? Of course not. One's ability to communi-cate and one's honesty are not synonymous. Similarly, the reports that indicate a wide spree of allegations of abuse from FC appear to be exaggerated, and many of the claims are corroborated with additional evidence. Reportedly, approximately 13 percent of the individuals with disabilities have made such reports, which is below the average for the general population (Hitzing, 1994).

What is perhaps more important is why FC appears to be a valid form of communication for some individuals but not for others. Cardinal and Hanson (1994) suggest that the traditional research methods used in evaluating FC are un-reliable and do not reflect its true validity. His work has consisted of developing a protocol for controlled studies that would be appropriate for evaluating the valid-ity of FC. The results thus far have been encouraging.

The second issue promulgated by Dr. Gerdtz refers to the presumed nega-tive consequences for persons with disabilities who use FC: "There are reports of significant decisions being made for persons with disabilities in such areas as ed-ucational placements, living arrangements, and even medications and other pro-cedures based on facilitation." If the FC is not valid, Dr. Gerdtz contends that the decisions made for an individual may be contrary to their wishes. He further sug-gests that to "act on" this information acquired from an invalid method such as FC would be unethical. Such a statement is not without merit, but let us present it in more definable terms. There are reported to be an estimated 350,000 individuals currently in the United States that meet the criteria for autistic disorder, and of those, approximately 70 percent have a disability that impairs the person's ability to communicate. Hundreds of decisions are made by social workers, educators, physicians, counselors, and others that affect the daily activities and lives of these individuals that seem to be "acted on" what is presumed to be in the individuals' best interest. What clothes they wear, what they eat each day, and their daily rou-tines are often predetermined for these individuals with regularity. From the time they awake each day until they retire in the evening, decisions that regulate and structure the lives of these individuals are benignly imposed.

Dr. Gerdtz's third implication, that the use of FC would prevent an individual from developing more functional communication skills and monopolize resources, is invalid. Proponents believe that FC may enhance other therapeutic methods and advocate the use of the technique in conjunction with other interventions.

As we claimed previously, we do not presume the effectiveness of FC, only that evidence seems to be contradictory and that the negative judgments regarding its use have been premature. Examinations on the validity of FC have been conducted on a few hundred subjects, and it appears to have been authenticated in some of the studies. The merits of an intervention should be determined by the direct improvement in the quality of life for an individual. While focusing solely on the validity of the authorship of the communication, opponents of FC seemingly discount evidence of significant improvements in the quality of life of those that use the technique. There are reports of individuals who were incapable of any sustained amount of behavioral concentration beyond a few minutes who now willingly facilitate undisturbed for much longer periods. Similarly, there are those individuals who have progressed from FC to full independent communication. Even if only 10 percent of the autistic individuals unable to communicate progress from FC and communicate independently, the improvement in the quality of life for those individuals could potentially number in the thousands. The roots of advocacy for the profession of social work are founded on maintaining an unbiased and nonjudgmental position. We certainly agree with Dr. Gerdtz, who reiterates that it is a social worker's responsibility to "foster the maximum self-determination on the part of clients." Dr. Gerdtz asks, "Why would any social worker recommend or support FC?" Indeed, why not?

REFERENCES

Cardinal, D., & Hanson, D. (1994, May). *Presentation of preliminary results of a validation study regarding facilitated communication.* Paper presentation at the Facilitated Communication Institute Conference, Syracuse, NY.

Hitzing, W. (1994). Reply to Levine et al.'s "plea to professionals." *Mental Retardation, 32,* 314–316.

Should Social Workers Support the Use of Neurolinguistic Programming?

Charles Zastrow, Ph.D., is Professor of Social Work with the University of Wisconsin–Whitewater. He is a member of the NASW Register of Clinical Social Workers and is a Certified Independent Clinical Social Worker in Wisconsin. He has received training in, and written two articles on, neurolinguistic programming. He is also the author of five social work textbooks.

M. Elizabeth Vonk, M.S.W., received her M.S.W. from Florida State University in 1980. She furthered her training by completing a clinical fellowship at the Judge Baker Guidance Center in Boston, MA, in 1983. For the past 11 years, she has practiced clinical social work at the Emory University Counseling Center in Atlanta, GA. She is currently a doctoral student in social work at the University of Georgia.

YES

CHARLES ZASTROW

Having received training in neurolinguistic programming (NLP), and having used NLP in psychotherapy, I am convinced that the approach has considerable usefulness for social workers in clinical practice and in other direct practice areas. NLP is a recently developed model of communication that promises to have substantial applications in assessing human behavior, in developing rapport, in influencing others (in public speaking, education, and sales), and in changing attitudes and behavior (counseling). NLP was developed by Richard Bandler and John Grinder (1975a, 1975b) and several other authorities (Lankton, 1980).

Bandler and Grinder are specialists in communication and linguistics. In the 1970s, Bandler and Grinder began developing NLP, partly by studying the nonverbal and verbal communication patterns between prominent therapists and their clients. The therapists included Salvador Minuchin (family therapist), Virginia Satir (family therapist), and Milton Erickson (a leading practitioner of using hypnosis in psychotherapy). Bandler and Grinder were able to describe in detail what these psychotherapists do, including what nonverbal and verbal cues they respond to, and how they go about helping clients make positive changes. Bandler and Grinder found that, although these psychotherapists have diverse theoretical perspectives, there are remarkable similarities in the communication patterns between these psychotherapists and their clients. Such descriptions of these patterns make it possible for others to learn how to repeat the same procedures and get similar results. This article briefly states some of the key principles of NLP and demonstrates with case examples how these principles can be used in clinical social work.

Change without Knowing Cause

NLP asserts that therapeutic change often occurs without knowing the cause of the problem. Most other psychotherapy approaches maintain that the causes of the problematic behavior must be assessed before positive changes in the problematic behavior will occur. NLP asserts that positive changes can occur without extensive attention being directed at the causes. Instead, the focus is on first identifying what the client wants and then on helping the client to identify the ways (and the resources he or she already has) to achieve his or her goals.

A client (26-year-old man) came in for a session, and appeared depressed. He had a slumped posture, downcast eyes, a sad facial expression, and he indicated that he had not slept very well for the past few nights. He said he was increasingly getting depressed because he was worried he would not be able to obtain a job when he graduated two years in the future with a major in English, and he stated he was also worried about how he would ever repay the college loans he had taken out. The following transactions then occurred:

Counselor: Can you currently do anything constructive about these two situations?

Client: No.

Counselor: Are you aware that worrying about something that you can't currently do anything about is making you more depressed?

Client: Yes.

Counselor: Let's see if we can lighten the air a bit. Could you think back to the last enjoyable vacation that you had, and tell me about that?

Client: Let's see. About three years ago I went to Glacier National Park in Montana and had a great time. (The client then proceeded to spend about ten minutes describing what he did and saw).

Counselor: Isn't it amazing that by thinking about an enjoyable time that you had, you now seem to be more relaxed, more energized, and less depressed than you were ten minutes ago?

Client: Yes-s-s, I guess that's the case.

Counselor: Are you also aware that it would be much more constructive for you to focus on what you want—currently, and in the future—than dwelling on worrying about things you have no control over?

Client: Perhaps.

Counselor: Let's give it a try. Can you tell me what you currently want?

Client: Yes, to be happy, and to again have the energy to focus on my studies this semester.

Counselor: Good. Now we're getting someplace. Tell me about some of the things you could do in the next few hours that are enjoyable for you and that will also stop you from worrying about things that you cannot currently change.

The client began talking about a variety of things he enjoyed doing—jogging, lifting weights, and calling some friends to get together for lunch. The more he talked about these things, the more relaxed he became. After about ten more minutes of talking, he smiled and said "You've been telling me for weeks that my thoughts determine my actions and emotions. I just proved it. By switching my thinking from worrying about something I can't control, to thinking about enjoyable activities I can do I feel better, and energized. I now get the message loud and clear. I think I'll go jogging for awhile, and then try studying. I want to do well with my grades, which will increase the chances of getting a job when I graduate. See you next week."

As counseling progressed over the next few sessions, the client learned that whenever he started thinking negatively (and thereby started to become depressed), he could rapidly counter the depression by getting involved in activities that he enjoyed or by focusing on his studies, which he now realized would help him achieve a number of his short- and long-term goals.

Communicating in Metaphor

A second principle of NLP is that positive therapeutic change can occur by the therapist communicating in metaphor. NLP uses the term *metaphor* to refer to the use of puns, stories, analogies, and anecdotes in therapy. Metaphors are particularly useful for clients who tend to resist direct suggestions. I have used metaphors with a variety of clients. I remember a seventeen-year-old high school student who was seriously contemplating suicide. I asked him to visualize the following scene:

> Let's assume you carry out your plan to take your dad's handgun and shoot yourself in the temple when no one is home. There will be blood all over. Let's also assume that the one who first discovers you after it happens is your younger brother. That will really leave a lasting impression on him. For months and years after, he will have nightmares about this. Eventually he may seek to end the terror of these nightmares in the same way you intend to end your life—that happens a lot in a family in which suicide occurs. After they find you, a funeral director will be called to embalm you, which involves draining your body of its fluids and a variety of other procedures. Your parents will be in a state of shock over you taking your life, and will forevermore be searching for why you did what you did. Often in families in which a suicide of a son or daughter occurs, the parents blame each other and eventually get a divorce. Friends and relatives will come to your funeral and say a variety of things, including it's really tragic that you chose a permanent solution to the temporary problems that you're now having. They'll also ponder why you didn't have the courage to face life's problems. After the funeral, you will be taken to the cemetery. You will be lowered into the ground, and slowly your body will deteriorate. If there is an air leak in the coffin, you will deteriorate very fast—perhaps worms may enter. Is this what you want?

This story is useful because it helps people contemplating suicide realize that what happens after suicide is worse than their present agony. (Most people who are contemplating suicide focus only on their current temporary emotional pain and do not think about what will happen if they complete suicide.) In this case, the student stopped thinking about taking his life, and instead started focusing on resolving the problems he was facing.

I have used metaphors in a variety of other ways in counseling. A few additional examples are described. For a twenty-one-year-old woman who was concerned about her future with being involved with a married man who was seventeen years older than she, I told a vividly detailed story about another client who had a miserable life for eight years while dating a married man. This story led this client to give her male friend an ultimatum—either you leave your wife or our relationship is over; the man refused to end the marriage, and the client then followed through in ending the relationship. For another sixteen-year-old female client who stated that she wanted to get pregnant to have a child who would love her, I related stories about two teenagers who did have children and then discovered that young children take love and give little affection in return; and that being a mother interferes with dating, partying, and forming a relationship with a male; and that it often plunges one into long-term poverty. After pondering these stories for awhile, the sixteen-year-old decided to wait to become a mother and made arrangements to receive contraceptives from a family planning clinic. Storytelling in such cases is often more effective than giving advice, because clients tend to react defensively to advice but tend to more readily accept the underlying messages conveyed with metaphors.

Reframing

A third principle of NLP that is very useful in counseling is reframing. NLP asserts that it is enduringly useful to presuppose a positive intent behind all behavior. The focus of reframing is to separate the positive intent from the negative behavior so that the positive intent then becomes linked to new positive behavior. NLP asserts that clients who are in problematic situations are generally making undesirable choices. Reframing is a way to help clients make better choices.

A thirty-two-year-old wife came into counseling asserting that she wanted her husband to stop drinking, which was creating major problems in the marriage. She was asked if her husband was willing to come in jointly to discuss this. She indicated she had asked him more than a dozen times, and he "flat out" refuses. She was asked for more details about her marriage and her husband's drinking. She mentioned their relationship was quite good, except when he went out drinking—which occurred one or two nights a week. She indicated when he came home drunk, she would begin chastising him for spending their money on "booze," and for acting foolishly while drunk. This usually led to a major argument between them, with her husband becoming verbally abusive, and she increasingly feared that he might actually hit her during these episodes. I praised her for her wanting to improve their relationship. I then asked if she really wanted to avoid the heated exchanges with her husband when he's drunk. She said, "Yes, definitely." I then asked if her actions of chastising him for drinking (when he was drunk) was achieving her desired result of improving their relationship. She said, "No—it's starting to build a wall between us." I then asked if she has the power to stop his drinking. She thought about it for awhile, and then said "No—but what can I do?" I then asked if there were other actions she could take when her husband came home drunk that would avoid a fight between the two of them—such as going shopping, taking a walk, or staying overnight with a female friend of hers. The wife thought about it for awhile and concluded she would try these suggestions. The focus in this case was to disconnect her positive intent (wanting to improve their relationship) from berating her husband when intoxicated. Instead, the positive intent was connected with new actions when the husband came home intoxicated, such as her leaving for a few hours so that the usual argument was avoided.

Joining and Leading

A fourth principle of NLP that is applicable to counseling is that the process of influencing another person involves two steps: (1) the influencer finds a way to "join" with the person to be influenced, and (2) the influencer then leads the person in a new (and preferably positive) direction. Once the influencee (customer or client) has joined with the influencer, the influencer is better able to lead the influencee in the direction desired. There are several ways to join with the person to be influenced, including talking knowledgeably with the person about subjects that interest the person; mirroring (without the person being consciously aware of the mirroring) the person's nonverbal communication—such as posture, gestures, and breathing patterns; and joining with the person's representational system. The latter involves the five sensory systems and is more fully described by Lankton (1980).

One of the major values for social workers who become trained in NLP is that the technique facilitates the worker attending to nonverbal and verbal communication. Personally, the approach has enabled me to better attend to paralanguage, eye-accessing cues, breathing patterns, the words that clients use, facial blushing, posture, gestures, signs of muscle tension, and other nonverbal cues. NLP has a number of intriguing conceptualizations in these areas, including sensory representational systems, representational system predicates, the map is not the territory, eye-accessing cues, the fourtuple, and the meaning of a communication is the response it elicits (Lankton, 1980).

I am convinced that training in NLP increases a social worker's perceptiveness, communication skills, and relationship skills. What proof is there that receiving training in NLP will increase these skills and capacities in a worker? Controlled studies in such an area are difficult to conduct. But an analogy may help. It is now widely assumed that receiving training in mathematics will develop one's mathematical capacities. Similarly, it makes sense that receiving training in communicative skills (through NLP) will develop one's communicative capacities.

Summary

I trust a summary of key principles of NLP, along with case illustrations, make the point that NLP has considerable usefulness for social workers in analyzing communication patterns of clients and in changing unwanted emotions and dysfunctional behaviors of clients. The concept of studying the verbal and nonverbal communication patterns between prominent therapists and their clients to identify what causes positive changes has considerable merit. NLP has developed a number of valuable concepts that are useful in explicating how a person (therapist, teacher, salesperson, public speaker) can influence another. Receiving training in NLP appears to increase a social worker's perceptiveness, communication skills, and relationship skills. The following principles have considerable application in direct practice/clinical social work: therapeutic change often occurs without knowing the cause of the problem, positive therapeutic change can occur by the therapist communicating in metaphor, reframing, and the therapist first joining with the client and then leading the client.

REFERENCES

Bandler, R., & Grinder J. (1975a). *The structure of magic* (Vol. 1). Palo Alto, CA: Science and Behavior Books.

Bandler, R., & Grinder, J. (1975b). *The structure of magic* (Vol. 2). Palo Alto, CA: Science and Behavior Books.

Lankton, S. (1980). *Practical Magic.* Cupertino, CA: Meta Productions.

Rejoinder to Dr. Zastrow
M. ELIZABETH VONK

After reading Dr. Zastrow's argument in support of the use of NLP, I am still unconvinced that social work should support the use of this approach. I would like to respond to four points that can be found in his summary. First, similar to other reports of clinical evidence, Dr. Zastrow's provision of a summary of NLP principles followed by case illustrations does *not* "make the point that NLP has considerable usefulness ... in analyzing communication patterns of clients and in changing unwanted emotions and dysfunctional behaviors of clients." As with other practice approaches, clinical evidence must be supported with empirical evidence to ensure effective and ethical practice. The lack of such evidence for NLP is not atttributable to its being a brand new untested approach, its extreme complexity, or to the difficulties of practice research. In spite of the difficulties involved in conducting controlled studies, evidence of the effectiveness of other practice approaches is accumulating.

Second, I do not agree that "NLP has developed a number of valuable concepts that are useful in explicating how a person can influence another." A review of the literature makes it very clear that the basic underlying concepts of NLP are faulty. Researchers have not even been able to show that a Preferred Representational System (PRS) exists, nor that matching a person's supposed PRS causes a desired influencing effect.

Third, Dr. Zastrow states that "receiving training in NLP appears to increase a social worker's perceptiveness, communication skills, and relationship skills." Once again, this claim of effectiveness is without empirical support.

Finally, Dr. Zastrow draws our attention to four NLP principles that he states "have considerable application in direct practice." Although these principles or techniques may be a part of NLP, they are certainly not original or unique to NLP. The use of metaphor, reframing, and the idea of change without knowledge of the root cause are a part of several therapeutic models. The idea of joining with one's client through the use of sensitivity toward verbal and nonverbal cues is a part of basic interviewing skills, not a magical NLP technique.

In conclusion, NLP has not been shown to be the effective practice model that its proponents claim. Although initial practice with the model seemed hopeful, supportive research evidence has not followed. It is alluring to think that a practice model might promise so much in the way of effecting change with our clients. It is our responsibility as a profession to turn away from that model when it fails to deliver.

NO

M. ELIZABETH VONK

Neurolinguistic programming (NLP), a "new model of human communication and behavior...developed by Richard Bandler and John Grinder..." (Bandler & Grinder, 1979, p. 3) has been applied in a variety of settings, including psychotherapy, education, and sales. Basing their work on extensive observations of well-known therapists (e.g., Salvador Minuchin, Fritz Perls, and Virginia Satir), Bandler and Grinder developed a model that is based on the idea that communication is most effective when people use the same sensory representational system. They contend that persons have a preferred representational system, meaning that each person tends to perceive the world primarily through one of five sensory modes that can be determined by observing predictable eye movements and by noting the person's use of language. NLP was widely promoted through expensive training workshops during the 1980s and was quickly adopted for use by members of many helping professions, including those in the field of social work. After briefly mentioning evidence of the use of NLP in the field of social work, I review claims of the therapeutic effectiveness of NLP, followed by a review of empirical evidence to the contrary.

As early as 1983 and as recently as 1995, NLP appears in the social work practice literature. In the *Handbook of Clinical Social Work,* Middleman (1983) briefly describes NLP as one of several clinical techniques that emphasizes nonverbal interactions. She goes on to report its enthusiastic use by clinicians who purport clinical evidence of its effectiveness despite a lack of empirical support for the basic tenants of the model. In spite of this early foreshadowing of the inability to produce empirical support for this model of treatment alongside of fervent claims of its power, NLP continues to find its way into the social work literature. For instance, NLP appears in both the first and second editions of Barker's *Social Work Dictionary* (1987 and 1991). Likewise, chapters on NLP appear in practice textbooks such as Turner's (1986) and Zastrow's (1995). In both of these texts, NLP techniques are described in detail and reported to be useful in social work practice.

Support for NLP is generally of two types. First are the effusive claims made by Bandler and Grinder themselves, along with other promoters. For example, the foreword of Bandler & Grinder's (1979) *Frogs Into Princes* states that

> using the principles of NLP...allows you to make many deep and lasting changes quickly and easily. A few specific examples of things you can learn to accomplish are: (1) cure phobias...in less than an hour, (2) help children and adults with learning disabilities overcome these limitations, often in less than an hour, (3) eliminate most unwanted habits...in a few sessions, (4) makes changes in the interactions of couples..., (5) cure many physical problems... in a few sessions." (Bandler & Grinder, 1979, p. ii)

The authors then attempt to back up these amazing claims by stating that practitioners who are experienced in the use of NLP can show such results from their work. In story after story, the authors then tell of quickly alleviating problems such as migraine headaches, various phobias, and obesity in their clients.

The second type of support for NLP is found in case studies. For instance, Hossack and Standidge (1993) describe the use of an NLP technique with an elderly male patient who suffered with debilitating depression. Although the patient showed improvement as measured both by the patient's subjective reporting of decreased symptomatology and by a rapid assessment instrument, the role of NLP is unclear because of concurrent treatment with antidepressant medication, relaxation training, and peer involvement with a retirement group. Davis and Davis (1983) report on two family therapy cases involving the use of two NLP techniques, anchoring and bridging. In both cases the authors describe improvement that they attribute to NLP, stating that "it enables clinicians to do what they previously could not" (p. 290). They go on to mention a series of other difficult clinical situations that improved dramatically and quickly using NLP, and then state their conviction that controlled outcome research will surely follow in the wake of "mounting clinical evidence" (p. 290).

Indeed, there is a need for empirical support as to the effectiveness of any intervention, including NLP. Although case studies such as the two above provide descriptions of interventions and suggest hypotheses about the effect of those interventions, they do not in and of themselves provide evidence that a particular intervention produces a particular result. Appropriately controlled outcome research, using single-subject or group designs, is necessary to provide evidence of an intervention's effectiveness. Such research provides a basis for effective and ethical social work practice. Without it, our practice is based solely on hopeful claims and clinical judgment that is vulnerable to bias and fallacies of reason (Nurius & Gibson, 1990). Although many practice interventions have been shown to be effective through the use of empirical research over the past fifteen years (Fisher, 1993), NLP is not among them.

A number of researchers have tested hypotheses related to NLP. These studies tend to be of two types. The first type tests hypotheses related to the basic tenets of the NLP model, and the second tests hypotheses related to the effectiveness of NLP interventions. Both are briefly reviewed.

First, related to the concepts underlying NLP, there have been several reviews of pertinent studies (Einspruch & Forman, 1985; Sharpley, 1984, 1987). In all, forty-four studies were reviewed in these three articles. The studies examined a variety of questions, including verification of the existence of the preferred representational system (PRS), ability to reliably identify the PRS in oneself or in another, ability to match a person's PRS for the purpose of an intervention, and the effect of matching the PRS during an exchange with another person. Sharpley (1987) provides a concise summary of the studies, reporting that of the forty-four, only six were supportive of NLP, versus twenty-seven that were nonsupportive and eleven that were mixed or only partially supportive. He goes on to state: "Data collected in 44 studies clearly indicate an overwhelming finding that (a) the PRS cannot be reliably assessed; (b) when it is assessed, the PRS is not consistent over time; therefore, (c) it is not even certain that the PRS exists; and (d) matching clients' or other persons' PRS does not appear to assist counselors reliably in any clearly demonstrated manner" (p. 105).

Interestingly, although Einspruch & Forman (1985) are in agreement with Sharpley (1984, 1987) that NLP concepts have not been shown to be valid and that NLP procedures have not been shown to be effective, they argue that these findings are attributable to methodological and design problems. From the thirty-nine articles they reviewed, they describe six problems that, for the most part, are attributable to the researchers' lack of knowledge and understanding of NLP, which they describe as "an extraordinarily complex model of human cognition and behavior" (p. 594). However complex NLP may be, it is difficult to dismiss the findings from forty-four studies, 85 percent of which failed to support even the most basic of NLP concepts.

Taking seriously Einspruch and Forman's (1985) description of methodological problems in prior research on NLP, Baddeley & Predebon (1991) reported on two studies designed to eliminate or control for those problems. In both experiments, the researchers tested the NLP eye-movement hypothesis that predicts particular eye movements to be associated with particular question categories (i.e., visual, auditory, or kinesthetic). The data from both experiments led the researchers to conclude that "even though the present research took Einspruch's objections into account, the findings do not support the validity of the NLP eye-movement hypothesis" and "the NLP account of eye-movements cannot be accepted" (p. 18).

Finally, regarding NLP concepts, the National Research Council, investigating NLP at the request of the U.S. Army (Swets & Bjork, 1990) found "little if any evidence . . . to support NLP's assumptions or to indicate that it is effective as a strategy for social influence" (p. 90). Consistently, findings from empirical research have failed to support the basic concepts that make up the NLP model. There are still those, however, who insist that the true test of NLP is in its clinical utility (e.g., Einspruch & Forman, 1985; Bandler & Grinder, 1979). Certainly, it is a possibility that the technique may be effective despite faulty theoretical or conceptual underpinnings. As Davis and Davis (1983, p. 290) state, "NLP makes no claim to truth; its highest criterion is utility." And, after all, it is its utility that is of most importance to social work practice.

In contrast to investigations of NLP concepts, there is little published research focused on outcome of NLP-based treatment techniques. As Melvin and Miller (1988) point out, this is surprising considering the claims that have been made about its effectiveness. They review three outcome studies. In all three studies, the researchers used an NLP treatment group versus a control group. In two of the studies, a comparison treatment group also was used. All three studies employed a pretest–posttest design using behavioral and self-report measures with snake-phobic or speech-anxious clients. Results from one of the studies indicated that there was no difference between groups after treatment. Similarly, in another study, no differences were found between groups in either *behavior or expression* of fear, but the NLP group members were more likely to *report* that they were over their fear of snakes. Although results of the third study indicated improvement in the NLP group versus the control group, the sample size was very small, and there was no comparison treatment group. Melvin & Miller (1988, p. 157) conclude that "the research support for NLP efficacy . . . is unconvincing."

Seven years later, there is still no strong empirical evidence that NLP techniques are effective. Although Davis and Davis (1983) were hopeful that outcome research on NLP would follow and corroborate claims of effectiveness based on clinical experience, this has simply not been the case.

Should social workers support the use of neurolinguistic programming? I would have to conclude that we should not. NLP concepts have been tested thoroughly and have been found to lack support. NLP techniques, though widely acclaimed, have not been empirically supported. To uphold high standards of effective and ethical social work practice, treatments must be backed with empirical support. In its fifteen or more years of existence, NLP has failed to meet this standard.

REFERENCES

Baddeley, M., & Predebon, J. (1991). Do the eyes have it? A test of neurolinguistic programming's eye-movement hypothesis. *The Australian Journal of Clinical Hypnotherapy and Hypnosis, 12*(1), 1–23.

Bandler, R., & Grinder, J. (1979). *Frogs into princes.* Moab, UT: Real People Press.

Barker, R. (1991). *Social work dictionary.* (2nd ed.). Silver Spring, MD: National Association of Social Workers.

Davis, S. L., & Davis, D. I. (1983). Neuro-Linguistic Programming and family therapy. *Journal of Marital and Family Therapy, 9,* 283–291.

Einspruch, E. L., & Forman, B. D. (1985). Observations concerning research literature on Neuro-Linguistic Programming. *Journal of Counseling Psychology, 32,* 589–596.

Fisher, J. (1993). Empirically-based practice: The end of ideology? *Journal of Social Service Research, 18,* 19–64.

Hossack, A., & Standidge, K. (1993). Using an imaginary scrapbook for Neurolinguistic Programming in the aftermath of a clinical depression: A case history. *The Gerontologist, 33,* 265–268.

Melvin, K. B., & Miller, H. L. (1988). Anchoring: Panacea or placebo? *Phobia Practice and Research Journal, 1,* 153–158.

Middleman, R. R. (1983). Role of perception and cognition in change. In A. Rosenblatt & D. Waldfogel (Eds.), *Handbook of clinical social work* (pp. 229–248). San Francisco, CA: Josey-Bass.

Nurius, P. S., & Gibson, J. W. (1990). Clinical observation, inference, reasoning, and judgment in social work: An update. *Social Work Research and Abstracts, 26,* 18–25.

Sharpley, C. F. (1984). Predicate matching in NLP: A review of research on the preferred representational system. *Journal of Counseling Psychology, 31,* 238–248.

Sharpley, C. F. (1987). Research findings on Neurolinguistic Programming: Non-supportive data or an untestable theory? *Journal of Counseling Psychology, 34,* 103–107.

Swets, J. A., & Bjork, R. A. (1990). Enhancing human performance: An evaluation of "new age" techniques considered by the U.S. Army. *Psychological Science, 1,* 85–96.

Turner, F. J. (Ed.) (1986). *Social work treatment: Interlocking theoretical approaches.* (3rd ed.). New York: Free Press.

Zastrow, C. (1995). *The practice of social work.* (5th ed.). Pacific Grove, CA: Brooks/Cole.

Rejoinder to Ms. Vonk

CHARLES ZASTROW

Ms. Vonk's review of the literature on outcome studies conducted on NLP is indeed impressive. One of her major assertions is that outcome studies have not demonstrated the effectiveness of many of the principles advanced by NLP. I heartily agree with that assertion. I do disagree, however, with her conclusion that because outcome studies have failed to document the effectiveness of many of the principles of NLP, social workers should not use concepts advanced by neurolinguistic programming.

Ms. Vonk is overlooking the fact that outcome studies have, at this point, failed to document (beyond a reasonable doubt) the effectiveness of most approaches to counseling and psychotherapy—including such approaches as psychoanalysis, transactional analysis, client-centered therapy, implosive therapy, psychodrama, play therapy, task-centered practice, feminist intervention, provocative therapy, Adlerian therapy, existential therapy, encounter therapies, Gestalt therapy, most family therapy approaches, and covert sensitization (Corsini & Wedding, 1989). There are a variety of reasons why there have been relatively few well-designed outcome studies on the various approaches to psychotherapy. A few of these reasons will be mentioned. Many theorists who have developed psychotherapy techniques are so convinced of the effectiveness of their techniques that they think case examples are sufficient to demonstrate their effectiveness. The length of therapy—sometimes two or three years—presents problems in following clients over a sufficient time frame to evaluate the results. Setting up criteria to evaluate the success of intervention techniques also presents problems. A review of the difficulties in designing outcome studies is contained in Lambert, Shapiro, & Bergin (1986).

Ms. Vonk's conclusion that NLP should not be used by social workers smacks of "throwing out the baby with the bath water." If we discarded all of the intervention techniques in the helping professions that have not as yet been deemed effective by outcome studies, then we would be discarding probably more than 90 percent of the intervention approaches that are being used.

Do I believe that all of the assertions made by NLP theorists are valid? No. Certainly claims of magically curing phobias and learning disabilities in less than an hour appear suspect to me. Do I believe that all the techniques advanced by NLP are effective? No. Some techniques, such as anchoring, may not be.

More outcome research on NLP (as well as on most intervention approaches) is needed to determine which principles, techniques, and assertions are valid, and which are not. Should the helping professions stop using intervention techniques until they are proven valid? Certainly not—to do so would leave us with only a few techniques, and result in clients failing to receive benefits from the approaches and techniques currently being used that are effective (but whose effectiveness has not as yet been documented).

What is a reasonable path for social workers and other helping professionals to take when most current intervention approaches have not undergone sufficient outcome studies to document their effectiveness? Helping professionals should advocate for, and hopefully become involved in, conducting outcome studies on intervention techniques that have promise in changing dysfunctional behaviors and unwanted emotions of clients. Secondly, with regard to the vast number of promising (but yet unproven) intervention techniques that are currently being used, helping professionals should carefully study the theoretical soundness of these approaches and select to use those that appear (from our current knowledge of human behavior) to be effective.

References

Corsini, R. J., & Wedding, D. (Eds.) (1989). *Current psychotherapies* (4th ed.). Itasca, IL: Peacock.

Lambert, M. J., Shapiro, D. A., & Bergin, A. E. (1986). The effectiveness of psychotherapy. In S. L. Garfield & A. E. Bergin (Eds.), *Handbook of psychotherapy and behavior change* (3rd ed., pp. 157–211). New York: Wiley.

Should Clinical Social Workers Support "Eye Movement Desensitization and Reprocessing" (EMDR) Therapy?

Sharman D. Colosetti, M.S.W., is a social work doctoral student at the University of Georgia, where she received her M.S.W. in 1989. She is employed as a mental health consultant by the Georgia Department of Corrections, providing individual and group therapy to incarcerated women. She also holds an appointment as a Clinical Instructor with the Department of Psychiatry and Health Behavior at the Medical College of Georgia.

Patrick S. Bordnick, Ph.D., received his M.S.W. from the University of Michigan in 1990, and his Ph.D. in social work from the University of Georgia in 1995. Dr. Bordnick is currently a research fellow at the University of Texas Medical Center, Department of Psychiatry and Behavioral Sciences, Substance Abuse Research Center. His research interests include behavioral and biological treatments for substance abuse and anxiety disorders.

YES

SHARMAN D. COLOSETTI

Licensed social workers trained in eye movement desensitization and reprocessing (EMDR) should use this form of therapy when clinically indicated. EMDR is a complex methodology that contains the following seven procedures: (1) dosed exposure to traumatic injury while the client follows the therapist's fingers in bilateral saccadic eye movements, (2) repeated exposure to, and dismissal of, traumatic imagery, (3) brief periods of attention to physical sensations associated with the traumatic memory, (4) identification of a negative self-assessment related to the trauma, (5) linkage of primary aspects of the trauma with emotionally corrective information, (6) sequential targeting of distressing material, and (7) interference with the client's fear (Shapiro, 1995). Training in the technique, followed by supervision, ensures positive outcomes. Pitman, Orr, Altman, Longpre, Poire, and Lasko (1993) demonstrated a direct correlation between the proper use of the methodology and the treatment outcome. Alternatively, improper use of EMDR, by limiting the number of eye movements and having the client relax after each set of eye movements, yields negligible results (Acierno, Tremont, Last, & Montgomery, 1994; Sanderson & Carpenter, 1992).

Research on EMDR has grown from anecdotal case studies to systematic evaluation using controlled studies. The literature on EMDR demonstrates its effectiveness with panic disorder, post–traumatic stress disorder (PTSD), phobias, excessive grief, burn victims, sexual dysfunction, dissociative disorder, and recurrent nightmares (EMDR Network, 1995).

Criticism of the methodology of early case studies has resulted in subsequently improved additional reports. Early studies were primarily outcome evaluations (do clients receiving EMD get better?), which precluded causal inferences (Does EMD *cause* these improvements) of treatment effects (Lohr et al., 1992). In a review of initial published cases using EMDR, the following additions were suggested to enhance future studies: (1) structured diagnostic interviews, (2) standardized pretreatment measures, (3) baseline clinical data, (3) standardized measures specific to client's symptoms, (4) psychophysiologic measures, (5) experimental manipulation using time-series designs, (6) comparison of EMDR with other trauma treatments, and (7) control for demand effects (Lohr et al., 1992; Herbert & Mueser, 1992). Later studies offered these additional suggestions: (1) control for random events, (2) control for unintentional experimenter bias, (3) use larger samples, (4) employ more treatment sessions, (5) use less chronic samples, and (6) conduct long-term follow-up assessments (Acierno et al., 1994; Boudewyns, Stwerka, Hyer, Albrecht, & Sperr, 1993).

Currently, no published studies appear to incorporate all of these suggestions, although nine controlled studies of samples employing more than ten subjects each use several of these recommendations. Eight of the studies used standardized measures, two used psychophysiological measures, four compared EMDR with other treatments, one used independent corroboration of outcome measures on follow-up, and two compared EMDR with alternate focusing methods. All nine studies, using clients who suffered from posttraumatic stress symptoms, reported positive results using EMDR (Shapiro, 1995). "EMDR has had more published case reports to support it than either systematic desensitization or flooding in the treatment of PTSD during a comparable time period" (Shapiro, 1995, p. 328).

The essential components of EMDR remain to be found. "It is clear that the eye movements are not unique in producing positive therapeutic effectiveness" (Shapiro, 1995, p. 328). They are, however, effective in monitoring the client's dissociation into dysfunctional material and orienting the client to maintain the dual-attention focus that may be responsible for the therapy's effectiveness (Shapiro, 1995).

The efficacy of EMDR may be attributed to (1) dosed exposure, which may facilitate Pavlovian extinction, (2) distraction provided by the eye movements, (3) brief exposure coupled with thought-stopping, (4) the object tracked in the eye movements functioning as a safety signal (Renfrey & Spates, 1994), (5) rhythmic activity, or (6) bilateral activation (Shapiro, 1995). Hopefully, accumulated published studies will fill in the gaps in our knowledge of EMDR (Wolpe & Abrams, 1991).

The research on EMDR provides a compelling justification for its use in clinical treatment. The Code of Ethics (COE) of the National Association of Social Workers (NASW, 1993) provides additional reasons. The Code of Ethics guides the conduct of social work professionals. The following four sections of the COE are relevant to the use of EMDR: (1) the social worker's conduct and comportment as a social worker; and the social worker's ethical responsibility (2) to clients, (3) to employers and employing organizations, and (4) to the social work profession.

The first section of the COE guides the social worker engaged in research to obtain the voluntary consent of clients and to protect clients from unwarranted harm. Because EMDR is a new technique that does not, as yet, have a proved theoretical base, social workers trained in EMDR can protect their clients by keeping abreast of the research and conducting outcome evaluations to identify EMDR's relevant components and demonstrate its usefulness with particular clinical diagnoses or psychosocial stressors.

Section Two of the COE addresses the social worker's primary responsibility to his or her clients' interests (NASW, 1993). The social worker is guided to demonstrate competency in his or her professional skill in service to clients. By participating in EMDR training and maintaining a supervisory relationship during the initial stages of learning, the social worker may attain such competency. Through training, he or she not only learns how to apply the technique but also obtains an overview of the research and development of EMDR. Consistent with the COE, the social worker is encouraged to accurately and thoroughly describe the technique, advise clients of the possible risks and opportunities in using the technique, and obtain supervision when needed. Both a sample "Acknowledgment and Consent Form" and a list of consultants and facilitators are provided in EMDR training workshops.

The final two sections of the COE add further credence to social workers' use of EMDR. They guide the social worker to improve the employing agency's efficiency and effectiveness of its services and to identify, develop, and fully use knowledge for professional practice. In the age of managed care, the use of EMDR as an effective brief intervention may improve agencies' efficiency and effectiveness. The treatment gains using EMDR take less time and are of a greater magnitude than what typically occurs with traditional treatment techniques. Real-life exposure therapy sessions to traumatic stimuli (e.g., sounds, photographs, movies, etc.) often last from two to two-and-one-half hours and take several sessions; implosive (intensive exposure solely in imagination) therapy may require eight to sixteen hours of exposure (Montgomery & Ayllon, 1994); however, EMDR clients receive only six to twelve minutes of exposure, following Shapiro's (1989) original protocol.

Through published research, practitioners are aided in their struggle to refine the procedures and identify the essential components that lead to EMDR's effectiveness. Suggestions from the research literature for future studies include investigating "other disrupting spatial/motor behaviors...the way images are 'blanked out' between sets...the modality in which the associated cognitions are experienced" (Bauman & Melnyk, 1994, p. 33) and designing a study of "endogenous opiates present in the cerebrospinal fluid" that are "negatively correlated with human anxiety states" (Hekmat et al., 1994, p. 128). EMDR has been shown to elicit cognitively linked traumas (Lipke & Botkin, 1992) and, therefore, may be an effective tool for studying the onset and maintenance of PTSD and other psychiatric disorders (Kleinknecht & Morgan, 1992).

Therefore, in the best interests of our clients and following the guidelines of our Code of Ethics, it is imperative that social workers add EMDR to their clinical armamentarium.

References

Acierno, R., Tremont, G., Last, C., & Montgomery, D. (1994). Tripartite assessment of the efficacy of eye movement desensitization in a multi-phobic patient. *Journal of Anxiety Disorders, 8,* 259–276.

Bauman, W., & Melnyk, W. T. (1994). A controlled comparison of eye movements and finger tapping in the treatment of test anxiety. *Journal of Behavior Therapy and Experimental Psychiatry, 25,* 29–33.

Boudewyns, P. A., Stwertka, S. A., Hyer, L. A., Albrecht, J. W., & Sperr, E. V. (1993). Eye movement desensitization for PTSD of combat: A treatment outcome pilot study. *The Behavior Therapist, 16*(2), 29–33.

EMDR. (1995). Efficacy of EMDR research and publications. *EMDR Network Newsletter, 1*(1).

Hekmat, H., Groth, S., & Rogers, D. (1994). Pain ameliorating effect of eye movement desensitization. *Journal of Behavior Therapy and Experimental Psychiatry, 25,* 121–129.

Herbert, J. D., & Mueser, K. T. (1992). Eye movement desensitization: A critique of the evidence. *Journal of Behavior Therapy and Experimental Psychiatry, 23,* 169–174.

Kleinknecht, R. A., & Morgan, M. P. (1992). Treatment of posttraumatic stress disorder with eye movement desensitization. *Journal of Behavior Therapy and Experimental Psychiatry, 23,* 43–49.

Lipke, H. J. & Botkin, A. L. (1992). Case studies of eye movement desensitization and reprocessing (EMDR) with chronic post-traumatic stress disorder. *Psychoperthy, 29,* 591–595.

Lohr, J. M., Kleinknecht, R. A., Conley, A. T., Dal Cerro, S., Schmidt, J., & Sonntag, M. E. (1992). A methodological critique of the current status of eye movement desensitization (EMD). *Journal of Behavior Therapy and Experimental Psychiatry, 23,* 159–167.

Lyons, J. A., & Keane, T. M. (1989). Implosive therapy for the treatment of traumatic stress. *Journal of Traumatic Stress, 2,* 137–152.

Montgomery, R. W., & Ayllon, T. (1994). Eye movement desensitization across subjects: Subjective and physicological measures of treatment efficacy. *Journal of Behavior Therapy and Experimental Psychiatry, 25,* 217–230.

National Association of Social Workers. (1993). *Code of ethics.* Washington, DC: Author.

Pellicer, X. (1993). Eye movement desensitization treatment of a child's nightmares: A case report. *Journal of Behavior Therapy and Experimental Psychiatry, 25,* 73–75.

Pitman, R. K., Orr, S. P., Altman, B., Longpre, R. E., Poire, R. E., & Lasko, N. B. (1993, May). *A controlled study of EMDR treatment for post-traumatic stress disorder.* Paper presented at the American Psychiatric Association Annual Meeting, Washington, DC.

Renfrey, G., & Spates, C. R. (1994). Eye movement desensitization: A partial dismantling study. *Journal of Behavior Therapy and Experimental Psychiatry, 25,* 231–239.

Sanderson, A., & Carpenter, R. (1992). Eye movement desensitization versus image confrontation: A single-session crossover study of 58 phobic subjects. *Journal of Behavior Therapy and Experimental Psychiatry, 23,* 269–275.

Shapiro, F. (1989). Eye movement desensitization: A new treatment for posttraumatic stress disorder. *Journal of Behavior Therapy and Experimental Psychiatry, 20,* 211–217.

Shapiro, F. (1995). *Eye movement desensitization and reprocessing: Basic principles, protocols and procedures.* New York: Guilford Press.

Wolpe, J., & Abrams, J. (1991). Post-traumatic stress disorder overcome by eye movement desensitization: A case report. *Journal of Behavior Therapy and Experimental Psychiatry, 22,* 39–43.

Rejoinder to Ms. Colosetti   Patrick S. Bordnick

Ms. Colosetti is obviously a well-trained EMDR therapist and puts forth the usual rhetoric in support of EMDR. Her position, like that of many other EMDR enthusiasts, seems fueled by a dream to have this therapeutic technique change the world overnight. The proponents of EMDR try to use case reports and studies with flawed methodology to support the widespread use and dissemination of this technique. Currently there does not appear to be any well-controlled outcome study clearly demonstrating that EMDR is an efficacious treatment for PTSD or any other psychiatric disorder. To the contrary, most of the outcome studies demonstrate that EMDR is *not* helpful in reducing symptomatology.

Ms. Colosetti states that "research on EMDR provides a compelling justification for its use in clinical treatment." This statement is completely groundless, if not unethical, in nature. The research on EMDR lends little if any scientific credence to this procedure. In fact, only anecdotal evidence exists with regard to EMDR efficacy. As I state in my original position, the use of interventions that have only anecdotal support has been condemned by the NASW (1992). Also, Ms. Colosetti tries to use the NASW *Code of Ethics* (1990) as justification and support for the use of EMDR by social workers. She does not clearly discuss the context in which EMDR will be performed. Is it for research or clinical practice? I would support social workers doing empirically controlled outcome research on EMDR. I would caution against the use of EMDR as a clinical intervention until empirically controlled studies demonstrating its efficacy have been completed.

The issue of intense training is discussed as if this were a proper substitute for clinical research. No matter how good the training on EMDR, if the intervention is harmful or not helpful, you are not increasing the efficacy of the intervention through this training process. Using excellent training techniques does not ensure that we are helping clients. The only way to do this is to train social workers in interventions that have been shown to be efficacious through empirically based outcome studies.

Lastly, the discussion of EMDR as a brief treatment technique that can increase our effectiveness and efficiency as practitioners represents a straw-man argument. EMDR has not been shown to be efficacious, so we need to stop acting as if this intervention has scientific support of its use before we make global statements regarding its use or potential benefits to clients and society. Again, we must remember that as social workers our ultimate goal is to help our clients. To ensure this, we need to use interventions that have been shown to be efficacious by empirical research and not anecdotal evidence. This is perhaps the only way we can ensure that we are not causing our clients undue harm.

REFERENCES

National Association of Social Workers (NASW Delegate Assembly) (1990). *NASW code of ethics* [Brochure]. Washington, DC: Author.

National Association of Social Workers (National Committee on Lesbian and Gay Issues) (1992). "Reparative" or "conversion" therapies for lesbian and gay men. *NASW Position Statement.* Washington, DC: Author.

NO

PATRICK S. BORDNICK

> Although a method becomes popular, it may not be based on sound research principles or even common sense (Gibbs, 1991, p. 16).

I wholeheartedly accepted the *no* position on this topic, because of social work being inundated with practitioners using methods that have never been put to rigorous scientific tests to determine their efficacy, and worse, using psychosocial interventions that research has already shown to be ineffective. In my response, I concentrate on two areas. First I present clinical research on the efficacy of EMDR, followed by a discussion of the relevance of professional ethics and practice standards to providing EMDR services at this point.

Research on the Efficacy of EMDR

Eye-movement desensitization and reprocessing therapy was developed and marketed by Francis Shapiro in the late 1980s as a purportedly highly effective and efficient cure for a wide variety of psychiatric syndromes. Since that time, Dr. Shapiro and her colleagues have developed an extensive organization, complete with a formal institute, a national system of (expensive!) training workshops, secret treatment manuals (not to be shared or discussed with those not trained!), official certifications, a newsletter, and an e-mail network.

More than a dozen case studies on the use of EMDR have been reported in the literature. Here are some examples. Shapiro (1989a) published a case on the treatment of a woman who was raped and experienced posttraumatic symptoms. The outcome measures were a SUDS scale (subjective units of distress, as rated by the client on a 0 to 10 scale) and a scale of positive cognitions, and at three month's follow-up this patient reported improvements on these scales. In another case report of a woman who experienced intrusive thoughts, it was found at six months posttreatment that she was almost completely free of these thoughts, and she had reduced SUDS ratings when the thoughts did recur (Puk, 1991). In another study, a woman who had been sexually abused was treated with one session of EMDR. At 12 months posttreatment she was found to be almost completely free of her nightmares and anxiety surrounding the abuse (Puk, 1991). And yet another report involved the one session of EMDR treatment of a ten-year-old girl suffering from nightmares. At six-month follow-up, she reported the absence of nightmares and reduced subjective anxiety ratings (Pellicer, 1993).

Lacking proper documentation of the numbers of treatment successes *and* failures, and of spontaneous improvements or deteriorations in the absence of treatment, case reports of the above nature, no matter how numerous, can, at best, be seen as *suggestive* of a new treatment's efficacy or ineffectiveness. Case studies are an excellent way to begin disseminating information about a promising new experimental treatment, but they do not serve as an adequate justification to begin the widespread adoption of that treatment. Moreover, case reports on using EMDR are plagued with various methodological problems, such as the use of self-reports of anxiety or other symptomatology, having the therapist conduct assessment of client improvements, the possible role of placebo influences, spontaneous remission, and so forth.

Fortunately for the purposes of science, there have been some group outcome studies on the effectiveness of EMDR, using a simple pretest–posttest design. One early one was reported by Marquis (1991), who treated seventy-eight patients suffering from a variety of anxiety-related disorders and complicating secondary diagnoses, using EMDR. The outcome measures were primarily self-report, but patients did report improvement, overall. However, the EMDR treatment was provided along with *other* interventions, complicating any claims for the unique efficacy of EMDR.

Forbes, Creamer, and Rycroft (1994) used standardized measures and self-report ratings as the dependent variables in a study of EMDR on eight patients diagnosed with PTSD. The results indicated that some of the PTSD symptoms were reduced, and half of the clients met the criteria for PTSD posttreatment and at three-month follow-up. Fifty percent success is not the same as a 100 percent cure.

In addition to the uncontrolled group outcome studies, there have been a few nomothetic investigations using various control groups. The first such investigation involved twenty-two patients who were randomly assigned to either EMDR or to an imaginal exposure treatment condition (Shapiro, 1989b). The results indicated that the patients who received EMDR reported greater improvement than patients in the imaginal exposure treatment. Several methodological problems exist in this investigation. First, the dependent variables were all subjective self-reports of distress, symptomatology, and cognition ratings. The experimenter completed the assessments and also conducted treatment sessions. The possibility of placebo effects may have accounted for the changes in the patients receiving EMDR.

In a study of fifty-eight phobia subjects, Sanderson and Carpenter (1992) compared EMDR with an exposure-control condition (image confrontation). Patients *within both* groups had reductions in SUDS ratings on exposure to the feared stimuli, but no SUDS differences were found *between* EMDR and imaginal exposure. This may potentially indicate that the eye-movement component of EMDR is an unnecessary element in this approach, superfluous to the exposure aspects of treatment.

Several other studies support this hypothesis. Renfrey and Spates (1994), in a study of 22 patients with PTSD, concluded that saccadic eye movements do not appear to be a factor in treatment efficacy, and that the agent responsible for change with EMDR is still unknown. In another investigation, it was determined that the reprocessing component of EMDR was not the cause of changes that are believed to occur with EMDR, and also that the effects of the EMD might simply be a form of counterconditioning (Hekmat, Groth, & Rogers, 1994).

Using a multiple-baseline design, Montgomery and Ayllon (1994) investigated EMDR with and without saccadic eye movements, and found that five out of six patients with PTSD had significant positive changes on self-report measures. However, improvements in psychophysiological measures (measures less amenable to placebo influences) did not occur. One interesting finding was that treatment without the saccadic eye movement component did not produce a significant change in clients' SUDS ratings. This could be because the eye-movement aspect is simply a more credible placebo treatment.

The first controlled investigation of EMDR that used standardized assessments and physiological measures was conducted on twenty patients diagnosed with PTSD (Boudewyns, Stwertka, Hyer, Albrecht, & Sperr, 1993). Patients were randomly assigned to either the experimental (EMDR) group, exposure therapy control group, or no-treatment control group conditions. Pre and post measurements consisted of self-report instruments, including the Clinician Administered PTSD Scale (CAPS), the Impact of Event Scale, Mississippi Scale for Combat-Related PTSD scale, and SUDS ratings. Physiological measures of heart rate, skin temperature, and skin conductance were also recorded. Significant changes were found on the SUDS ratings *during* treatment sessions for the EMD group, but pretreatment and posttreatment ratings did not significantly improve. All of the groups did not show any significant changes on the other measures. The absence of changes on the standardized psychometric measures or on physiological responses to imaginal confrontation with feared stimuli among the EMDR patients is a telling omission, raising the possibility that the effects of EMDR are primarily placebolike in nature, mainly influencing client self-reports.

Bates, Montgomery, McGlynn, and Mattke (1995) assigned fourteen spider-phobic clients either to EMDR treatment or to a no-treatment control condition. Subjective, behavioral (approach test measures) and physiological measures of fear were assessed during exposure to a live spider, before and after treatment. Those receiving EMDR reported greater reductions in fear (the ubiquitous SUDS ratings again!) but evidenced no improvements in physiological responding or in behavioral avoidance. The authors concluded that "The efficacy of EMD with specific phobias was not established in this experiment. Additional experimentation that controls for demand effects might show that EMDR effects are, in fact, no more than poorly controlled demand–placebo effects on experimental measures" (Bates et al., 1995, p. 11).

On balance, the evidence that EMDR therapy produces clinically significant improvements, much less complete "cures," for posttraumatic stress disorder and other behavioral problems is weak. Many of the positive outcomes can be attributed to EMDR simply being a more credible placebo treatment. What has been lacking are blind evaluators, unconnected with providing treatment, assessing the presence or absence of diagnostic criteria pretreatment and posttreatment. Such would be the true litmus test of the efficacy of EMDR and other psychosocial treatments. Formal assessments of the degree of credibility that clients ascribed to their individual treatments is also necessary to control for the placebo-value of EMDR. Simply having a so-called placebo control group is insufficient. It must be an equivalently credible placebo treatment.

Informed clinical researchers, including social workers, have concluded that the widespread application of EMDR in clinical settings is premature (e.g., Steketee & Goldstein, 1994), because of the lack of adequate supportive evidence of efficacy. The secrecy heretofore surrounding EMDR training has hindered clinical research on the procedure and has been held by some to be a contradiction of the canons of the scientific method (e.g., Aceirno, Hersen, Van Hasselt, Tremont, & Meuser, 1994).

Several recently published review articles discuss the research literature on EMDR, and here is what these authors have concluded:

> EMDR at this point in time, does not have prescriptive treatment status (Acierno et al., 1994, p. 297)

> While the interest and enthusiasm which EMD has generated is substantial, the amount of empirical research evaluating the procedure is small (Lohr et al., 1992, p. 166)

Ethical Issues

It is becoming increasingly recognized that if a given intervention is known to be effective in the treatment of a given problem/disorder, then social workers have an ethical obligation to offer that treatment as a first choice and to provide less well-supported interventions only after those with a stronger empirical foundation have been given a fair trial and shown not to be effective (cf. Thyer, 1995). Moreover, anecdotal evidence alone is no longer an adequate empirical foundation. Here is what the NASW recently proclaimed with respect to one psychosocial "treatment":

> Proponents of reparative therapies claim—without documentation—many successes. They assert that their processes are supported by conclusive scientific data which are in fact *little more than anecdotal...* empirical research does not demonstrate that... sexual orientation (heterosexual or homosexual) can be changed through these so-called reparative therapies. (NASW, 1992, p. 1, emphasis added)

The NASW position statement then goes on to assert that social workers providing reparative therapy are engaging in an *unethical* practice, in part because of the lack of an adequate empirical foundation. The phrase "EMDR" could be substituted into the above quote with accuracy.

This is not a new point of view. Consider the statement by Steven Segal:

> ... any new program established by an agency is unproven. A control study design therefore seems not only ethical but mandatory to allow an accurate evaluation.... It is not unethical to deprive someone of a treatment when that treatment is not an established one within the agency. It is *unethical* to grant such treatment when no systematic assessment for possible negative effects has been carried out. (Segal, 1972, p. 10, emphasis added)

More succinctly put: "Before widespread use, a method should be carefully evaluated" (Gibbs, 1991, p. 8).

Such views, if widely adopted, would have far-reaching implications for social work practice and education. They certainly seem to apply to EMDR and raise troubling questions as to the mad rush to disseminate (expensive) training in the procedure before thoroughly testing it.

According to the NASW Code of Ethics (1990), "Social workers should base practice upon recognized knowledge relevant to social work" (p. 9), and "Social workers should critically examine and keep current with emerging knowledge relevant to social work" (p. 9). Furthermore, the NASW's (1989) *Standards for the Practice of Clinical Social Work* state that "Clinical social workers shall have and continue to develop specialized knowledge and understanding of individuals, families and groups and of therapeutic and preventive interventions" (p. 6). Failure to use this emerging knowledge, and continuance of using ineffective methods or untested methods, including EMDR, would be an apparent violation of NASW standards. Of course, if credible empirical research supporting the efficacy of EMDR arises, then future social work practitioners would be ethically bound to use this intervention.

In closing, using interventions that have not been shown to be efficacious in scientifically controlled research is comparable to unleashing a potentially harmful psychological virus on our patients. There is no justification for exposing our patients, who place their trust in us, to the potential risks of interventions primarily supported by anecdote, such as EMDR.

REFERENCES

Acierno, R., Hersen, M., Van Hasselt, V. B., Tremont, G., & Meuser, K. T. (1994). Review of the validation of eye-movement desensitization and reprocessing: A scientific and ethical dilemma. *Clinical Psychology Review, 14,* 287–299.
Bates, L. W., Montgomery, R. W., McGlynn, F. D., & Mattke, T. G. (1995, May). *Experimental investigation of eye movement desensitization (EMD) with*

spider phobics. Paper presented at the annual meeting of the Association for Behavior Analysis, Washington, DC.

Boudewyns, P. A., Stwertka, S. A., Hyer, L. A., Albrecht, J. W., & Sperr, E. V. (1993). Eye movement desensitization for PTSD of combat: A treatment outcome pilot study. *The Behavior Therapist, 16,* 29–33.

Forbes, D., Creamer, M., & Rycroft, P. (1994). Eye movement desensitization and reprocessing in posttraumatic stress disorder: A pilot study using assessment measures. *Journal of Behavior Research and Experimental Psychiatry, 25,* 113–120.

Gibbs, L. (1991). *Scientific reasoning for social workers.* New York: MacMillan.

Hekmat, H., Groth, S., & Rogers, D. (1994). Pain ameliorating effect of eye movement desensitization. *Journal of Behavior Therapy and Experimental Psychiatry, 25,* 121–129.

Lohr, J. M., Kleinknecht, R. A., Conley, A. T., Dal Cerro, S., Schmidt, J., & Sonntag, M. E. (1992). A methodological critique of the current status of eye movement desensitization (EMD). *Journal of Behavior Therapy and Experimental Psychiatry, 23,* 159–167.

Marquis, J. N. (1991). A report on seventy-eight cases treated by eye movement desensitization. *Journal of Behavior Therapy and Experimental Psychiatry, 22,* 187–192.

Montgomery, R. W., & Ayllon, T. (1994). Eye movement desensitization across subjects: Subjective and physiological measures of treatment efficacy. *Journal of Behavior Therapy and Experimental Psychiatry, 25,* 217–230.

National Association of Social Workers, National Committee on Lesbian and Gay Issues. (1992). *"Reparative" or "conversion" therapies for lesbian and gay men* (Position Statement). Washington, DC: Author.

National Association of Social Workers. (1989). *NASW Standards for the practice of clinical social work.* Washington, DC: Author.

National Association of Social Workers. (1990). *NASW code of ethics.* Washington, DC: Author.

Pellicer, X. (1993). Eye movement desensitization treatment of a child's nightmares: A case report. *Journal of Behavior Therapy and Experimental Psychiatry, 24,* 73–75.

Puk, G. (1991). Treating traumatic memories: A case report on the eye movement desensitization procedure. *Journal of Behavior Therapy and Experimental Psychiatry, 22,* 149–151.

Renfrey, G., & Spates, C. R. (1994). Eye movement desensitization: A partial dismantling study. *Journal of Behavior Therapy and Experimental Psychiatry, 25,* 231–239.

Sanderson, A., & Carpenter, R. (1992). Eye movement desensitization versus image confrontation: A single-session crossover study of 58 phobic subjects. *Journal of Behavior Therapy and Experimental Psychiatry, 23,* 269–275.

Segal, S. P. (1972). Research on the outcome of social work intervention. *Journal of Health and Social Behavior, 13,* 3–17.

Shapiro, F. (1989a). Eye movement desensitization: A new treatment for post-traumatic stress disorder. *Journal of Behavior Therapy and Experimental Psychiatry, 20,* 211–217.

Shapiro, F. (1989b). Efficacy of eye movement desensitization procedure in the treatment of traumatic memories. *Journal of Traumatic Stress, 2,* 199–223.

Steketee, G., & Goldstein, A. J. (1994). Reflections on Shapiro's reflections: Testing EMDR within a theoretical context. *The Behavior Therapist, 17,* 156–157.

Thyer, B. A. (1995). Promoting an empiricist agenda in the human services: An ethical and humanistic imperative. *Journal of Behavior Therapy and Experimental Psychiatry, 26,* 93–98.

Rejoinder to Dr. Bordnick SHARMAN D. COLOSETTI

> The results of studies by researchers who have never been trained in the use of EMDR (Sanderson & Carpenter, 1992; Tallis & Smith, 1994; Acierno, Tremont, Last & Montgomery, 1994) cannot provide definitive conclusions about the efficacy of the method as it is actually used in clinical practice (Shapiro, 1995, p. 333).

Just as equivalently credible placebo treatments are necessary to control for the placebo value of EMDR, so is the correct use of the EMDR procedures in its evaluation. Now that EMDR is out of the closet with the publication of the book by Shapiro (1995), it will be easier to accurately evaluate its efficacy and discover its relevant components.

The first study using EMDR was a controlled study published in the *Journal of Traumatic Stress,* a peer-reviewed journal (Shapiro, 1989). The first controlled study using systematic desensitization was eight years after it was first introduced; seven years for imaginal flooding (Puk, 1994). As anyone who has submitted an article for publication knows, there is often a gap between an article's acceptance and its publication. However, thanks to the EMDR Network, research studies are more readily available to facilitate future refinements.

One study by Wilson, Tinker, and Becker (1994) provides a true litmus test of the efficacy of EMDR. Eighty subjects with traumatic memories were given three one-and-a-half-hour sessions of EMDR by one of five EMDR-trained, licensed therapists. Subjects were randomly assigned to a therapist and to a treatment or a delayed treatment condition. Before receiving treatment, the delayed treatment group showed no improvement. After three sessions of EMDR, the treatment subjects demonstrated statistically significant change in reduction of anxiety and presenting complaints and an increase in positive cognitions. The delayed treatment group also showed statistically significant change on all measures. At the ninety-day follow-up, effects were maintained. In this study, the principal investigator did not provide the treatment, and an independent assessor collected all of the pretest and posttest measures. In conclusion, the question remains:

> Should the rapid treatment effects of EMDR be denied to a client who is informed it is an experimental procedure, particularly when the treatment may take only a few sessions in some cases as compared to several months or more with other modalities? I think this is a choice for an informed client. (Puk, 1994, p. 201)

REFERENCES

Acierno, R., Tremont, G., Last, C., & Montgomery, D. (1994). Tripartite assessment of the efficacy of eye-movement desensitization in a multi-phobic patient. *Journal of Anxiety Disorders, 8,* 259–276.

Puk, G. (1994). EMDR: The utility of clinical observation. *The Behavior Therapist, 17,* 201–202.

Sanderson, A., & Carpenter, R. (1992). Eye movement desensitization versus image confrontation: A single-session crossover study of 58 phobic subjects. *Journal of Behavior Therapy and Experimental Psychiatry, 23,* 269–275.

Shapiro, F. (1989). Efficacy of eye movement desensitization procedure in the treatment of traumatic memories. *Journal of Traumatic Stress, 2*(2), 199–223.

Shapiro, F. (1995). *Eye movement desensitization and reprocessing: Basic principles, protocols, and procedures.* New York: Guilford Press.

Tallis, F., & Smith, E. (1994). Does eye movement desensitization facilitate emotional processing? *Behaviour Research and Therapy, 32,* 459–461.

Wilson, S. A., Tinker, R. H., & Becker, L. A. (1994, November). *Efficacy of eye movement desensitization and reprocessing (EMDR) treatment for trauma victims.* Paper presented at the annual meeting of the International Society for Traumatic Stress Studies.

Should Social Workers Attempt to Apply Specific Interventions for Clients with Specific Problems?

Betty J. Blythe, Ph.D., is a Professor with the Boston College Graduate School of Social Work. Her research interests are in the areas of intensive family preservation services and child welfare. She has published extensively in practice evaluation, conducting research in social agencies, and social work programs and practice for children and families.

Geraldine Jackson-White, Ed.D., is an assistant professor of social work with the University of Georgia. Dr. Jackson-White received her MSW and her Ed.D. in adult education from the University of Georgia. Her primary academic interest is in developing professional education programs that prepare social work practitioners for competent practice in unique and complex settings.

YES

BETTY J. BLYTHE

Helping clients deal with specific problems calls for a thorough assessment of the problem, some form of contractual client–worker agreement on goals and objectives, thoughtful development of an intervention or treatment plan, and ongoing monitoring of the implementation of the intervention plan and its effects. The entire process is noted by continual data gathering, analysis, and decision making as the social worker seeks to find the most effective method of helping the client achieve the desired outcomes.

To address this question regarding the importance of specific interventions, we must first examine what is meant by "specific problems." As a social worker helps a client define the reasons for seeking help, a process of continually refining the description of the problem ensues. This process involves gathering information about the onset and duration of the problem, the frequency with which the problem occurs, and the magnitude or severity of the problem (Blythe & Tripodi, 1989). It also involves determining such things as conditions or factors that seem to maintain the problem and previous attempts to address the problem. *Problem* is a general term used by social workers, but it can actually refer to any of a number of conditions, situations, or issues that a client may face. The specification of the "problem" is further influenced by the extent to which the client is voluntary or involuntary and the aegis and constraints under which the worker is operating. The following examples help to clarify the range of possibilities.

At one extreme, we might have a client who self-refers for a substance abuse problem, drinking. The social worker works at an outpatient community mental health center, and the client is able to pay for his treatment with health insurance, without his employer being informed of the situation. The frequency of the client's drinking has escalated from social drinking, to heavy social drinking, to heavy drinking on evenings and weekends. The client, a middle-aged man, is concerned that his drinking is beginning to affect his relationships with his partner and his two children, who live with him. On occasion, he also has noted that the drinking is affecting his performance at work. The client, with the help of the worker, defines the problem as the effects his drinking is having on his personal and professional life, and he seeks a goal of eliminating alcohol consumption. The worker gathers additional information, such as the client's previous attempts to control his drinking, his urges to drink, and his family members' and friends' responses to his drinking. On additional assessment and analysis, this client's situation will be further specified into a series of objectives that must be accomplished to meet this goal, and other goals also might be identified.

As another example offering some contrast, this client is a young woman whose two children are being removed from her because she left them unattended to make a telephone call from a nearby phone booth (she cannot afford a phone in her apartment). The social worker is a public child welfare worker who is seeing the client as a result of an investigation of neglect based on a report from a neighbor. The client has previously been investigated for neglect on two occasions. The client apparently uses crack, and the allegation is that she made the telephone call about a drug deal, although the client maintains that she was trying to call her sister to secure transportation to her WIC appointment. There have been other situations in which the children have not had adequate supervision. The worker and the client decide that the immediate problem is that the children need to have a stable, safe living situation, although the client is not able or willing to admit to a substance abuse problem at this time. Because the client obviously loves her children and wants them to be safe and healthy, she is able to see that their safety is a "problem," although she cannot acknowledge her substance abuse. The worker gathers information about possible resources and the client's network of supports to determine an appropriate placement for the children. Work with this client will likely result in specification of additional treatment goals and objectives over time so that her children can return home.

Although these examples are meant to depict somewhat extreme instances, they nonetheless demonstrate some of the many facets of the term *problem*. Both clients suffer from substance abuse, yet several other variables such as their life circumstances, level and type of abuse, ability to acknowledge their abuse, and the degree to which they are voluntary or involuntary clients all lead to extremely different specific definitions of the problem and to different treatment goals and objectives.

It is important to consider treatment goals and objectives at this juncture, because they are the link between assessment data and treatment plans. A treatment goal is the long-term outcome that is sought, whereas the practice objective (also known as a subgoal) is more temporally proximate and directly related to the imminent work with the client (Ivanoff, Blythe, & Tripodi, 1994). Goals might be oriented to maintenance of a current situation (such as keeping a job), prevention (such as preventing unplanned pregnancy), or change (such as increasing parenting skills). In any case, goals and objectives should develop out of the assessment data collected and analyzed by the social worker. Any given client typically has several goals, some that must be accomplished earlier in treatment and some that will be acknowledged and/or adopted later in treatment. The timing of working on these goals relates to such factors as the potential for crisis surrounding attainment of the goal, the necessity of time ordering goal attainment, and the readiness of the client to work on specific goals. For example, the client who appears to be addicted to crack but unable to admit it may eventually be willing and able to address her substance abuse problem, but the more immediate goal relates to the problem of the children's safety.

Just as client problems cannot be simplistically defined as "substance abuse" or "child abuse" and treatment goals are highly specific, operational definitions of the client's "problem," specific interventions must be carefully detailed to address the specific conditions present in each case. Interventions cannot be simplistically defined as "social skills training" or "family therapy" or "gestalt therapy." And, an intervention must be backed by a plan for implementing it.

Rosen (1993) describes "systematic planned practice," which is a framework for organizing practice decisions and activities, regardless of theoretical framework. In systematic planned practice, client problems are formulated, outcomes (or goals) are identified, and priorities for treatment are selected. At all times, the worker is concerned about the client's best interests. Accordingly, the worker's actions are purposefully directed toward selecting and implementing a treatment plan that will achieve the identified outcomes.

Specific interventions are worker-directed activities or tasks that are undertaken to achieve the outcomes identified in the treatment goals or objectives. Rosen's (1993) description of three levels of defining interventions is of particular interest here. The first, intervention responses, describes such worker actions as the use of specific interviewing skills. Intervention strategies are more complex and describe a set of specific responses that are intended to accomplish a specific outcome. Finally, intervention programs describe an entire treatment effort, a more complex plan including a range of intervention strategies and responses. With each level of intervention, the degree of complexity increases. Ideally, a treatment plan for an individual client will identify the intervention strategies that a worker intends to use for each client goal.

There are several reasons for defining interventions as specifically as possible, at least at the level of intervention strategies. To begin, a well-defined intervention is necessary to assess treatment integrity (Yeaton & Sechrest, 1981). Treatment integrity means that an intervention plan is implemented as intended. If the intervention is not implemented as planned, then the intended outcomes cannot realistically be expected (in other words, the goal is not likely to be achieved). Workers, supervisors, and others cannot determine if a vague or ill-defined intervention has been implemented as intended, because the intervention responses and strategies and the exact conditions of implementation have not been defined. Treatment integrity typically is assessed by such means as reviewing audiotaped or videotaped treatment sessions to determine compliance with the treatment plan.

As the work with the client unfolds, the social worker will monitor the client's response to the treatment plan as implemented. Assuming that the intervention is being implemented as intended, the social worker will expect to see that the client is making progress toward the intended goal. If progress is not being made, the social worker will consider the following options: continue the intervention because it is expected that the effect will be somewhat delayed, alter the treatment to add or subtract selected interventive responses or strategies, increase the dose or strength of the intervention, or replace the treatment plan with an entirely new one. Obviously, the social worker is not able to make such careful decisions and to modify treatment plans in response to monitoring data unless the treatment is sufficiently specific to allow for such analysis.

Monitoring client progress allows the social worker to determine if the treatment plans need to be altered, as described above. At the end of treatment or after a follow-up interval, this monitoring also allows the worker to consider whether the intervention was effective. If the monitoring data suggest that the intervention was effective, the worker will want to consider using this intervention again with another client having the same goal and similar circumstances surrounding the description of the client problem. If the worker is able to replicate these results with two or more clients, the findings should be shared with colleagues in an effort to develop new practice knowledge (Blythe & Briar, 1985). The treatment plan must be very carefully specified to enable the social worker to implement the same intervention with another client or to describe the intervention to colleagues in sufficient detail, such that they can implement the intervention with their clients.

Finally, there are instances in which the entire intervention plan cannot be articulated at the outset of the intervention phase. These are likely to be cases that have some unusual circumstances surrounding the problem, the worker has limited experience in dealing with such a problem, or the knowledge base for addressing the problem is insufficient. In these cases, the worker will develop the intervention plan in a methodical fashion, in response to ongoing assessment and monitoring data. A specific intervention plan is essential in such cases. Granting that it may not always be easy to define the particular components of an intervention or to determine what is a sufficient level of detail, this author nonetheless maintains that failure to do so will result in intervention that can only be viewed as a black box.

REFERENCES

Blythe, B. J., & Briar, S. (1985). Developing empirically-based models of practice. *Social Work, 30,* 483–488.
Blythe, B. J., & Tripodi, T. (1989). *Measurement in direct practice.* Newbury Park, CA: Sage.
Ivanoff, A., Blythe, B. J., & Tripodi, T. (1994). *Involuntary clients in social work practice: A research-based approach.* Hawthorne, NY: Aldine de Gruyter.
Rosen, A. (1993). Systematic planned practice. *Social Service Review, 67,* 84–100.
Yeaton, W. H., & Sechrest, L. (1981). Critical dimensions in the choice and maintenance of successful treatments: Strength, integrity, and effectiveness. *Journal of Consulting and Clinical Psychology, 49,* 156–186.

Rejoinder to Dr. Blythe   GERALDINE JACKSON-WHITE

Dr. Blythe has developed an argument for specific interventions that clearly illustrates the traditional epistemology of practice. The social worker is the expert who assumes the leadership role in problem identification and resolution. Although her argument for specific interventions is based on tried and true approaches to social work practice, I still maintain that this approach to practice denies the uniqueness of the individual, has inherent dangers of malpractice, and reduces the art of practice to a series of methodical steps.

Throughout her discussion, Dr. Blythe consistently refers to the tasks of the social worker in the intervention process. The social worker has to assume the responsibility for gathering data, assessing the information, developing treatment goals and objectives, and monitoring the accomplishment of all of these. Social workers, as professional helpers, should be involved with all of these processes; however, the manner in which they are implemented is the issue at hand. Rather than the social worker assuming the leadership role in all of these activities, I am suggesting that the approach to practice be less prescriptive and more interactive. Why not let the client work more closely with the worker in framing the problem and determining the most appropriate ways to reach solutions? If clients are allowed to assume ownership of the problem, they will probably assume ownership of the solution as well. Although two very different clients may present with the same "problem," such as substance abuse, as Dr. Blythe discusses, the social worker must be able to work with that individual client to determine how this is a problem for him or her and also to determine how the client may want to approach resolution or elimination of the problem. Throughout her discussion, Dr. Blythe suggests that the social worker must take on the responsibility for assessment, developing goals and objectives, and monitoring accomplishment of the intervention. This approach places all responsibility on the social worker and implies that if the client does not improve, there may be a problem with the intervention, or there is a problem with the client's adherence to the "plan," or that perhaps the worker made a wrong selection of intervention. In either instance, the worker does all of the work, and the client is the "beneficiary." This approach to practice clearly denies the uniqueness of the individual, runs the risk of malpractice, and reduces the art of social work practice to applications of methodical steps. Dr. Blythe asserts that the reasons for using specific interventions is to assess treatment integrity, to determine client progress, to have a basis for changing the intervention, and to evaluate if the intervention was effective. These are noble reasons, and I do not disagree. I believe that social workers can apply these same evaluative tools to any intervention to determine effectiveness. I contend that the problem is not with the evaluative processes; rather, it is with how the problem is defined and how the client is involved in the treatment interaction that will support the uniqueness of the individual, reduce the potential for incorrect treatment, and provide for the inclusion of the art of practice with the science of practice.

NO

GERALDINE JACKSON-WHITE

I am opposed to the method of practice suggested by this question because it means that social workers will deliver what I consider to be "robot practice"— practice that does not consider the dynamic and powerful interaction that occurs between worker and client in the helping encounter. Applying specific interventions to specific client problems is prescriptive and immediately places the worker in a position of power that does not consider the client's role in identifying and solving the problem. I am opposed to this approach to practice because I believe (1) it ignores the uniqueness of the individual and relies on prescriptions for practice; (2) it can potentially increase the occurrence of malpractice suits against social workers; and (3) it removes the art from social work practice and suggests that it should only be scientific.

Uniqueness of the Individual

Throughout my career as a social worker, and I might add, even before I became a professional social worker, the one consistent aspect of this profession that was appealing to me was the emphasis on respect for the uniqueness of the individual. "Honoring the uniqueness of the individual is central to social work practice.... Traditional models of helping are based on practice assumptions that restrict the practitioner's ability to appreciate unique aspects of clients" (Pray, 1991, p. 80). The application of specific interventions to specific problems suggests that the social worker who has the expert theoretical knowledge is the expert and will solve the client's problem. This assumption, however, does not allow for the client to accept ownership of the problem nor of the solution. I do not think this is the intent of practitioners, but using this method of social work practice certainly would lead to this result. As Bisman (1994, p. 13) indicates, "Social work practice cannot be reduced to an easy set of rules.... Every client is a special and unique individual and must not be treated as a member of a class of persons."

Prescriptive practice does not take into account the diverse experiences and cultures clients may bring into the helping relationship. Iglehart and Becerra (1994) address the increasing numbers of culturally diverse populations in this country and challenge the profession to become more ethnically sensitive in the entire spectrum of social work service delivery. They state, "In the era of the mosaic society, social service providers are charged with the task of responding to the needs of diverse groups in ways that recognize, respect, and tolerate group differences"(Iglehart & Becerra, 1994, p. 2). Applying specific interventions to specific problems also presents the danger of drawing generalizations about clients who may share similar characteristics but very different problems (Bisman, 1994).

Prescriptive practice is the direct result of traditional professional education. Traditional professional education is based on the scientific method. "Academia's positivist, technical rational outlook has influenced social work's educational traditions and tasks" (Papell & Skolnik, 1992, p. 18). Suggesting that specific interventions should be applied to specific client problems is clearly in accordance with the traditional method of the philosophical underpinnings of professional social work education. I contend that this approach to practice not only denies the uniqueness of the individual client, but it also denies the unique life experiences and culture of the practitioner. Social workers are not robots interacting with clients. The interaction between worker and client should be dynamic, and it should allow for the client to assume a leadership role in identifying the problem and framing alternative solutions. This will result in the client exercising his or her right to self-determination. As Saleeby (1992, p. 7) points out, "A helper may be best defined as collaborator or consultant; . . . but definitely not the only one in the situation to have relevant, important, even esoteric knowledge."

Some social workers are evaluating the efficacy of the traditional episte- mology of practice and suggesting that the profession begin to move into the di- rection of practice modalities that are more in accordance with the values and ethics of social work (Bisman, 1994; Papell & Skolnik, 1992; Saleeby, 1992). As the profession continues to explore alternative ways to improve practice, I believe we will see more exploration into practice modalities that are less prescriptive and more responsive to the unique and dynamic qualities of each client.

Increase in Malpractice Cases

Although confirmed information about the frequency of malpractice cases was not available, the *NASW News* recently reported that "The largest percentage of malpractice suits stem from incorrect treatment and sexual misconduct . . ." (Law- suits, 1995). If social workers are being sued for incompetent practice, perhaps it is because practitioners applied a specific intervention to a specific problem with- out consideration of the peculiarities of the particular case. One could assume that the intervention(s) selected in these cases was not appropriate to helping the client resolve or eliminate the problem.

Some may take the position that the occurrence of malpractice cases in so- cial work is a mere reflection of the increase in malpractice cases in all profes- sions, and that we are living in a litigious society. I am not so quick to accept this generic excuse. Rather, I believe that consumers of services, including the con- sumers of social work services, have become more astute in identifying problems with the help they receive, and, therefore, have become more assertive in demand- ing competent professional intervention. The active involvement of the recipients of these services in judging quality and effectiveness is another reason not to ap- ply specific interventions to specific problems.

The occurrence of malpractice cases also implies that perhaps the education and training social workers receive may be inadequate for the tasks they are per- forming. This point is emphasized by Thyer (1994), when he discusses the role of theory for practice in social work. Thyer points out that schools of social work provide only "sketchy familiarity" with theories of human behavior. He goes on to state that many of the theories students learn in social work schools have not been empirically supported, and that the practice models that are derived from them are often ineffective. If this point of view is accepted, then it becomes even more critical that social workers expand their repertoire of skills to respond to the range of complexities one case may present and not be too quick to apply a prescriptive intervention that may not be effective. The purpose of this article is not to judge the efficacy or validity of theories of human behavior. Rather, this information is used to illustrate the potential problems with some of the specific interventions that may be applied to specific client situations.

Donald Schon (1983, 1987) suggests that professionals are being challenged to provide competent services and to be accountable to the consumers of their services. He suggests that one way to decrease the occurrence of malpractice and increase the competence of professional practice is to develop a new epistemology of practice that allows for effective practice in the "swamp" of professional practice. This "swamp" of professional practice is what Schon refers to as the indeterminate zones of uniqueness, uncertainty, and value conflict. According to Schon, it is within these indeterminate zones that the professional practitioner has to bring theoretical knowledge and intuition together to develop the art of professional practice. If professionals can accomplish this, then Schon posits they will be better equipped to perform the roles and tasks of professional problem solving.

Developing the Art of Practice

Although the scientific paradigm seems to be in direct contradiction to the tradition of the profession, Weick (1992) asserts that this has been the underlying paradigm of social work practice for some time. She suggests that although the profession did not accept the scientific paradigm wholeheartedly, it still was very much present. Some social workers, however, are challenging the traditional/scientific approach to practice and are offering alternative practice models that encourage partnership between the worker and client (Bisman, 1994; Pray, 1991).

Pray (1991) examined Schon's reflective practice model in terms of the model's usefulness in recognizing the uniqueness of the individual. "The reflective model offers the possibility of a conceptualization of social work practice wrought from assumptions that clearly inspire efforts to respond to uniqueness in each practice interaction" (p. 83). To respond to the uniqueness of each case, social workers must develop the art of their practice. Like a work of art, the worker has to approach each case as a new experience. I reject the position of applying specific interventions to specific client problems because it does not allow for the complete expression of the dynamic interaction with a client.

Papell and Skolnik (1992) examined the suitability and applicability of Schon's conceptual framework of the reflective practitioner to social work education and practice. They compare Schon's conceptualization with key practice models used in social work from its early history to the current time. Papell and Skolnik conclude that Schon's concept of the reflective practitioner is indeed suitable and applicable to social work. They state, "for social work education in academic settings, Schon's work has the potential to elevate the teaching of action to a level of importance comparable to the teaching of theory" (Papell & Skolnik, p. 25).

Social workers have always addressed the art of professional practice, and it has been encouraged and developed with the consistent emphasis in social work education on the practicum (Bisman, 1994). "Social work practice encompasses both art and science. . . . Just as painters approach a blank canvas each day, so social workers need to start each client contact as a fresh beginning" (Bisman, 1994, p. 290). I agree.

REFERENCES

Bisman, C. (1994). *Social work practice: Cases and principles.* Pacific Grove, CA: Brooks/Cole.

Iglehart, A. P., & Becerra, R. M. (1994). *Social services and the ethnic community.* Boston, MA: Allyn & Bacon.

Lawsuits: No more immunity. (1995, January). *NASW News, 40*(1), 7.

Papell, C. P., & Skolnik, L. (1992). The reflective practitioner: A contemporary paradigm's relevance for social work education. *Journal of Social Work Education, 28,* 18–26.

Pray, J. E. (1991). Respecting the uniqueness of the individual: Social work practice within a reflective model. *Social Work, 36,* 80–85.

Saleeby, D. (Ed.) (1992). *The strengths perspective in social work practice.* New York: Longman.

Schon, D. A. (1983). *The reflective practitioner.* New York: Basic Books.

Schon, D. A. (1987). *Educating the reflective practitioner.* San Francisco, CA: Jossey-Bass.

Thyer, B. A. (1994). Are theories for practice necessary? No!. *Journal of Social Work Education, 30,* 148–151.

Weick, A. (1992). Building a strengths perspective for social work. In D. Saleeby (Ed.), *The strengths perspective in social work practice* (pp. 18–26). New York: Longman.

Rejoinder to Dr. Jackson-White   BETTY J. BLYTHE

It is somewhat difficult to respond to Dr. Jackson-White's paper as she reframed the idea of applying specific interventions to specific problems as prescriptive practice or "robot practice." My paper clearly defines the process of applying specific interventions for specific problems as one that could not be termed as prescriptive. Thus, many of her comments seemed irrelevant to the issue we were asked to discuss.

Early in her paper, Dr. Jackson-White suggests that "applying specific interventions to specific client problems . . . places the worker in a position of power that does not consider the client's role in identifying and solving the problem." This is in direct contradiction to my conception of the process of applying specific interventions to specific client problems in which the social worker is in a position of *responsibility*, not power. I offered two case illustrations in which the client and the social worker collaboratively defined the problems to be addressed. Elsewhere, I have described how clients must be consulted as treatment plans are developed, to ensure that the plans are sensitive to the unique needs of the client and the context (i.e., the client's environment) in which the interventions are implemented (Blythe, 1990). To accomplish a highly specific intervention plan, it is absolutely necessary to involve clients in the process of defining the problems, selecting goals, and specifying intervention plans.

Dr. Jackson-White further argues that prescriptive practice ignores the uniqueness of the individual. That may be true for the type of practice she is imagining, but it does not apply to the process of developing specific interventions that I described. In fact, the uniqueness of the individual is the underpinning of a highly specific intervention plan.

Fortunately, I do find some points of agreement with Dr. Jackson-White. I concur with her comments about the importance of the interactions between the worker and the client. I also agree that these interactions should be addressed when defining interventions as worker-directed intervention responses, and that we should attend to theories of human behavior in specifying interventions, particularly when these theories are supported by research.

I find Dr. Jackson-White's comments about malpractice to be puzzling and based largely on conjecture. She appears to take a leap from "incorrect treatment" which the *NASW News* cited as a frequent basis for malpractice suits to applying specific interventions to specific cases. How did "incorrect treatment" come to be defined as applying specific interventions to specific cases? Unfortunately, Dr. Jackson-White fails to explain this, and we are left with what appears to be a definitional flight of fancy. I suspect that "incorrect treatments" are more likely to occur when social workers *do not* take the time to conduct thorough, specific assessments and to develop specific interventions tailored to the unique needs of the client.

Perhaps most disappointing was Dr. Jackson-White's failure to help us understand the art of practice. It would have been extremely helpful to have an explication of the process so that we could see how it is different from the process I described. Without this specificity, approaching each case like a "work of art" sounds like a more likely candidate for a malpractice suit than does the process I outlined.

Reference

Blythe, B. J. (1990). Applying practice research methods in intensive family preservation services. In J. K. Whittaker, J. Kinney, E. M. Tracey, & C. Booth (Eds.), *Reaching high-risk families: Intensive family preservation in human services* (pp. 147–164). New York: Aldine de Gruyter.

Should Social Workers Support the Inpatient Treatment of Substance Abusers Who Do Not Need Detoxification?

Cheryl Davenport Dozier, D.S.W., is currently an Assistant Professor at the University of Georgia School of Social Work in Athens, Georgia. She currently teaches chemical dependency, cultural diversity, human behavior, and practice courses in the M.S.W. program. Dr. Dozier received her D.S.W. from Hunter College, at the Graduate Center of the City University of New York in 1994. She received an M.S.W. Degree from Atlanta University in 1980. Her previous position was Associate Director, Outpatient Alcoholism Treatment Programs of Yonkers General Hospital, Yonkers, New York. She was the founding Program Director of the Archway Alcoholism Treatment Program in Mt. Vernon, New York, from 1982 to 1994.

David A. Patterson, Ph.D., is an Assistant Professor of social work with The University of Tennessee at Knoxville. Dr. Patterson currently teaches substance abuse treatment, human behavior, and research. He is the lead author/developer of *HyperCDTX*, interactive, multimedia software for substance abuse treatment education. Dr. Patterson received his M.S.W. from the University of Utah in 1981, and his Ph.D. in Social Work from the University of Utah in 1991.

YES

CHERYL DAVENPORT DOZIER

To this question, I believe that a "yes," with some precautions, is appropriate. My response is centered around three major conditions that indicate that inpatient treatment is necessary for: (1) certain types of substance abusers, (2) the initial elimination of environmental triggers, and (3) the intense immersion of treatment services in the initial recovery phase. I will address each of these points individually after a brief historical overview. Much of the research for this response was based on the literature regarding treatment of alcoholism, heroin and cocaine addictions. However, the findings can be applied to support most of the other substances of abuse. As a director of an outpatient alcoholism/substance abuse treatment program for more than ten years, I recognized that many clients benefited greatly from inpatient treatment. However, this modality must be recommended by social workers on an individual basis, with clinical justifications for this costly treatment.

Historically, substance abuse treatment for alcoholism and heroin often included some form of inpatient treatment. Treatment for opiate addictions, primarily heroin addiction, began back in the 1920s to include hospitalization, and by the 1960s there was the development of long-term residential therapeutic communities (TCs). Alcoholism treatment often included hospitalization for detoxification followed by inpatient rehabilitation for more intensive treatment. Many inpatient programs were based on the "Minnesota Model," which was developed by alcoholism treatment centers in Minnesota during the 1940s and 1950s. It was based on an abstinence-oriented, comprehensive, multidisciplinary approach to the treatment of addictions, based on the principles of Alcoholics Anonymous. Minnesota Model services included: an intense educational component about chemical dependency, individual and group counseling/therapy, and self-help orientation. Other inpatient programs followed a more cognitive–behavioral model of intensive inpatient treatment followed by aftercare and self-help (Cook, 1988; Keso & Salspuro, 1990).

Social work practitioners should use the least intrusive method of treatment, including self-help programs, outpatient treatment, detoxification, and then inpatient treatment. Some of these methods may be combined initially; for example, inpatient detoxification may be combined with outpatient treatment before sending the client to inpatient treatment.

Severely Impaired Substance Abusers

Inpatient treatment is necessary for certain types of substance abusers (i.e., chronic, violent, dually diagnosed, homeless, and suicidal clients), who often need more intensive treatment in the initial recovery phase. When developing a treatment plan for cocaine abusers, the decision to use inpatient treatment is not based on the need for detoxification (unless the client is polyaddicted to alcohol and is currently going through withdrawal). Inpatient treatment for cocaine is usually determined based on the following clinical factors: (1) greater severity of cocaine use with a diminished ability to achieve an initial period of abstinence from cocaine; (2) heavier use of other drugs, particularly alcohol; (3) severity of cocaine-associated impairments, particularly social functioning, limited social supports for attaining a drug-free state; (4) more severe psychopathological condition, particularly suicidality and depression, which may place the patient at risk if inpatient supervision is not given; or (5) previous failures at outpatient treatment, indicating that more intense treatment may be necessary for this episode (Budde, Rounsaville, & Bryant, 1992, pp. 337–338). Many of these justifications would be a similar rationale for inpatient treatment of alcoholism and other drugs when detoxification is not indicated.

There have been empirical studies whose findings are that inpatient substance abuse treatment programs are not more effective than outpatient treatment. However, many of these studies did not include patients who are clinically determined to require inpatient treatment (Pettinati et al., 1993). A research study by Dougherty and Lesswing (1989) indicated that 72 percent of their sample were polyaddicted, and 90 percent were dually diagnosed with an Axis II diagnosis (most commonly being narcissistic and borderline personality disorders). Budde et al. (1992) obtained similar findings that inpatients present with more severe problems than outpatients. This would suggest a rational basis for the patients' need for inpatient versus outpatient treatment.

A number of studies reviewed by Harrison, Hoffman, and Streed (1991) compared inpatient treatment with outpatient treatment, and they found that studies that compare intake characteristics of inpatients and outpatients reported a consistently higher prevalence of factors associated with poorer prognosis. Even though these studies show no difference in recovery results, what might actually be interpreted is that there is no significant difference in the outcomes of less impaired substance abusers in outpatient treatment as compared with more impaired substance abusers in inpatient treatment. Miller and Hester (1986), who also reviewed research that found there is no substantive difference in inpatient and outpatient treatment of alcoholics, stated that "predictor data do provide modest evidence that inpatient settings may be differentially advantageous for the more severely deteriorated alcoholic, whereas outpatient settings may be more effective for those who are less impaired and more socially stable" (p. 802).

Environmental Triggers

The second reason was the removal of chronic substance abusers from the environmental triggers that prevent them from maintaining abstinence in the early treatment phase. Some of these environmental triggers include the ready access to alcohol and other drugs by living in drug-infested communities or households. Even though the old "3 Rs" model (remove from society, repair the problem, and replace in society) of alcohol treatment is outmoded (Miller & Hester, 1986), there is clinical evidence that some clients recover better initially when they are removed for a brief period. In practice, when treating clients for chronic relapse, an inpatient stay often provides clients an opportunity to obtain twenty-eight days of abstinence. This is often the longest period of abstinence that many of these clients have had in years. My experience with these clients in an outpatient day treatment setting indicated that it may take these clients up to six months to obtain their initial thirty days of abstinence. Recovery cannot truly begin until clients can have a minimal period of thirty days, and preferably ninety days, of abstinence.

Inpatient treatment is an appropriate treatment alternative for clients who have repeatedly failed at outpatient treatment. Some of these clients lack stable support systems in their communities or have medical problems. The general purpose of an inpatient rehabilitation program "is to help individuals gain understanding of their problems and to prepare them for long term recovery" (Lewis, Dana, & Blevins, 1994, p. 25). The rehabilitation setting should provide clients with the opportunity to develop personal recovery goals, to learn relapse prevention skills, to prepare for resocialization into the community, and to plan and rehearse an abstinent and drug-free lifestyle (Lewis, Dana, & Blevins, 1994).

Intensive Treatment Services

The third reason is the immersion of treatment that an inpatient stay can impose for a limited time. Inpatient programs can differ from outpatient programs in a number of ways, including: level of care, content, format, or context, with inpatient offering more intensive observations, programming, and structure in a secure environment (Harrison et al., 1991). Inpatient rehabilitation provides a positively reinforcing, round-the-clock, drug-free environment. At most inpatient programs, clients must participate in twelve-step meetings, Alcoholics Anonymous (AA) or Narcotic Anonymous (NA), which has proved to be significant to successful recovery outcomes. There has been evidence that inpatient care is necessary for a number of substance abuse clients. Studies have reported findings of "no significant difference" in inpatient versus outpatient treatment, which is often related to the very high relapse rates in both groups (Pettinati et al., 1993). These authors further suggest that other factors such as poorly designed treatment programs, extremely impoverished client groups, or some grossly insensitive outcome measures may have a significant effect on the findings. Alterman and McLellan (1993) agreed that one must look at the distinctive characteristics of inpatient and outpatient programs, such as program history, staff structure, program leadership, and environmental stressors of the clients when interpreting the findings.

Conclusion

As social workers, we must be concerned about the billions of dollars being spent in inpatient treatment, specifically for those clients without clinical justification for this intense level of care. Too often social workers, especially those in employee assistance settings, opt for the most costly inpatient treatment because the client's health insurance plan would reimburse. This decision should have been based on what was clinically the most appropriate treatment for this specific client. In addition, private inpatient programs often marketed their services to social workers and gave positive personal and agency incentives for the referral of clients. Social workers' limited knowledge and understanding of addiction and appropriate treatment modalities often prevented them from challenging this unethical practice of referring blocks of clients to the same service despite their individual treatment needs.

Another justification against the use of inpatient treatment are the current cutbacks in insurance reimbursements, especially with managed care and the high cost of this treatment at private agencies. As social workers, we always need to be concerned with the costs of health care, but not to the extent that we ignore the sound reasoning and therapeutic justifications for this level of care. We cannot refuse to use inpatient treatment because of its cost when it may be clinically more effective for certain clients. Further research is needed to evaluate the cost of repeated outpatient treatment and medical hospitalization of clients with severe physical, psychological, and social factors versus the combined inpatient and outpatient treatment use for this client population.

REFERENCES

Alterman, A. I., & McLellan, T. (1993) Inpatient and day hospital treatment services for cocaine and alcohol dependence. *Journal of Substance Abuse Treatment, 10,* 269–275.

Budde, D., Rounsaville, B., & Bryant K. (1992). Inpatient and outpatient cocaine abusers: Clinical comparisons at intake and one-year follow-up. *Journal of Substance Abuse Treatment, 9,* 337–342.

Cook, C. C. H. (1988). The Minnesota Medel in the management of drug and alcohol dependency: Miracle, method, or myth? Part I. The Philosophy and the programme. *British Journal of Addictions, 83,* 625–634.

Dougherty, R. J. & Lesswing, N. J. (1989). Inpatient cocaine abusers: An analysis of psychological and demographic variables. *Journal of Substance Abuse Treatment, 6,* 45–47.

Harrison, P. A., Hoffman, N., & Streed, S. (1991). Drug and alcohol addiction treatment outcome. In N. Miller (Ed.), *Comprehensive handbook of drug and alcohol addiction* (pp. 1163–1197). New York: Marcel Dekker.

Keso, L. & Salspuro, M. (1990). Inpatient treatment of employed alcoholics: A randomized clinical trial on Hazelton-type and traditional treatment. *Alcoholism: Clinical and Experimental Research, 14,* 584–589.

Lewis, J. A., Dana, R. Q., & Blevins, G. A. (1994). *Substance abuse counseling.* Pacific Grove, CA: Brooks/Cole Publishing.

Miller, W. R., & Hester, R. K. (1986). Inpatient alcoholism treatment: Who benefits? *American Psychologist, 41,* 794–805.

Pettinati, H., Meyers, K., Jensen, J. M., Kaplan, F., & Evans, B. D. (1993, Summer). Inpatient vs. outpatient treatment for substance dependence revisited. *Psychiatric Quarterly, 64,* 173–182.

Rejoinder to Dr. Dozier
DAVID A. PATTERSON

Dr. Dozier's arguments in support of use of inpatient hospitalization of substance abusers not requiring detoxification are replete with the common "clinical wisdom" of the substance abuse treatment community. The espoused position is, however, remarkably void of any empirical evidence supporting such wisdom or demonstrating the superiority of inpatient substance abuse treatment (ISAT) over outpatient alternatives. This is not surprising given the fact that such evidence from controlled studies cannot currently be found in the research literature.

Case Severity

It is clear from a careful reading of Dr. Dozier's argument, and it should be stated from the outset, that we agree on some of the conditions that justify the limited use of inpatient substance abuse treatment (ISAT). For instance, we both agree that suicidal clients (an immediate threat to health) who are substance abusers may require ISAT. Dr. Dozier asserts that ISAT is appropriate for dually diagnosed clients. Unfortunately, the term *dual diagnosis* is nonspecific and overly inclusive. For instance, the inpatient hospitalization of a client dually diagnosed with substance abuse and narcissistic personality disorder is likely unjustifiable. I would suggest instead that ISAT is appropriate when there is a comorbid major psychiatric disorder that represents an immediate threat to health and safety. This is far more specific and appropriate justification for the limited use of ISAT.

Dr. Dozier contends that ISAT is "necessary" for substance abusers who are either chronic, violent, or homeless. It is noteworthy that this assertion is made without any citation of any research that ISAT is in fact effective for substance abusers with any one of these three features.

In attempting to justify ISAT for severely impaired substance abusers, Dr. Dozier cites Miller and Hester (1986) with a quote suggesting that inpatient treatment may be more advantageous for more severely impaired alcoholics. Omitted, however, is Miller and Hester's (1986) next sentence: "Nevertheless, the controlled research to date, ranging across a variety of kinds of treatment and patient populations, has yielded *not a single study* (emphasis added) to point to superior overall effectiveness of treatment in intensive residential settings" (p. 802). Dr. Dozier goes on to cite Pettinati et al. (1993), who point to differences in levels of case severity between treatment settings in an attempt to refute Miller and Hester's (1986) findings. It should be noted that in Pettinati et al.'s report they disregard all of the studies reviewed by Miller and Hester that compared partial hospitalization with ISAT. In Pettinati et al.'s attempt to discredit Miller and Hester's findings, they omitted a significant portion of the data.

Environmental Triggers

In my initial statement, I provide a detailed refutation of the environmental triggers argument. It is interesting that Dr. Dozier suggests that some clients have improved recovery when removed initially from their environments and the associated triggers and placed in ISAT. If this is in fact the case, why has the difference not appeared in the controlled studies of ISAT versus nonresidential treatment? Nor is there evidence put forth by Dr. Dozier to support her assertion that recovery does not begin until there are thirty to ninety days of abstinence.

Intense Immersion

Dr. Dozier's third rationale for ISAT is "intense immersion of treatment services." Implicit here is the assumption that partial hospitalization/day treatment programs cannot provide equally intense treatment as ISAT programs. It is noteworthy that Pettinati et al. (1993), often cited by Dr. Dozier in support of her position, state that "partial hospital programs . . . provide all-day treatment services at the same intensity as residential (ISAT) programs" (p. 174). Clearly, the rationale of differential intensity between ISAT and partial hospitalization programs is untenable.

Conclusion

Given the overwhelming evidence from thirty years of research that ISAT is no more effective than nonresidential treatment, the burden of proof falls on proponents of ISAT to back up their justifications for the use of ISAT with empirical evidence. That evidence has not been provided by Dr. Dozier. If the social work profession is to play a defining role in substance abuse treatment, we can no longer justify our actions with "clinical wisdom." We must use the empirical evidence no matter how it conflicts with our long-held "clinical wisdom." The truth is that ISAT has not been found to have superior efficacy. Therefore, social workers must be extremely reticent to recommend its use. Otherwise, we are knowingly espousing more restrictive and costly interventions that are no more effective than less restrictive and less costly procedures. Conversely, we also must engage in the development of nonresidential treatment approaches and carefully evaluate their effectiveness.

REFERENCES

Miller, W. R. & Hester, R. K. (1986). Inpatient alcoholism treatment: Who benefits? *American Psychologist, 41,* 794–805.

Pettinati, H. M., Meyers, K., Jensen, J. M., Kaplan, F., & Evans, B. D. (1993). Inpatient vs. outpatient treatment for substance dependence revisited. *Psychiatric Quarterly, 64,* 173–182.

NO

DAVID A. PATTERSON

The use of inpatient hospitalization for the treatment of substance abusers is, with few exceptions, both unsupported by the research literature and clinically unjustified. Inpatient substance abuse treatment (ISAT) is best viewed as an anachronistic practice that persists today more as a function of clinical tradition, failure to develop alternative resources, and institutional (public and private) economic pressures for continued operations of inpatient facilities. Social workers should *not* support the use of ISAT, except for a very limited number of reasons, which are detailed below. ISAT is antithetical to social work's history of understanding and working with individuals in their environmental context and the profession's movement to empirically based practice.

Efficacy of Inpatient Treatment: The Failure of Evidence

Any justification for the use of ISAT cannot be supported by the empirical literature. There is now a thirty-year history of studies finding that ISAT is no more efficacious than outpatient treatment alternatives (Edwards & Guthrie, 1966, 1967; Valliant, 1983). In the largest review of the literature on inpatient alcoholism treatment to date, Miller and Hester (1986) examined both uncontrolled and controlled studies of inpatient care. They found that a number of uncontrolled studies supported inpatient treatment, whereas others came to the opposite finding. The correlational designs of these uncontrolled studies presented significant methodological problems that rendered their positive findings insupportable. Miller and Hester further reviewed twenty-six controlled studies in which there was either random assignment or matching used to compare inpatient alcohol treatment with nonresidential care. They found that inpatient care was no more effective than nonresidential care and in some studies, the outcomes for clients receiving partial hospitalization was superior to those of clients receiving inpatient care.

In a more recent report, McLellan, O'Brien, Metzger, Alterman, Cornish, and Urschel (1992) cite findings from two ongoing studies comparing ISAT with partial hospitalization. One study compares the outcomes for alcohol-dependent veterans randomly assigned to either inpatient care or partial hospitalization. In the second study, cocaine-dependent veterans were assigned randomly to one of the two treatment conditions. In both studies, there were no significant differences in outcomes for clients receiving inpatient care versus partial hospitalization. The authors conclude "... There has been no evidence to date indicating that patients show more or broader changes in any particular setting or modality" (McLellan et al., 1992, p. 243).

The most widely used form of ISAT in this country is the Minnesota Model (Cook, 1988). The Minnesota Model has traditionally used a twenty-eight-day length of treatment in which clients receive education about the harmful effects of substance abuse, confrontational group therapy, an introduction to Alcoholics Anonymous (AA), and family therapy (Weiss, 1994). Hester (1994) evaluated the limited literature on the Minnesota Model using weighted evidence index (WEIn) created by Holder, Longabaugh, Miller, and Rubonis (1991). Hester concluded that there was "insufficient evidence of effectiveness" (1994, p. 36) of the Minnesota Model, because there has been only one study in which the Minnesota Model was compared with another inpatient treatment model (Keso & Salspuro, 1990). Clearly, the Minnesota Model needs to be compared with nonresidential treatment alternatives in a controlled study.

In a "special article" on substance abuse appearing in the *American Journal of Psychiatry,* authored by the Committee on Alcoholism and the Addictions, recommendations were made regarding when ISAT was appropriate. These recommendations are reviewed here. What is perhaps most noteworthy is that not a single study was cited in support of their recommendations nor of the efficacy of ISAT over nonresidential treatment. Weiss (1994), writing on ISAT in the *American Psychiatric Press Textbook of Substance Abuse Treatment,* failed to cite a single controlled study supporting the use of ISAT instead of nonresidential treatment. Finally, in a recent publication (NIAAA, 1992), even the National Institute of Alcohol Abuse and Alcoholism (NIAAA), was only able to cite one controlled study in which ISAT was found to have a superior outcome to nonresidential treatment. The study found inpatient alcohol treatment with an AA component more effective than outpatient AA. Given the fact that the outcome of referral to AA was found to be equivalent to no treatment, AA's comparison to ISAT hardly seems valid (Miller, 1992).

It is striking that prominent committees of psychiatrists, national institutes, extensively published researchers, and major textbooks are unable to offer evidence of the superior treatment efficacy of ISAT. Given the weight of evidence suggesting that ISAT is largely unwarranted and cost-inefficient, one must wonder what possible rationale is used to support ISAT (Institute of Medicine, 1990; Miller & Hester, 1986). As someone who conducted hundreds of utilization reviews of ISAT admissions across the country in the late 1980s, the answer I most often heard was that ISAT was justified by pressing clinical reasons. It is to those clinical rationales that we now turn our attention.

A Refutation of Clinical Rationales

In a recently published rationale for ISAT, Weiss (1994) set forth a number of clinical reasons for the use of inpatient treatment. Weiss argued that ISAT is justified for clients who have not responded to less restrictive alternatives (prior nonresidential care). There is no evidence that increasing the restrictiveness of a treatment approach increases its efficacy. A more fruitful response to repeated treatment failure is to examine with the client the triggers (cognitive, behavioral, situational, and affective) that precipitated the most recent relapse (Beck, Wright, Newman, & Liese, 1993). Then, in collaboration with the client, a treatment plan can be formulated to address the identified relapse triggers. Miller's (1995) motivational interviewing techniques may be particularly helpful in this collaborative process. Additionally, a review of treatment modalities provided in earlier treatment episodes may reveal a prior failure to use interventions with known efficacy, e.g., behavioral martial therapy, community reinforcement approach (CRA), self-control training, social skills training, and stress management (Hester, 1994; Miller, 1992). Incorporation of one or more of these interventions into a treatment plan formulated with the client's participation and provided in an intensive outpatient setting is a far more empirically sound treatment approach than simply putting the client in the hospital because of prior treatment failure.

Weiss (1994) has argued for the use of ISAT on the grounds that it may increase clients' "awareness of the internal triggers that place them at risk to return to substance abuse" (p. 361). He suggests that if clients experience the urges to use, cued by internal triggers, in the safety of an inpatient unit, it may increase their ability to recognize and effectively cope with theses urges. This rationale is offered without any evidence that in the "safety" of an inpatient setting, clients do learn to effectively recognize internal triggers and effectively cope with the resultant urges. An inpatient unit is essentially an artificial environment in which there is no opportunity to satisfy an urge to use substances short of leaving against medical advice. The suggestion that clients learn to effectively cope with internal triggers is partially negated by the fact that clients know the urge to use cannot be rewarded. Stated more succinctly, without the risk of use, the potential to learn new coping skills that will generalize to clients' external environments is diminished.

Weiss also fails to mention that urges are not only activated by internal triggers, but that clients also must cope with external triggers, such as objects, people, and places, which constitute equally powerful stimuli capable of triggering urges (Beck et al., 1993). Newly learned behaviors that are practiced in an environment that has previously triggered problematic behaviors are more likely to both generalize and endure (Stokes & Baer, 1977). Clients ultimately benefit from learning to cope in the context of substance abuse cues and nonresidential treatment, as opposed to ISAT, makes this coping skill acquisition and generalization possible.

Weiss further suggests that inpatient treatment interrupts a cycle of drug use to allow the user to consider the consequences of continued use and the advantages of engaging in treatment. The empirical evidence just reviewed, demonstrating the equivalent efficacy of partial hospitalization and inpatient treatment, mitigates this justification. Intensive outpatient treatment can allow for the same interruption of drug use cycles while allowing clients to return each day for support to learn new skills for dealing with environmental conditions to which they may return upon completion of treatment.

Limited Clinical Justification

Given the weight of the empirical evidence reviewed here, it seems clear that social workers should support ISAT only for very limited clinical reasons. ISAT may be indicated when (1) there are immediate threats to health secondary to major psychiatric or medical problems, and (2) when an adequate social support network is either absent or cannot be arranged to support nonresidential care (Kissen, Platz, & Su, 1970; Pettinati, Meyers, Jensen, Kaplan, & Evans, 1993). These recommendations are partially based on the proposals of the Committee on Alcoholism and the Addictions (GAP, 1991). The Committee on Alcoholism and the Addictions list also includes "a high degree of chronicity and severe addiction, with polysubstance abuse" (GAP, 1991, p. 1296) as a justification for ISAT. Referral to a therapeutic community/halfway house, as opposed inpatient hospitalization, will likely be a more productive environment for clients with severe and chronic polysubstance addiction after detoxification (Gerstein, 1994).

In summary, social workers should not support the inpatient treatment of substance abusers who do not need detoxification. This position is supported by both a large body of controlled studies and by the absence of valid clinical justifications for this treatment modality, with few exceptions. The dramatic increase in ISAT in the 1970s and 1980s was driven not by its therapeutic effectiveness, but by substance abuse treatment facilities that arose in response to increased coverage of substance abuse treatment by public and private insurers (Institute of Medicine, 1990; Weiss, 1994). Given the continuing fiscal constraints on health care, social workers must support interventions that are empirically based, clinically justifiable, and cost-efficient. ISAT meets none of these criteria.

REFERENCES

Beck, A. T., Wright, F. D., Newman, C. F., & Liese, B. S. (1993). *Cognitive therapy of substance abuse.* New York: Guilford.

Cook, C. C. H. (1988). The Minnesota Model in the management of drug and alcohol dependency: Miracle, method, or myth? Part 1. The philosophy and the programme. *British Journal of Addictions, 83,* 625–634.

Edwards, G., & Guthrie, S. (1966). A comparison of inpatient and outpatient treatment of alcohol dependence. *Lancet, 1,* 467–468.

Edwards, G., & Guthrie, S. (1967). A controlled trial of inpatient and outpatient treatment of alcohol dependence. *Lancet, 1,* 555–559.

GAP Committee. (1991). Substance abuse disorders: A psychiatric priority. *American Journal of Psychiatry, 148,* 1291–1300.

Gerstein, D. R. (1994). Outcome research, drug abuse. In M. G. Galanter & H. D. Kleber (Eds.), *American Psychiatric Press textbook of substance abuse treatment* (pp. 45–64). Washington, DC: American Psychiatric Press.

Hester, R. K. (1994). Outcome research, alcoholism. In M. G. Galanter & H. D. Kleber (Eds.), *American Psychiatric Press textbook of substance abuse treatment* (pp. 35–44). Washington, DC: American Psychiatric Press.

Holder, H., Longabaugh, R., Miller, W. R., & Rubonis, A. V. (1991). The cost effectiveness of treatment for alcoholism: A first approximation. *Journal of Studies on Alcohol, 52,* 517–540.

Institute of Medicine (1990). *Broadening the base of treatment for alcohol problems.* Washington, DC: National Academy Press.

Keso, L., & Salspuro, M. (1990). Inpatient treatment of employed alcoholics: A randomized clinical trial on Hazeldon-type and traditional treatment. *Alcoholism: Clinical and Experimental Research, 14,* 584–589.

Kissen, B., Platz, A., & Su, W. H. (1970). Social and psychological factors in the treatment of chronic alcoholism. *Journal of Psychiatric Research, 8,* 13–27.

McLellan, A. T., O'Brien, C. P., Metzger, D., Alterman, A. I., Cornish, J., & Urschel, H. (1992). How effective substance abuse treatment—Compared to what? In C. P. O'Brien & J. H. Jaffe (Eds.), *Addictive Studies* (pp. 231–252). New York: Raven Press, Ltd.

Miller, W. R. (1992). The effectiveness of treatment for substance abuse: Reasons for optimism. *Journal of Substance Abuse Treatment, 9,* 93–102.

Miller, W. R. (1995). Increasing motivation for change. In R. K. Hester & W. R. Miller (Eds.), *Handbook of alcoholism treatment approaches: Effective alternatives* (2nd ed., pp. 89–104). Boston, MA: Allyn and Bacon.

Miller, W. R., & Hester, R. K. (1986). Inpatient alcoholism treatment: Who benefits? *American Psychologist, 41,* 794–805.

NIAAA. (1992). Treatment outcome research. *Alcohol Alert, 17*(322).

Pettinati, H. M., Meyers, K., Jensen, J. M., Kaplan, F., & Evans, B. D. (1993). Inpatient vs. outpatient treatment for substance dependence revisited. *Psychiatric Quarterly, 64,* 173–182.

Stokes, T. F., & Baer, D. M. (1977). An implicit technology of generalization. *Journal of Applied Behavior Analysis, 10,* 349–367.

Vaillant, G. M. (1983). *The natural history of alcoholism: Causes, patterns, and paths to recovery.* Cambridge, MA: Harvard University Press.

Weiss, R. D. (1994). Inpatient treatment. In M. G. Galanter & H. D. Kleber (Eds.), *American Psychiatric Press Textbook of Substance Abuse Treatment* (pp. 359–368). Washington, DC: American Psychiatric Press.

Rejoinder to Dr. Patterson Cheryl Davenport Dozier

Dr. Patterson raises many reasons why inpatient treatment for substance abusers may not be the most effective intervention. I concur with his assessment that social workers must support treatments that are clinically justifiable and cost-efficient.

However, I am unpersuaded by his arguments that there are no valid clinical justifications for inpatient treatment.

Dr. Patterson primarily bases his opposition to inpatient substance abuse treatment (ISAT) on the research studies reviewed by Miller and Hester (1986), who concluded that ISAT is no more efficacious than outpatient care. Analysis of those studies indicated that many of them were methodologically flawed (Sell, 1995), calling into question their conclusions. Many inpatient treatment programs around the country over the past two decades were based on the Minnesota model. "The Miller–Hester studies were not relevant to determining inpatient versus outpatient effectiveness or length of stay issues in Minnesota model treatment settings" (Sell, 1995, p. 21).

There have been two controlled, randomized studies of the Minnesota model treatment that contrasted inpatient results with outpatient results. The Keso and Salaspuro (1990) study examined Finnish alcoholics assigned to a Minnesota model program or to a standard Finnish, psychiatric/social work–oriented program. The results were unequivocally in favor of the Minnesota model regarding abstinence and other outcome measures. The second study, by Walsh et al. (1991), was a randommized, controlled investigation involving three groups of employee assistance program (EAP)-referred patients. Using the criteria of abstinence, inpatient treatment was favored (Sell, 1995).

The question is not whether inpatient treatment is more effective than outpatient treatment, as Dr. Patterson suggested; it is, "Should social workers support the use of inpatient treatment?" I again say yes, especially for certain types of clients based on an individual assessment of their clinical needs. Even the Institute of Medicine (1992, p. 12), in their discussion of the effectiveness of treatment modalities, stated, "there is no guidance . . . from the literature indicating a single superior treatment approach for all persons with alcohol related problems."

Dr. Patterson fails to acknowledge the literature on patient-matching for improving the effectiveness and efficiency of substance abuse treatment. He challenges Weiss's premise that inpatient treatment is necessary for certain types of clients. Even Miller and Hester (1986, p. 801) state that "available data . . . suggest that indicators of severity and social stability may be predicative of differential response to alternative treatment settings . . . More severe and less socially stable alcoholics seem to fare better in inpatient (or more intensive) treatment, whereas among less severe and more socially stable (married, employed) alcoholics, outpatient (and less intensive) treatment yields more favorable outcomes than inpatient treatment." Most ISAT programs referrals were primarily from EAPs. However, the acceptance criteria was largely based on the patient's insurance plan and not on the clinical needs of the patient.

Many of the EAP-referred clients had the necessary support systems (work, family, community) and motivation (returning to job/career) to recover in outpatient treatment. However in urban, inner-city treatment programs such as the one I directed, patients usually had very limited support systems, no insurance resources, and had repeatedly failed in prior attempts at outpatient treatment. An intensive inpatient program would be initially appropriate for this type of client. It is important to note that these clients often need to return to an intensive outpatient program. Inpatient treatment cannot be viewed in isolation of the necessary and available aftercare or community-based treatment resources. Miller (1992) emphasizes patient matching to achieve treatment effectiveness and offering clients a menu of alternative treatment strategies. Social workers armed with the knowledge, skills, and abilities to assess and treat substance abusers will be better equipped to make these choices. Among these options should be inpatient treatment.

REFERENCES

Institute of Medicine. (1992). Prevention and treatment of alcohol-related problems: Research opportunities. *Journal of Studies on Alcohol, 53,* 5–16.

Keso, L. & Salspuro, M. (1990). Inpatient treatment of employed alcoholics: A randomized clinical trial on Hazeldon-type and traditional treatment. *Alcoholism: Clinical and Experimental Research, 14,* 584–589.

Miller, W. R. & Hester, R. K. (1986). Inpatient alcoholism treatment: Who benefits? *American Psychologist, 41,* 794–805.

Miller, W. R. (1992). The effectiveness of treatment for substance abuse: Reasons for optimism. *Journal of Substance Abuse Treatment, 9,* 93–102.

Sell, J. J. (1995). A critique of outcome studies misapplied: The Minnesota model and managed care. *Alcoholism Treatment Quarterly, 13,* 17–31.

Walsh, D. C., Hingson, R. W., Merrigan, D. M., Levenson, S. M., Cupples, L. A., Heeren, T., Coffman, G. A., Becker, C. A., Barker, T. A., Hamilton, S. K., McGuire, T. G., Kelly, C. A. (1991). A randomized trial of treatment options for alcohol-abusing workers. *New England Journal of Medicine, 325,* 775–782.

Should Social Workers Support the Inpatient Psychiatric Treatment of Nonpsychotic Adolescents?

Raymond Jefferson Waller, M.S.W., is the assistant director of the Phillip Grace Group Home, a residential treatment facility for adjudicated adolescents. His primary area of practice has been with behaviorally disturbed children and adolescents. He received his M.S.W from the University of Georgia in 1993, where he is a social work doctoral student.

Wayne K. Carson, M.S.W., is the Director of Social Services for the All Church Home for Children in Ft. Worth Texas, and a doctoral candidate in social work at the University of Texas at Arlington. He is also grant manager for the Community Policing Evaluation Project at the Center for Research, Evaluation, and Technology.

Richard F. Dangel, Ph.D., is Professor of Social Work and chairperson of the Doctoral Program in Social Work at the University of Texas at Arlington. He is the developer of the "Tri-Guard System," the first comprehensive approach to organizational child abuse risk management.

YES

RAYMOND JEFFERSON WALLER

The question of whether social workers should support the inpatient psychiatric care of nonpsychotic adolescents is not one that lends itself readily to a polarized response. Treatment in the least restrictive environment is a fundamental tenant of mental health practice, and, as is intuitively obvious, preliminary attempts to measure "restrictiveness" of children's living environments indicate that inpatient psychiatric care is a treatment response that is highly restrictive (Thomlison & Krysik, 1992). Effective therapeutic intervention for adolescents, however, has been applied in settings that range from rooftops—for clients undergoing exposure therapy for acrophobia (or fear of heights)—to inpatient psychiatric care for adolescents whose behavior has become so severely impaired, disruptive, or dangerous that outpatient intervention is not practical. It is for this reason that I maintain that social workers should support the inpatient psychiatric care of non-psychotic adolescents.

Longitudinal studies on the mental health of children and adolescents indicate that particular disorders are likely to exacerbate as the teenage years progress. Affective disorders, anorexia nervosa (and other eating disorders), suicide, and attempts to commit suicide have been shown to increase in intensity and duration during adolescence (Rutter, 1989), as have the childhood disruptive behavior disorders—attention deficit hyperactivity disorder, oppositional–defiant disorder, and conduct disorder (Loeber, Lahey, & Thomas, 1991). Furthermore, as the research base on these disorders advances, it becomes increasingly apparent that they are more prevalent than once was assumed. It is estimated that more than 7 million youth in this country are in need of intervention services (LeCroy, 1992), and inpatient psychiatric care will address the needs of a small percentage of these youth. For our profession to ethically support the inpatient care of non-psychotic adolescents, though, it is incumbent on us to engage in two activities. The first of these is a systematic determination of appropriate, client-specific intervention, and the second is insurance that the selected intervention modality is supported by empirically based outcome studies (for a thorough enumeration of systematic treatment selection, see Beutler & Clarkin, 1990). A brief summarization of the considerations that should be paramount to social workers when attempting to design a treatment plan or recommendation based on the least restrictive environment is offered by LeCroy (1992):

> To assess the restrictiveness of various systems of care, social workers must be familiar with the alternatives: outpatient treatment, day treatment, foster care, group home care, and so forth. They must also be acquainted with local programs and their treatment philosophies, because these philosophies will affect the restrictiveness of the programs. (p. 228)

Thus, the decision to employ inpatient care should be a result of systematically ruling out less restrictive treatment alternatives, remaining focused on maintaining the primary goal of providing an appropriate intervention that serves the best interests of the youth. The treatment facilities' philosophical standpoint mentioned above is tantamount, and this refers to not only the written philosophy, but the philosophy that becomes apparent through the services provided. One way that a facility can demonstrate unequivocally that they are dedicated to the provision of the highest quality of service to clients is through evaluation of their programs. Without methodical outcome evaluations, a prospective client has little more than the word of the clinician or administrator with whom they talk that the particular intervention is effective. This practice not only is scientifically indefensible, it may be a violation of the National Association of Social Workers's *Code of Ethics*.

The question of empirical support for the inpatient care of nonpsychotic adolescents is a stickier consideration, because the research base for mental health of children and adolescents is more replete with gaps and consists of fewer well-controlled outcome studies than does the research base for adults. Current evidence suggests that the usage of inpatient care for nonpsychotic adolescents is promising. For example, a review of twenty-four inpatient programs found that each program had demonstrated positive behavioral change of some magnitude (Blotcky, Dimperio, & Gossett, 1984). Furthermore, self-reports of parents and teachers have indicated that significant behavioral change can occur during hospitalization and that this behavioral change is maintained at a one-year follow-up (Kazdin & Bass, 1988).

Another point that warrants exploration is the nature of the problem that often results in an inpatient placement. Youth who manifest affective or psychotic disorders are more likely to be hospitalized than those who do not (Pottick, Hansell, Gutterman, & White, 1995), and the risk of suicide has been shown to be the best predictor of inpatient placement (Morissey, Dicker, Abikoff, Alvir, De-Marco, & Koplewicz, 1995). Among nonpsychotic adolescents, those often receiving inpatient care manifest severe behavioral disorders for which less restrictive interventions have failed, or whose behavior is such that it can no longer be managed by parents or primary caregivers (Kazdin & Bass, 1988). Inpatient treatment has repeatedly been shown to ameliorate harmful, acutely disruptive, or antisocial behavior in children and adolescents (Kazdin, Bass, Siegel, & Thomas, 1989). Inpatient treatment also provides a level of supervision and behavioral control that parents and outpatient interventions will be unlikely to match. The example of anorexia nervosa is illustrative of a nonpsychotic condition that can be problematic from an outpatient standpoint. Anorexia nervosa is a condition that has been described clinically since 1689, though it seems to have existed since earlier times (Sours, 1979). It is primarily a problem seen in females who are generally perceived as "perfectionistic, well-behaved, and competitive" (Foreyt & Kondo, 1985, p. 319) and is characterized by refusal to maintain normal body weight, an intense fear of gaining weight, and a significant disturbance of body image (American Psychiatric Association, 1994). Many physiological manifestations may be associated with anorexia nervosa, including renal dysfunction, cardiovascular disorders, anemia, and osteoporosis. Intervention for this complicated problem has been encouraged to be multidisciplinary, multidimensional, and flexible and should include professionals from the medical, mental health, and nutritional fields (Foreyt & Kondo, 1985). Obviously, inpatient care is an accessible forum in which this combination of professionals can be found, and a person whose physical condition has significantly declined may need inpatient placement. People who evince this disorder are not always cooperative with a treatment regimen and have shown remarkable creativity in circumventing the attempts of involved professionals. Behaviors such as water loading or filling one's shoes with pennies before weigh-ins are arduous enough to monitor by trained inpatient staff members who can provide a high level of supervision. Occurrences of this type would be extremely difficult to prevent on an outpatient basis.

One argument that might be reasonably proposed against inpatient care is that it is difficult to assess behavioral changes resulting from the multimodal or milieu therapy offered by many inpatient programs (Blotcky, Dimperio, & Gossett, 1984), and this has hindered attempts to determine exactly what it is about inpatient care that helps people to get better. In the absence of such identified variables, I would argue that the important qualifier is that, by many indicators, people who receive inpatient care get better, and this is a primary concern of the profession of social work.

Indeed, one of the strengths of inpatient care may lie in milieu therapy. Such care may, by its diverse application, increase the chance for improvement through individual therapy, music and activity therapy, interpersonal interaction with similarly situated peers, medication, family therapy, and group therapy. We as social workers know that in issues of mental health, even highly successful interventions such as exposure therapy for simple phobias are not successful for everyone. It therefore seems unwise to begin to preclude empirically promising interventions from our therapeutic repertoire.

Thus I conclude that, within the parameters of careful selection of treatment and positive empirical evidence, inpatient care for nonpsychotic adolescents is a reasonable component of a hierarchy of alternatives. Inpatient care for young people should not be viewed as a panacea, and an intrinsic concern regarding the delivery of inpatient care is the possibility of an abusive overusing of inpatient care when a less restrictive alternative might suffice. However, this is possible any time caregivers are tied to a cash register instead of to the best interests of clients; it is certainly not constrained to happening only with inpatient caregivers. Social workers should not shy away from empirically supported interventions because of such fears but should endeavor to ensure that such abuse does not occur. This, too, is a historical (and contemporary) goal of our profession. Social work is strengthened, and our code of ethics honored, when we embrace interventions that are guided by empirical outcomes. At this point, there is no compelling evidence that indicates our clients would best be served by removing inpatient care from our treatment hierarchy, and much evidence suggests the contrary. On this premise, I say yes, let us support this method of intervention.

REFERENCES

American Psychiatric Association. (1994). *Diagnostic and Statistical Manual of Mental Disorders (4th ed.)*. Washington, DC: Author.

Beutler, L. E., & Clarkin, J. F. (1990). *Systematic treatment selection: Toward targeted therapeutic interventions.* New York: Brunner/Mazel.

Blotcky, M. J., Dimperio, T. L., & Gossett, J. T. (1984). Follow-up of children treated in psychiatric hospitals: A review of studies. *American Journal of Psychiatry, 141,* 1499–1507.

Foreyt, J. P., & Kondo, A. T. (1985). Eating disorders. In P. Bornstein & A. Kazdin (Eds.), *Handbook of behavior therapy with children* (pp. 309–344). Homewood, IL: Dorsey Press.

Kazdin, A. E., & Bass, D. (1988). Parent, teacher, and hospital staff evaluations of severely disturbed children. *American Journal of Orthopsychiatry, 58,* 512–523.

Kazdin, A. E., Bass, D., Siegel, T., & Thomas, C. (1989). Cognitive-behavioral therapy and relationship therapy in the treatment of children referred for antisocial behavior. *Journal of Consulting and Clinical Psychology, 57,* 522–535.

LeCroy, C. W. (1992). Enhancing the delivery of effective mental health services to children. *Social Work, 37,* 225–231.

Loeber, R., Lahey, B. B., & Thomas, C. (1991). Diagnostic conundrum of oppositional defiant disorder and conduct disorder. *Journal of Abnormal Psychology, 100,* 379–390.

Morissey, R. F., Dicker, R., Abikoff, H., Alvir, J. M. J., DeMarco, A., & Koplewicz, H. S. (1995). Hospitalizing the suicidal adolescent: An empirical investigation of decision-making criteria. *Journal of the American Academy of Child and Adolescent Psychiatry, 34,* 902–911.

Pottick, K., Hansell, S., Gutterman, E., & White, H. R. (1995). Factors associated with inpatient and outpatient treatment for children and adolescents with serious mental illness. *Journal of the American Academy of Child and Adolescent Psychiatry, 34,* 425–433.

Rutter, M. (1989). Isle of Wight revisited: Twenty-five years of child psychiatric epidemiology. In S. Chess & M. Hertzig (Eds.), *Annual Progress in Child Psychiatry and Child Development* (pp. 131–175). New York: Brunner/Mazel.

Sours, J. A. (1979). The primary anorexia nervosa syndrome. In J. Noshpitz (Ed.), *Basic handbook of child psychiatry* (Vol. 2, pp. 568–580). New York: Basic Books.

Thomlison, B., & Krysik, J. (1992). The development of an instrument to measure restrictiveness of children's living environments. *Research on Social Work Practice, 2,* 207–219.

Rejoinder to Mr. Waller

Wayne K. Carson
Richard Dangel

Waller claims social workers should use inpatient hospitalization because anorexics put pennies in their shoes to weigh more; because hospitals provide milieu therapy; and because inpatient care has been shown to be an effective treatment for at least some problems.

The "pennies in the shoes" argument falls prey to the fallacy of composition error described by Gambrill (1990, p. 131). The fallacy of composition error occurs when a case is made that what is true for the part is true for the whole. In this case, Waller seems to be trying to argue that because a very small number of extreme cases of anorexia nervosa resort to dramatic tactics, all anorexics must be hospitalized. In fact, most anorexics respond successfully to outpatient interventions.

Although he admits that there is no clear evidence to support milieu therapy, Waller would like the reader to believe that milieu therapy works and that only in a hospital setting can milieu therapy be provided. He goes on to suggest that such "promising modalities" as individual therapy, music and activity therapy, medication, interaction with similarly situated peers (does he mean situated in the hospital?), and family and group therapy can only be received as an inpatient. Obviously, a client could receive all of these services as an outpatient and with less risk of a conflict in a treatment setting where different ideologies, theoretical foundations, and fundamental beliefs exist.

Finally, Waller seems to misconstrue the so-called evidence that hospitalization is empirically supported. After describing the research base as "replete with gaps" and as consisting of few "well-controlled studies," he goes on to conclude that inpatient treatment has "repeatedly been shown to ameliorate harmful behaviors." He cites two studies to support this statement. A closer look at the first (Kazdin, Bass, Siegel, & Thomas, 1989) contradicts Waller's claim. The study was not an evaluation of the effects of hospitalization. Rather, it was a study of the effects of cognitive–behavioral therapy in treating antisocial behavior. Both inpatient and outpatient youth were included in the study, and the authors clearly state that they found "no reliable differences" between inpatient and outpatient treatment (p. 528). In fact, the study challenges the need for hospitalization by providing direct evidence that inpatient treatment is no more effective than outpatient treatment.

Waller also describes a study by Kazdin and Bass (1988) as suggesting that inpatient treatment for adolescents is promising. However, the study was based entirely on self-report data. The hospital teachers who worked with the children reported almost no improvement in the youth during treatment, and parents and teachers disagreed about the severity of the children's problems. These findings seem more puzzling than promising. Waller cites a meta-analysis of twenty-four follow-up studies conducted from 1936 to 1982 on hospital and residential treatment programs (Blotcky, Dimperio, & Gossett, 1984). Rather than supporting the effectiveness of hospitalization, the authors concluded that the studies failed to differentiate between the effects of treatment and the "natural course of psychiatric illness" (p. 1505).

Some cultures chop off the hands of thieves. One might argue that because this treatment produces profound effects, its use should be widespread. Conversely, one might argue that the unrecoverable costs of such an intervention greatly outweigh the benefits. The same could be said for hospitalizing adolescents. Instead of blindly supporting inpatient treatment for nonpsychotic adolescents, social workers should put up their hands and demand the least harmful, most cost-effective treatment available.

REFERENCES

Blotcky, M. J., Dimperio, T. L., & Gossett, J. T. (1984). Follow-up of children treated in psychiatric hospitals. *American Journal of Psychiatry, 141,* 1499–1507.

Gambrill, E. (1990). *Critical thinking in clinical practice: Improving the accuracy of judgments and decisional about clients.* San Francisco, CA: Jossey-Bass.

Kazdin, A. E., & Bass, D. (1988). Parent, teacher and hospital staff evaluations of severely disturbed children. *American Journal of Orthopsychiatry, 58,* 512–523.

Kazdin, A. E., Bass, D., Siegel, T., & Thomas, C. (1989). Cognitive-behavioral therapy and relationship therapy in the treatment of children referred for antisocial behavior. *Journal of Consulting and Clinical Psychology, 57,* 522–535.

NO

WAYNE K. CARSON
RICHARD DANGEL

Is your teen driving you crazy?

Does your teen talk on the phone constantly? Does he not do his schoolwork? Is his room a mess? Does he argue? Backtalk? Does he think he knows it all? If you answered "yes" to any of these questions, maybe it's not you who are crazy; maybe it's your teen! Why not send him for a short stay at The Villages of Shimmering Brooks? Our inpatient hospital will medicate him and give you the vacation you need. Best of all, it's free—your insurance will pay for it! But don't wait too long. Call 555-HELP! before your teen outgrows his problems.

Scandal erupted in the psychiatric industry in the 1990s (Lodge, 1994) when hundreds of former patients began telling horror stories of torture, forced drug use, involuntary treatment, denial of civil rights, and separation from loved ones, all sanctioned as "necessary for the good of the patient" and administered in hospitals under the supervision of psychiatrists, physicians, nurses, and, social workers. Hundreds of parents, guardians, and children described being dismissed from care the instant insurance benefits expired, with complete disregard for patient well-being. Psychiatric hospitals set up screening booths in shopping centers, where parents were encouraged to have their children "tested" for mental illness. Hospitals offered "free counseling" to students in the schools and hosted an array of "educational seminars" that were open to the public. Ostensibly, these charitable services were provided to promote mental health awareness. However, the real motivation was much more insidious: the hospitals were casting forth their fishing nets to lure unsuspecting individuals, with alarming prognostications of future drug addiction, suicide, and crime for those who disavowed themselves of the services, and false promises of unbridled happiness to those who subscribed. A quick telephone review of insurance benefits determined whether the applicant had a need for hospitalization. The hospitalized adolescents were not the only victims of these schemes. Well-intentioned parents spent their life savings, depleted college funds, and mortgaged their homes and their futures to pay for these unnecessary, and usually destructive, services.

Adolescence is a time of conflict (Broughton, 1987). The normal developmental issues of individuation and separation, coupled with the extraordinary demands placed on todays' teens to be academically successful, socially popular, physically attractive, financially well-off, appropriately dressed, coifed, and pierced, sexually abstinent, drug free, and laid back, all within communities rife with discrimination, poverty, hatred, sex, drugs, and violence, present a formidable challenge to families. However, dumping adolescents into psychiatric hospitals is not the answer. Social workers should not support the inpatient treatment of adolescents, for four reasons: (1) inpatient care hurts children; (2) inpatient care does not work; (3) inpatient care undermines the development of community-based services; and (4) inpatient care costs too much. Each of these reasons is discussed below.

Inpatient Hospital Care Hurts Youth

The deinstitutionalization literature of the 1960s and 1970s vividly describes the multiple problems associated with a system that depends on hospitalization as a treatment for mental health issues (Lamb, 1979; Paul, 1969; Stein and Test, 1979). A few of the more commonly cited problems included the labeling and stigmatization resulting from a hospital admission; the isolation from social support systems; the unnecessary loss of client liberty; the dehumanizing effects; and the inflexibility of inpatient treatment to meet individual needs. More than two decades ago, awareness of these issues prompted an outcry by professionals for more humane and effective alternatives to treat mental health issues (Bentley, 1994).

These outcries spurred the development of new and innovative community-based treatments. Individuals in the community previously thought to be untreatable outside the locked walls of a hospital unit were effectively served by some programs (Borland, McRae, & Lycan, 1989; Dintz, 1979). Although critics of the deinstitutionalization movement are quick to point out its problems (Belcher, 1994; Lamb, 1988), the solutions to these problems do not lie in a reenactment of past mistakes.

Should one argue that some of the references mentioned are almost thirty years old and that the state of the art in inpatient care has vastly improved, they need only again look to the recent scandals that again exposed immense injustices existing within the modern system (Deener, 1994; Everbach, 1994). Investigations showed that little has changed in the way hospitalized patients are treated. Lawsuits alleging insurance fraud, kickback schemes, unnecessary treatment, coerced hospitalizations, and malpractice continue to flood the courts. Despite past abuses, youth continue to be labeled, overmedicated, isolated from support systems, and deprived of liberty, all in the name of quality care.

Supporters of inpatient treatment for nonpsychotic youth claim that youngsters who exhibit problems such as aggressiveness, suicidal thinking, drug use, and truancy are not suitable for inclusion in the community. This position makes a convenient twenty-second sound bite for politicians: "Keep our streets safe. Lock 'em up." Mental health professionals surely must know that the issue is much more complex than confinement without regard to individual freedom or program effectiveness.

One significant flaw in the argument for hospitalization is the assumption of homogeneity. Homogeneity assumes that all youth who demonstrate similar behaviors require the same treatment, in this case, hospitalization. In much the same way as two individuals with a cough may require two different treatments, so might two adolescents who run away from home. One cough may be a cold, the other may be lung cancer; chemotherapy would not be appropriate for both coughers. Recommending hospitalization for all adolescents who exhibit similar behaviors would be analogous to assuming that all male adolescents who pierce their ears are gay or that all teens who wear red are Bloods. Because the population of adolescents who exhibit similar behaviors is heterogeneous, some youth need less intrusive treatment, structure, and supervision than others. Community-based programs have demonstrated effectiveness in caring for youth with a wide range of difficulties without compromising the safety of the community (Kinney, Haapala, & Booth, 1991; National Research Council, 1993; Whittaker, Kinney, Tracy, & Booth, 1990).

Finally, the concept of grouping together adolescents with seemingly similar problems in an effort to decrease their problem behaviors is by itself dangerous. The power that social groups have on social behavior, particularly during adolescence, is widely known (Worchel & Austin, 1986). Dynamics such as conformity to group norms and groupthink (Janis, 1983) actually help hospitalized teens learn new, more problematic behaviors than those they had at the time of admission. During investigative hearings into the psychiatric industry, one mother recounted how her sixth-grade son had been hospitalized because of poor school performance. After four months of treatment at a cost of almost $100,000, he returned to school and immediately failed three subjects. However, he now failed these classes proudly and with a cigarette in his mouth, attitudes he picked up from the older kids in his hospital unit. Inpatient settings provide youth with the perfect environment to see modeled, then practice, then get reinforced for acquiring unproductive, unhealthy, and dangerous behaviors.

Inpatient Care Does Not Work

Studies experimentally evaluating the effectiveness of inpatient treatment for adolescents are missing, largely because the purveyors of such services are proprietary and not eager to undergo scientific scrutiny. The inability of hospitals to successfully address the long-term functioning of adult clients has been discussed (Anthony, 1972; Stein & Test, 1979). However, despite the countless dollars that have been spent to hospitalize children, scientific evidence supporting this modality is virtually nonexistent.

The lack of demonstrated effectiveness of inpatient treatment is not surprising considering its implicit theoretical underpinnings. Inpatient treatment is most often based on the medical model. The model emphasizes disease, not health (Pardeck & Murphy, 1993), and treatment involves "doing something to the person," in isolation from the day-to-day environment (Weick, 1983). The medical model sees the physician as the expert who tells the client what is wrong and how to fix it, thus disregarding the client as a knowledgeable participant in the healing process. Client problems are seen as existing within the person, and treatment ignores environmental contingencies such as poverty, crime, and unemployment. Instead, youth are removed from their environment, treated in the sterile setting of the hospital unit, and then suddenly returned to the environment where the problems were occurring.

The problems associated with treating youth in isolation from their support systems and apart from their usual environment are widely discussed in the literature (Carman & Small, 1988; Pecora, Whittaker, & Maluccio, 1992; Wells, Wyatt, & Hobfoll, 1991; Whittaker, 1979). Treatment models that focus on client strengths, client empowerment, family involvement, and environmental conditions have been shown to be effective, often without removing children from the home (Feldman, 1991; Kinney et al., 1991; Pecora et al., 1992).

Inpatient Care Undermines the Development of Community-Based Services

Social workers who support the inpatient treatment of adolescents unwittingly undermine the development of more effective, more humane, community-based mental health services (Stein & Test, 1979). The process of simply placing problematic youth behind locked doors is a "quick-fix" response to a much larger community problem. Yes, this approach is "quick." Unfortunately, nothing gets "fixed." Instead, the approach kicks in "revolving door" treatment: in the hospital, back to the community, in the hospital, back to the community, and so on (Borland et al., 1989). Repeated hospitalizations do nothing but contribute to problem resilience and parent and adolescence hopelessness. Communities that fail to develop alternative services are caught in a Catch-22: if they do not have the services, social workers use hospital care. If social workers use hospital care, they drain the impetus and financial resources necessary to develop community services. Community-based services provide an alternative to hospitalization and, more importantly, produce better quality of life for clients involved (Borland et al., 1989).

Some critics contend that a move away from hospital care has done nothing but transinstitutionalize: people moved from hospitals to the streets or jail. The worn-out argument goes that because communities fail to develop outpatient and local services, hospital care is better than no care at all. Carried further, this argument says that because a community fails to provide immunizations for infants it should forbid childbirth or slaughter newborns. Support for the inpatient treatment of adolescents equates with relinquishing support for comprehensive outpatient mental health services.

Inpatient Care Costs Too Much

Skyrocketing health care costs have dramatically changed the health care delivery system. Insurance companies now set prices, limit reimbursement rates, insist on copayments, require that determinations of need be made by their own representatives, and routinely seek the most rapid, least expensive treatment. For example, since 1980, the average length of time mothers spend in the hospital after childbirth has been reduced by 75 percent. During the peak of the inpatient hospital scandal, the average daily cost for inpatient treatment was $700, with an average length of stay of about sixty days. This translates to a cost of $42,000, which will buy more than 1,500 hours of parent training, twelve months of residential treatment, eighteen months of extended day treatment, twenty-four months of family preservation services, thirty-six months of paraprofessional mentoring, or about fifteen years of outpatient therapy. Although the comparative effectiveness of these interventions has not been experimentally decided, few individuals knowledgeable of adolescent development and treatment would in good conscience support sixty days of incarceration. The exorbitant costs of inpatient care, the lack of demonstrable effectiveness, and the availability of less expensive and more theoretically sound services may make this debate purely academic. Insurance companies will simply stop purchasing a product that is prohibitively expensive and just as likely to do harm as good.

Conclusion

Should inpatient hospitalization play a part in a comprehensive continuum of community services for adolescents? By its very nature, a continuum includes an array of services, each with defined purposes and intents, and each presumably with measurable effectiveness. For some teens who engage in chronic suicidal behavior or for those whose psychosis is so severe that confinement for safety is necessary, inpatient care could provide a useful service. However, even under these narrowly defined conditions, several important safeguards are necessary to avoid sanctioned organizational child abuse. First, admission decisions should not be made by one person, nor should they be made by someone with a proprietary interest in the hospital. Second, a full explanation of the purposes, risks, and benefits of the hospitalization should be given to the adolescent in clearly understood language, free from technical jargon, and to his or her legal representative. Third, specific treatment objectives with timeframes should be articulated at admission. These objectives should be closely monitored by an independent reviewer who holds the primary caregiver responsible. Fourth, discharge planning should begin at admission, and quality assurance measures should insure the provision of transition and aftercare services. With these parameters in place, inpatient treatment may assume its place on the continuum of care of services for adolescents.

REFERENCES

Anthony, W. A. (1972). Efficacy of psychiatric rehabilitation. *Psychological Bulletin, 78,* 447–456.

Bentley, K. J. (1994). Is community-based mental health care destined to fail? No. In H. J. Karger, & J. Midgley, (Eds.), *Controversial issues in social policy* (pp. 176–181). Needham Heights, MA: Allyn and Bacon.

Belcher, J. R. (1994). Is community-based mental health care destined to fail? Yes. In H. J. Karger & J. Midgley (Eds.), *Controversial issues in social policy* (pp. 171–175). Needham Heights, MA: Allyn and Bacon.

Borland, A., McRae, J., & Lycan, C. (1989). Outcomes of five years of continuous intensive case management. *Hospital and Community Psychiatry, 40,* 369–376.

Broughton, J. (1987). *Critical theories of psychological development.* New York: Plenum Press.

Carman, G. O., & Small, R. W. (1988). *Permanence and family support: Changing practice in group child care.* Washington, D.C.: Child Welfare League of America.

Deener, B. (1994, April 15). Psychiatric hospital chain agrees to pay millions to settle fraud cases. *Dallas Morning News,* p. 1.

Dintz, S. (1979). Home care treatment as a substitute for hospitalization: The Louisville experiment. In Lamb, H. R. (Ed.), *Alternatives to acute hospitalization* (pp. 1–15). San Francisco, CA: Jossey-Bass.

Everbach, T. (1994, September 27). Hospital sues company, cites anti-trust laws and alleges scheme involving psychiatric patients. *Dallas Morning News,* p. 22.

Feldman, L. H. (1991). Evaluating the impact of intensive family preservation services in New Jersey. In K. Wells & D. E. Biegel (Eds.), *Family preservation services: Research and evaluation* (pp. 47–71). Newbury Park, CA: Sage.

Janis, I. L. (1983). Groupthink. In Blumberg H. H., Hare, A. P., & Dent, V. (Eds.). *Small groups and social interaction* (pp. 39–46). New York: John Wiley & Sons.

Kinney, J., Haapala, D., & Booth, C. (1991). *Keeping families together: The homebuilders model.* New York: Aldine de Gruyter.

Lamb, H. R. (Ed.). (1979). *Alternatives to acute hospitalization.* San Francisco CA: Jossey-Bass.

Lamb, H. R. (1988). Deinstitutionalization at the crossroads. *Hospital and Community Psychiatry, 39,* 941–945.

Lodge, B. (1994, June 28). Ex-psychiatric hospital exec admits bribing physicians. *Dallas Morning News,* p. 1.

National Research Council. (1993). *Losing generations: Adolescents in high risk settings.* Washington, DC: National Academy Press.

Pardeck, J. T., & Murphy, J. W. (1993). Postmodernism and clinical practice: A critical analysis of the disease model. *Psychological Reports, 72,* 1187–1194.

Paul, G. L. (1969). Chronic mental patients: Current status—future directions. *Psychology Bulletin, 71,* 81–84.

Pecora, P. J., Whittaker, J. K., & Maluccio, A. N. (1992). *The child welfare challenge: Policy, practice, and research.* New York: Aldine deGruyter.

Stein, L. I., & Test, M. A. (1979). From the hospital to the community: A shift in the primary locus of care. In Lamb, H. R. (Ed.), *Alternatives to acute hospitalization* (pp. 15–32). San Francisco CA: Jossey-Bass.

Weick, A. (1983). Issues in overturning a medical model of social work practice. *Social Work, 28,* 467–471.

Wells, K., Wyatt, E., & Hobfoll, S. (1991). Factors associated with adaptation of youths discharged from residential treatment. *Children and Youth Services Review, 13,* 199–216.

Whittaker, J. (1979). *Caring for troubled children: Residential treatment in a community context.* San Francisco, CA: Jossey-Bass.

Whittaker, J. K., & Pfeiffer, S. (1994). Research priorities for residential group care. *Child Welfare, 73,* 583–601.

Whittaker, J. K., Kinney, J., Tracy, E. M., & Booth, C. (1990). *Reaching high-risk families.* New York: Aldine de Gryuter.

Worchel, S., & Austin, W. G. (1986). *Psychology of intergroup relations.* Chicago: Nelson-Hall.

Rejoinder to Mr. Carson and Dr. Dangel   Raymond Jefferson
Waller

In response to Carson and Dangel, I will address the major assertions of their argument, rather than attempt to reiterate my position that social workers should support the inpatient care of nonpsychotic adolescents. Rather than propose additional empirical evidence, I will honor the debate format of this text, and respond directly to the apparent flaws of their position.

Our colleagues have demonstrated both the incisive ability to identify important precautionary measures that we should consider before the consideration of using inpatient hospitalization for nonpsychotic adolescents as well as a flair for the dramatic. Scandal erupts when the gross tragedy of the failure of a 39-cent lightbulb results in the crash of a jet liner and the accompanying loss of life. Such occurrences are indeed tragedies, even though air travel is among the safest, most convenient methods of transportation. These scandals often result in new safety techniques and new technology that ultimately improve, rather than terminate, service delivery. Carson and Dangel have, quite aptly, appealed to our emotions in an attempt to dissuade those of us who are actually engaged in practice with troubled adolescents that we should immediately discontinue our professional support for inpatient care for those clients for whom it is indicated.

What a careful reading of the argument offered by Carson and Dangel does show is that, despite their plea and presentation, they failed to cite one empirical outcome study that corroborates their statement that inpatient hospitalization actually fails to help adolescents who receive care in inpatient settings. They propose tentative evidence that hospitalization might not help adults, even though there is a tremendous developmental difference in adolescents and adults that should preclude such comparisons. They further suggest that abuses that have occurred during hospitalization are harmful. I doubt, however, that professional social workers support these abuses.

I agree that hospitalization can result in adolescents modeling aberrant behaviors, but our colleagues have, in my opinion, missed the point. Adolescents whose behavior has deteriorated to such a degree that hospitalization is warranted are not likely to be typically middle-class, engaged in developmentally appropriate legerdemain or exhibiting the behavioral manifestations of adolescent "conflict." Adolescents who have reached the point of being considered for hospitalization are likely to have been, by virtue of extreme behaviors, already rejected by their "normal" peers. Therefore, they are likely to be already bereft of appropriate peer modeling and to be within the influence of a "deviant" peer group.

Carson and Dangel suggest that the average hospitalization of an adolescent may cost $42,000, and they describe less expensive services that could be purchased with that amount of money, such as fifteen years of outpatient therapy. With the same amount of money, one could also purchase 1,400,000 peppermint candies, but this would not necessarily be helpful unless one had hypoglycemia or severe halitosis. A breakdown such as that offered by our colleagues has little relevance to those who need inpatient care. Indeed, they conclude their argument by providing a group of circumstances and conditions that they believe might warrant hospitalization. I find this strange. If I truly believed that inpatient care was as dangerous as our colleagues propose, I cannot fathom any circumstance that would allow me to support this method of care.

Apparently, Carson and Dangel are of the impression that hospitalization is the intervention of choice for all adolescents who have emotional or behavioral problems. Were this the case (and it is not), then social workers should mount the steed of justice and ride swiftly toward abolishing inpatient psychiatric treatment of nonpsychotic adolescents with Carson and Dangel. However, this method of intervention has been shown to help kids, does fill a needed space on the hierarchy of service delivery, and should, with judicious consideration, be supported for these reasons as a viable treatment alternative by the profession of social work.

Should Clinical Social Workers Support the Use of Outpatient Commitment to Mental Health Treatment?

Walter Gott, M.S.W., is a doctoral student with the School of Social Work at the University of Georgia, where he received his M.S.W. in 1974. Mr. Gott is a licensed clinical social worker and licensed marital and family therapist in Georgia and has spent most of his professional career coordinating an intensive case management program and coordinating social work services on a short-term inpatient psychiatric unit.

Ruta Wilk, D.S.W., is Associate Professor and Chair of the M.S.W. program at the University of South Florida. She received her D.S.W. in social welfare from the University of California at Berkeley, and has a long-standing interest in the public mental health system and the protection of the legal rights of patients.

YES

WALTER GOTT

In the past three decades, many states have revised their civil commitment statutes to include outpatient commitment. This form of civil commitment allows the client to live in the community while following a prescribed treatment program. At least twenty-six states and the District of Columbia explicitly provide outpatient commitment by statute, and it is permitted in some form in virtually all states (McCafferty & Dooley, 1990). Statutes allow outpatient commitment to be used when a client is mentally ill or alcohol or drug dependent, in need of treatment to prevent further disability or deterioration, and will not seek treatment voluntarily. A history of noncompliance with outpatient treatment leading to multiple hospitalizations is usually required, and some states require evidence of prior dangerousness. Outpatient commitment is used to encourage compliance with treatment plans and as a preventative measure for rehospitalizations.

Procedures vary from state to state but generally follow this pattern: A hearing is held to determine if the client meets the requirements for outpatient commitment and to establish a treatment plan. At appointed times, outpatient committed clients are required to report to their community mental health center. However, the client can then refuse medications or other forms of treatment. The center can take action only if the client fails to report. Should the client miss an appointment, the center can petition the court to order the police to bring the client to the center for an evaluation. Hospitalization occurs if the client meets established criteria for involuntary hospitalization. If not, another appointment is made, and the client remains in the community.

Social workers should support the use of outpatient commitment for mental health treatment for the following reasons: Research indicates that, under certain conditions, it can be an effective intervention. It can be a factor in the effective treatment of the most recidivistic clients. It provides both the client and the treatment program the opportunity to form a working relationship. It is consistent with social work values. Each of these issues is described more fully below.

Research on the Effectiveness of Outpatient Commitment

Since 1982, there have been at least ten studies evaluating the influence of outpatient commitment on a variety of outcome variables in the treatment of the mentally ill. With one exception (Bursten, 1986), the authors of each study concluded that outpatient commitment had a positive impact on treatment outcome. Table 9.1 on page 112 presents a summary of the types of studies and the results of this research. Most of the studies have been pretest–posttest designs (O-X-O) without a comparison with control groups. Two studies with comparison groups (Bursten, 1986; Hiday & Scheid-Cook, 1989) showed outpatient commitment not to be effective in reducing hospital admission rates. However, Bursten points out that his result may have been attributable to inconsistent enforcement by outpatient clinics. Hiday and Scheid-Cook point out that their results are favorable when the sample is limited to those who were outpatient committed and actually began outpatient treatment (n = 31). They conclude that outpatient commitment was a success.

The body of research varies in number in sample, ranging from three to 4,140; enforcement procedures, ranging from inconsistent enforcement to strict enforcement; selection of clients, ranging from those judged likely to succeed to

TABLE 9.1 Outpatient Commitment Outcome Studies

Authors	Number	Design	Measures	Results
Hiday and Scheid-Cook (1991)	31	X-O Y-O O	Compliance	Increased
Fernandez and Nygard (1990)	4,140	O-X-O	Admission rate Inpatient days	Decreased Decreased
Hiday and Scheid-Cook (1989)	38	X-O Y-O O	Admission rate Inpatient days Functioning Continuance*	No difference No difference Increased Increased
Schmidt and Geller (1989)	8	O-X-O	Admission rate Length of stay	Decreased Decreased
Van Putten, Santiago, and Berren (1988)	35	X-O O	Length of stay Continuance	Decreased Increased
Hiday and Scheid-Cook (1987)	114	X-O Y-O O	MHC visits Compliance Dangerousness Countinuance	Increased Increased No difference Increased
Bursten (1986)	78	O-X-O O O	Admission rate	No difference
Geller (1986)	3	O-X-O	Admission rate Compliance Quality of life	Decreased Increased Increased
Zanni and de Veau (1986)	42	O-X-O	Admission rate Length of stay	Decreased No difference
Hiday and Goodman (1982)	167	O-X-O	Admission rate	Decreased

*Continuance indicates remaining in treatment past the expiration of outpatient commitment court orders.

the most recidivistic; treatment and community support provided, ranging from appointments for medications to assertive case management; and length of study, ranging from three months to three years. Results must be interpreted cautiously and more research encouraged. Swartz et al. (1995) make suggestions for additional research that include studying outpatient commitment in settings that offer high-quality community treatment, standardizing enforcement procedures, and studying subpopulations. This research suggests a positive impact and justifies the use of outpatient commitment for additional research and clinical evaluation purposes.

Recidivistic Clients

The late 1970s saw the emergence of revolving-door patients, who typically have a chronic mental illness, are noncompliant with outpatient treatment, and are frequently admitted to inpatient hospitalization (Geller, 1992). This is a difficult population to treat and a population that many mental health centers had failed to help (Gronfein, 1985). Outpatient commitment offers mental health centers a means to offer treatment to this population. Its criteria is designed specifically for the recidivistic client, and several studies (see Table 9.1) have shown decreases in hospitalization rates.

Some patient advocates argue that use of outpatient commitment can obscure inadequacies in service systems and can become a substitute for developing high-quality services and support systems (Schwartz & Costanzo, 1987). However, the development of community support systems and services has been a major focus in community mental health treatment. Swartz et al. (1995) report that case management has become essential in state-of-the-art mental health services and recommends assertive case management for the most seriously disabled individuals. They suggest future outpatient commitment research in treatment systems that include aggressive case management and outreach. Hiday and Scheid-Cook (1989) found that centers that had the most success with outpatient commitment used assertive case management. Clinicians in those centers viewed outpatient commitment as an important component of a comprehensive support program for the revolving door client. From the results of their study, Fernandez and Nygard (1990) conclude that the impact of outpatient commitment on the revolving door syndrome is strong.

Opportunities

Outpatient commitment provides an opportunity for the clinician and the client to develop a working relationship. The clinician has a chance to offer support services to the client and to offer counsel and recommendations regarding these services, perhaps permitting the development of a therapeutic relationship. Geller (1986) provides some good examples of this relationship. Missed appointments require follow-up, and the client does not get lost in the caseload. Hendrickson (cf. van Putten, Santiago, & Berren, 1988) believes that outpatient commitment works because it "not only commits the patient but also the treatment team" (p. 958). Three studies (see Table 1) found that clients who were outpatient committed were more likely to continue in treatment months beyond the expiration of their commitment orders than comparison groups. These clients had developed a working relationship with their clinicians, realized the benefits of treatment, and continued treatment voluntarily.

Social Work Values

The issues of patient rights, advocacy, liability, social control, paternalism, and autonomy have been well discussed in the literature (see Geller 1986; Rubenstein, 1986; Schwartz & Costanzo, 1987; and Scheid-Cook, 1991 for a few examples). There are good arguments for and against outpatient commitment based on these issues. The concept of self-determination is fundamental to social work values (National Association of Social Workers, 1980). However, Reamer (1980) provides guidelines to justify paternalism in special circumstances. Two of the guidelines are particularly applicable to outpatient commitment: "Clients are likely to consent to the paternalistic intervention subsequent to the interference" (p. 264), and "A wider range of freedom for the client can be preserved only by restricting it temporarily" (p. 266). Outpatient committed clients are likely to continue treatment voluntarily after their orders expire, and outpatient commitment is time limited and can be discontinued if ineffective. Social workers have traditionally assumed a duty to aid (Reamer, 1990). Commitment to outpatient treatment, combined with high-quality treatment, and using appropriate guidelines such as those suggested by Geller (1990), is consistent with social work values and a social worker's duty to aid.

References

Bursten, B. (1986). Posthospital mandatory outpatient treatment. *American Journal of Psychiatry, 143,* 1255–1258.

Fernandez, G., & Nygard, S. (1990). Evaluation of involuntary outpatient commitment in North Carolina. *Hospital and Community Psychiatry, 41,* 1001–1004.

Geller, J. L. (1986). Rights, wrongs, and the dilemma of coerced community treatment. *American Journal of Psychiatry, 143,* 1259–1264.

Geller, J. L. (1990). Clinical guidelines for the use of involuntary outpatient commitment. *Hospital and Community Psychiatry, 41,* 749–755.

Geller, J. L. (1992). A historical perspective on the role of state hospitals viewed from the era of the "revolving door." *American Journal of Psychiatry, 149,* 1526–1533.

Gronfein, W. (1985). Incentives and intentions in mental health policy: A comparison of the Medicaid and community mental health programs. *Journal of Health and Social Behavior, 26,* 192–206.

Hiday, V. A., & Goodman, R. R. (1982). The least restrictive alternative to involuntary hospitalization, outpatient commitment: Its use and effectiveness. *Journal of Psychiatry and Law, 10,* 81–96.

Hiday, V. A., & Scheid-Cook, T. L. (1987). The North Carolina experience with outpatient commitment: A critical appraisal. *International Journal of Law and Psychiatry, 10,* 215–232.

Hiday, V. A., & Scheid-Cook, T. L. (1989). A follow-up of chronic patients committed to outpatient treatment. *Hospital and Community Psychiatry, 40,* 52–59.

Hiday, V. A., & Scheid-Cook, T. L. (1991). Outpatient commitment for "revolving door" patients: Compliance and treatment. *The Journal of Nervous and Mental Disease, 179,* 83–88.

McCafferty, G., & Dooley, J. (1990). Involuntary outpatient commitment: An update. *Mental and Physical Disability Law Reporter, 14,* 277–287.

National Association of Social Workers. (1980). *Code of Ethics.* Washington, DC: Author.

Reamer, F. G. (1980). The concept of paternalism in social work. *Social Service Review, 57,* 254–271.

Reamer, F. G. (1990). *Ethical dilemmas in social service.* New York: Columbia University Press.

Rubenstein, L. S. (1986). Treatment of the mentally ill: Legal advocacy enters the second generation. *American Journal of Psychiatry, 143,* 1264–1269.

Scheid-Cook, T. L. (1991). The validity of social control critiques: Psychiatric medication, side effects, and outpatient commitment. *Sociological Focus, 24,* 59–76.

Schmidt, M. J., & Geller, J. L. (1989). Involuntary administration of medication in the community: The judicial opportunity. *Bulletin of the American Academy of Psychiatry and the Law, 17,* 287–292.

Schwartz, S. J., & Costanzo, C. E. (1987). Compelling treatment in the community: Distorted doctrines and violated values. *Loyola of Los Angeles Law Review, 20,* 1329–1429.

Swartz, M. S., Burns, B. J., Hiday, V. A., George, L. K., Swanson, L K., & Wagner, H. R. (1995). New directions in research on involuntary outpatient commitment. *Psychiatric Services, 46,* 381–385.

Van Putten, R. A., Santiago, J. M., & Berren, M. R. (1988). Involuntary outpatient Commitment in Arizona: A retroactive study. *Hospital and Community Psychiatry, 39,* 953–958.

Rejoinder to Mr. Gott

RUTA WILK

Mr. Gott cites ten studies in his argument that involuntary outpatient commitment is an effective treatment. I applaud his use of empirical research to validate his position; however, the very research he cites is replete with conditions and qualifications that affect the outcome of treatment. They may be summarized as, "Yes, some individuals might avoid commitment to an inpatient setting, if conditions are just so." But when one considers just a few of the many unique factors, alluded to by Mr. Gott, that can affect successful treatment—the clients must be just the right clients, the courts must make appropriate decisions in situations where knowledge is not perfect, the court orders must be interpreted accurately and enforced with enthusiasm by professionals who strongly believe in outpatient commitment as an intervention, the clients must show up for treatment, there must be support from collaterals in the community—one is not surprised that results are mixed and success rates are lower than proponents might have hoped. I believe that the outcomes of the studies cited have not made the case for effectiveness of this approach. Instead, because we operate in a "messy," rather than ideal, world, we see disappointing results in which yet another mental health treatment breakthrough falls short of the promises made by professionals because we cannot control all of the players in the system—judges, therapists, psychiatrists, clients, family members, and taxpayers as well.

I find it difficult to agree with Mr. Gott's final two arguments—opportunity to develop a working relationship and consistency with social work values. Regarding the first, I am reminded of the old saw, "You can lead a horse to water but you can't make him drink." In involuntary treatment, therapist and client are thrown together, and as Mr. Gott says, "*perhaps* permitting the development of a therapeutic relationship" (emphasis mine). Client participation by choice is, I believe, the *sine qua non* of a working relationship for the purposes of therapy. How can a relationship be therapeutic when it is based on coercion, and when the client knows that not showing up for treatment can result in having the police show up at your doorstep and haul you off for an "evaluation"? Even Mr. Gott suggests, in his section entitled "Opportunities," that the epitome of success is the case in which the client continues treatment *voluntarily.*

In addition, Mr. Gott himself states that "the concept of self-determination is fundamental to social work values." It is frightening to me to think that we as social workers are so willing to ignore this value while we decide what is for someone elses own good. This is the paternalism that I thought our profession gladly left behind decades ago. Unless an individual is a minor, or is found to be legally incompetent (which is not the case for persons ordered to involuntary community treatment), or has given up certain rights to freedom by breaking the law, there should be no exception, no matter how well intentioned, to ones right to self-determination. The social workers duty to aid, in my opinion, does not apply in a situation in which adults are mentally capable of making a choice about whether they want our aid.

Mr. Gott states that recidivistic clients are the focus of the outpatient commitment approach, and I agree that these individuals present a dilemma for mental health professionals. He points to studies that have found a decrease in hospital admission rates where involuntary outpatient commitment is used. Of the ten studies, seven looked at admission rates, and among these, the results were mixed.

Even if all of the studies showed success, however, the question for social workers wondering whether to support involuntary outpatient commitment still remains: does the end justify the means?

NO

Ruta Wilk

Although receiving mental health treatment, even involuntarily, on an outpatient basis seems like an arguably better alternative than involuntary commitment to a psychiatric hospital, I argue that it is not an alternative that social workers should support.

Background

Before presenting that arguments, it is necessary to define the term *outpatient commitment,* because it is frequently misunderstood and confused with other related terms, such as "conditional release" or "least restrictive alternative." For the purposes of this debate, "outpatient commitment" refers to a "judicial order, entered pursuant to a states civil commitment scheme, which compels a person to participate in mental health programs and to comply with a court-approved treatment regimen outside of the walls of a mental institution" (Schwartz & Costanzo, 1987, pp. 1332–1333).

Two predominant scenarios involve outpatient commitment: first, after a period spent in a mental hospital, an individual is legally required to continue outpatient treatment; this is similar to the common practice of conditional release or trial visits, except that in those cases one is technically still a patient of the hospital; and second, at time of initial judicial disposition, outpatient commitment used as an alternative to commitment to a hospital. The latter scenario has been observed to have inherent contradictions; in other words, if one is ill enough for the hospital, one cannot be well enough to be in the community. In a study of family members opinions about civil commitment, McFarland, Faulkner, Bloom, and Hallaux (1990) found that "In relation to their relative's last commitment, family members indicated that their mentally ill relative was too dangerous (50 percent) or too sick (45 percent) for outpatient commitment at that time" (p. 539). Indeed, this judicial scenario involves a dilemma regarding legal standards for commitment that must be either resolved through legislative change or ignored in violation of state law. Although many states have had some form of noninstitutional involuntary treatment, for example, conditional release, written in existing law for a long time, the most recent debates about involuntary commitment have revolved around the desirability of aggressively increasing the use of this alternative, and consequently increasing the number of individuals under the control of the state and the courts.

For involuntary outpatient commitment to work, there must be sufficient community-based treatment alternatives in place. In most cases, treatment would be provided under the auspices of a community mental health center. Because social workers form an important component of the staffing in community mental health centers, they would play a pivotal role in the implementation of any system of outpatient involuntary treatment. Therefore, it is important for social workers to understand what such involuntary treatment would involve.

States that have revised their mental health legislation over the past few years to specifically authorize involuntary outpatient commitment have gone beyond a simple commitment order on the part of the judge to a much more complicated system of judicial approval of individualized plans that would make up the treatment program with which an individual must comply. These plans could include medication (where the psychiatrist would play the primary role), regular therapy sessions, day programs, residence in a specified community setting, and the like. As one practitioner using involuntary outpatient commitment put it, "Treatment is anything that keeps them out of the hospital and functioning" (Scheid-Cook, 1991, p. 50). All of these activities would be legally mandated, and the patient would be subject to sanctions for not participating in the required treatment.

Why should social workers reject the use of outpatient commitment for mental health treatment? Given the administrative and implementation problems that arise from this approach, I propose three broad reasons: the professional role dilemmas that result, the liability and insurance concerns that emerge, and most importantly, the social work value conflicts inherent in a coercive system of intervention.

Reasons to Oppose Outpatient Commitment

Legally mandated treatment in the community is virtually unenforceable, and puts social workers into difficult and untenable professional positions if they try to enforce it (Wilk, 1988a, 1988b). It raises many unanswerable questions, such as who decides when treatment is successful, and what evidence will be required? Who is responsible if the patient does not comply with treatment, and what should the response be? Automatic hospitalization? With or without another court hearing? What activities must be relinquished to make time for monitoring patients, providing reports to the court, dealing with judges regarding problematic and "unsuccessful" patients, or removing "successful" patients from judicial oversight?

Professional Role Dilemmas

Any treatment that goes beyond simple forced medication, and there are those who suggest that outpatient commitment really comes down to nothing more than this (Schmidt & Geller, 1989), requires a willingness on the part of the patient to engage in a relationship. One cannot force another to participate in therapy, and the phrase "coercive therapy" is an oxymoron. The very image of coercion is antagonistic to the helping relationship. Miller and Fiddleman (1984) state, "While is it certainly possible that requiring attendance at CMHCs for nonmedical treatment might prove effective, to our knowledge there are no data to support such a hypothesis" (p. 150).

Instead of focusing on providing treatment, social workers are put in the role of "mental health police," or perhaps probation officers, rather than mental health providers. In North Carolina, for example, "If the patient refuses treatment or misses schedules appointments, the primary therapist may ask the local sheriff to forcibly bring the patient to the CMHC to try to induce patient treatment compliance." (Scheid-Cook, 1991, p. 47). One can envision situations in which, at the mental health center, an outpatient who is refusing medication may have to be physically restrained, perhaps in the view of other, truly voluntary, patients attending treatment programs. At the very least, this type of involuntary outpatient treatment would require more aggressive, directive case management.

Liability and Insurance Concerns

One of the most serious issues for social workers who treat seriously mentally ill individuals is dangerousness—the patients dangerousness to self or to others. Remember, the patients participating in involuntary outpatient commitment would otherwise be hospitalized; because dangerousness is a necessary criterion for commitment in virtually every state, their degree of disorder is, at least at times, serious enough to require twenty-four-hour supervision. In the community, absent such supervision, the social workers and other mental health providers assume a major risk should their patient harm another or himself. As Lefkovitch, Weiser, and Levy (1993) wryly point out, "It is, after all, asking a great deal of psychiatrists that they assume the burden of caring in the community for individuals whom they have just characterized as dangerous to themselves or others" (Lefkovitch et al., 1993, p. 214). Unless the state's involuntary outpatient commitment law specifically grants sovereign immunity to mental health providers in community mental health centers, the social worker may be subject to legal liability if a patient on involuntary outpatient commitment status harms himself or herself or others. Likewise, the social workers may be liable for damages if the patient or patients family sues the worker.

Social Work Value Conflict

Most importantly, social workers should not support involuntary outpatient commitment because coercion in any sense conflicts with social work values. Why do people argue in favor of involuntary outpatient commitment? Because it is seen as "for the patients own good." But who decides this? What happens to self-determination, and the expressed choices made by clients/patients? Social work professionals do not do things against peoples will because we think its "for their own good." We do not impose our values on our clients. Involuntary outpatient commitment removes the option of self-determination from adults who aré *legally competent* to make decisions about their lives. Remember, if they were deemed legally incompetent they would not even have the option of community treatment; instead, they would be hospitalized to prevent harm, abuse, or exploitation. Involuntary outpatient commitment can be a means of massive expansion of state control over people. It places limitations on one's physical freedom, and on "the fundamental right to control one's body" (Schwartz & Costanzo, p. 1357). This latter phrase has haunting echoes of the arguments made to preserve women's rights to abortion, which the social work profession supports as congruent with its value base.

Another value conflict for social workers deals with resource issues. Given the scarcity and limitations of public mental health services in our society, social workers should think carefully about the impact of numbers of new patients who must be treated, and legally may not be turned away. Who would be turned away for lack of space, and what would be lost? Should social workers support a program that results in further dilution of already scarce community resources? In a national survey of state outpatient commitment practices, Miller concludes that "The major difficulty continues to be the lack of community resources and the reluctance of many community-based clinicians to work with committed patients" (Miller, 1992, p. 81).

Conclusion

There is no doubt that this is a complicated issue. It is true that some people do better when they take medication faithfully, and it would be nice to have a way to *make* them do this. And yes, recidivism is a fact in the lives of many chronically ill people. But taking away choice and self-determination from a competent individual "for their own good" is so paternalistic and in such conflict with the values of professional social work that it seems to me impossible for social workers to support such a concept.

REFERENCES

Lefkovitch, Y., Weiser, M., & Levy, A. (1993). Involuntary outpatient commitment: Ethics and problems. *Medicine and Law, 12,* 213–220.
McFarland, B., Faulkner, L., Bloom, J., & Hallaux, R. (1990). Family members' opinions about civil commitment. *Hospital & Community Psychiatry, 41,* 537–540.

Miller, R. (1992). An update on involuntary civil commitment to outpatient treatment. *Hospital & Community Psychiatry, 43,* 79–81.

Miller, R., & Fiddleman, P. (1984). Outpatient commitment: Treatment in the least restrictive environment? *Hospital & Community Psychiatry, 35,* 147–151.

Scheid-Cook, T. (1991). Outpatient commitment as both social control and least restrictive alternative. *Sociological Quarterly, 32,* 43–60.

Schwartz, S., & Costanzo, C. (1987). Compelling treatment in the community: Distorted doctrines and violated values. *Loyola of Los Angeles Law Review, 20,* 1329–1429.

Schmidt, M. & Geller, J. (1989). Involuntary administration of medication in the community: The judicial opportunity. *Bulletin of American Academy of Psychiatry and Law, 17,* 283–292.

Wilk, R. (1988a). Involuntary outpatient commitment of the mentally ill. *Social Work, 33,* 133–137.

Wilk, R. (1988b). Implications of involuntary outpatient commitment for community mental health agencies. *American Journal of Orthopsychiatry, 58,* 580–591.

Rejoinder to Dr. Wilk   WALTER GOTT

Dr. Wilk makes compelling arguments against outpatient commitment. However, her arguments are of a general nature and can be easily countered when examined specifically. My reaction is, "Hey, let's not throw out the baby with the bath water here!"

First, before examining Dr. Wilk's main points, a picky detail: She states that the patient will be subject to sanctions for not participating in the required treatment. Just what are these "sanctions"? The patient can be brought to the center for evaluation, and that is all. The patient is rehospitalized only if he or she meets the usual established criteria; if not, the patient is returned to the community. The only sanction is an evaluation.

Unanswerable Questions

The "unanswerable questions" that Dr. Wilk raises are answerable. Outpatient commitment is enforced by having the patient brought in for evaluation. Can we make a patient take medication or participate in other treatment? No. However, being brought in for evaluation is effective, as the research indicates. Who enforces and decides if the treatment is effective? The clinician/treatment program, of course. Hopefully, this is done in collaboration with the patient. Outpatient commitment is time limited and in Georgia can be discontinued by the clinician/treatment program before the allotted time expires if the clinician determines that it is no longer needed. A petition for continuing outpatient commitment can be filed by the clinician/treatment program if needed.

Professional Role Dilemmas

Those of us with experience in the treatment of children, in the treatment of involuntarily hospitalized patients, or in assertive case management know that a therapeutic relationship does not necessarily have to begin with a "willingness on the part of the patient to engage in a relationship," as Dr. Wilk states. Therapeutic relationships often begin by exploring resistance and confronting the patient's unwillingness to participate. The role dilemma of "police" versus "therapist" is not insurmountable. Of course, unskilled clinicians could function as "mental health police" when implementing outpatient commitment. That potential is there, but hopefully, clinicians will use this intervention to explore resistance, confront and support behavior, offer a wide range of program options, and build a treatment relationship. Three studies (see Table 9.1) have found that clients who were outpatient committed were more likely to continue in treatment months beyond the expiration of their commitment orders than comparison groups. These clients had developed a working relationship with their clinicians and continued treatment voluntarily. Effective clinical relationships can be built using outpatient commitment.

Liability and Insurance Concerns

This issue is a tough one because there are legitimate concerns in states in which the statutes do not clearly distinguish between the criteria for hospitalization and the criteria for outpatient commitment. Fortunately, many states make this distinction by clarifying that the criteria for hospitalization is imminent dangerousness, and the criteria for outpatient commitment is a history of dangerousness or involuntary hospitalization. Georgia and North Carolina are two states that make such a distinction. Dr. Wilk confounds the issue by blurring the criteria for dangerousness and involuntary hospitalization. This issue, however, calls for clinical clarity. Patients who are imminently dangerous should be treated in a hospital. Statutes, however, do not allow patients to be kept involuntarily in the hospital when there is no imminent danger. These patients must be discharged. Outpatient commitment offers an alternative to discharge without mental health contact; it is not an alternative to involuntary hospitalization. If the patient is imminently dangerous, hospitalization is required, and should the patient with a history of dangerousness, living in the community, become dangerous, this person, if participating in outpatient commitment, will likely be hospitalized sooner because the imminent dangerousness will be detected by the regular evaluations at the mental health center. I am aware of no liability suits arising from outpatient commitment. I can more readily imagine cases arising out of the failure to outpatient commit.

Social Work Value Conflict

There is a social work value conflict arising from outpatient commitment. Any paternalistic intervention engenders a social work value conflict and requires careful consideration. However, in my opinion, a social worker's duty to aid and other arguments presented in my initial statement win out. Outpatient commitment can be effective in building positive treatment relationships and in keeping the most recidivistic out of the hospital. If, in a particular situation, it is not, then, because it is time limited, it can be discontinued. Research has shown that outpatient commitment's potential for effectiveness is high. Our clients, when qualified, deserve a trial with this intervention.

Should Social Workers Rely on Repressed Memories of Childhood Incest "Recovered" during Therapy?

David Prichard, Ph.D., is an assistant professor of social work at the University of New England. He has worked as a senior mental health crisis clinician for the Chesterfield County (VA) Mental Health Center, where he was also a member of the Sexual Abuse Task Force. He received his Ph.D. in social work from Virginia Commonwealth University, where his dissertation focused on the primary and secondary inpact of trauma. His major professional interest is in the primary and vicarious impact of trauma.

J. Timothy Stocks, Ph.D., is an Assistant Professor at the Michigan State University School of Social Work. He has worked as a protective services worker and child abuse intake investigator for the Florida Department of Health and Rehabilitative Services. Before this he was on staff at the Sex Offender Unit of the North Florida Evaluation and Treatment Center. He received his M.S.W. and Ph.D. from Florida State University.

YES

DAVID C. PRICHARD

It is a pleasure for me to present the "yes" side of the debate on whether social workers should rely on repressed memories of childhood incest recovered during therapy. This issue has been simmering for years. Research indicates that many women have experienced sexual abuse in childhood (Finkelhor, Hotaling, Lewis, & Smith, 1990). However, there is convincing evidence in support of illusory "recovered memories." With the publications of recent popular books on incest and recovery (e.g., Bass & Davis, 1988; Frederickson, 1992) and the subsequent outcry by others about "false memories," the topic is likely to be among the most emotionally heated and publicly debated controversies in social work in the 1990s.

Although the issue has become polarized, there is increasing evidence (e.g., Herman & Schatzow, 1987; Williams, in press) that strongly supports the validity of repressed memories of childhood incest recovered during therapy. Social work practitioners must not shy away from exploring this issue because of the fear of encouraging false memories. That is not to say that we need to go on a fishing expedition for these memories or necessarily believe without question everything that we hear from clients. Neither should we diminish or invalidate their reality and experience as we listen and encourage the emergence of memories associated with bodily sensations or conscious recollections. Client body memories may be vague, and narratives are often tentative, cautious, and confused. Both, however, will emerge in due time as the client is ready to process and deal with the memories recovered.

Fortunately, there is a developing body of research that supports the veracity of recovered memories and makes a strong case for social workers to develop competence in this area of practice. The fuss about "false memories," although a documented and legitimate area of concern, should not deter the competent, qualified social work practitioner. False memories need to be treated as the exception and not the rule.

My argument is twofold. First, I offer an overview of supportive evidence related to general concepts in the debate—implicit and explicit memory encoding and retrieval processes in children. Second, I present the most current evidence in support of validity of recovered memories of repressed childhood sexual abuse. In conclusion, I discuss the place of body work and narrative with this population forms of therapy in the clinical setting when memories of incest emerge.

Recollection of Childhood Events

There is general agreement that adults forget at least some traumatic events experienced in childhood. Research on childhood amnesia suggests that if a child experiences a trauma before a fully functioning autobiographical memory system has developed, retrieval of explicit memory of the event may be lost (Schactel, 1947; Usher & Neisser, 1993). What is the process by which children encode and later retrieve memories? Siegel (1995) summarizes research that suggests that children have excellent coding and retrieval capacities for implicit memory (behavioral, bodily memory processes), but those for explicit memory (subjective conscious experience of "recalling" a fact or event) are immature and may lead to inconsistencies in cued and spontaneous recall for personally experienced events. It is not unusual for children older than age five (range, three to seven) years to experience amnesia around non–trauma-related events.

Children, then, encode both bodily sensations and autobiographical narrative; however, their ability to recall is limited to the bodily sensations with no narrative context. The recalling of such traumatic events, then, often occurs initially through retrieval of those memories related to body memories. Various types of body work in the therapy setting may trigger or unlock some memories stored in the unconscious part of the brain. Thus, we see the use of body work as a means to recall early childhood traumatic events that may be encoded implicitly but are lost to explicit memory recall.

Repressed Memories of Incest

There is substantive literature supporting the validity of repression of sexual abuse memories and their recovery (Briere & Conte, 1993; Herman & Schatzow, 1987; Williams, 1994). A common symptom of repressed memories of childhood sexual abuse, cited in both scientific and popular literature, is significant gaps in the client's memory of childhood (Bass & Davis, 1988; Sgroi, 1989). The false memory/recovered memory debate centers around the possible relation between gaps in a client's memory and the recollection of childhood sexual abuse: is repressed sexual abuse a valid or even likely explanation for these gaps, and are the memories *created* (often with the help of the therapist) to fill the gaps?

At least two professional journals have recently covered this issue extensively. *Consciousness and Cognition* (1994, *3*[3/4]) published a special issue titled "The Recovered Memory/False Memory Debate"; and *Applied Cognitive Psychology* (1994, *8*[4]) titled its special issue "Recovery of Memories of Childhood Sexual Abuse." Each explores both sides of the debate. Research suggests clearly that some adult clients who report experiencing sexual abuse in childhood have gone through periods of forgetting that abuse occurred.

Gold, Hughes, & Swingle (1995) present data based on interviews with 160 woman survivors of childhood sexual abuse. Their sample consists of 26.3 percent women who retained fairly complete recollection both in the past and currently, 36.9 percent who lost and subsequently recovered sexual abuse memories, and 36.8 percent with vague or incomplete degrees of memory. If repression is taken to mean some degree of forgetting the details of the abuse, most of the sample (71.9 percent) could be considered to have "repressed" their sexual abuse experiences. These findings are impressive support for the repression that occurs among women sexually abused as children.

So what about "false memories"? The "false memory" side of the debate questions the veracity of recovered memories, but relies on contrary anecdotal evidence and general studies on memory and suggestibility to determine claims of recovered memory (Wakefield & Underwager, 1992). There is compelling evidence on recovered memories of abuse in women with documented child sexual victimization histories. Although some studies may be open to attack from proponents of the "false memory syndrome," because of an inability to corroborate the abuse, more recent research address this concern by building into the methodology independent corroboration of the occurrence of abuse (Herman & Schatzow, 1987; Williams, in press).

Williams (in press) provides convincing corroborative evidence on recovered memories of sexual abuse and suggests that many women recalling sexual abuse in childhood had periods in the past when they did not remember what had happened to them. What is interesting about this study is that the recollection of abuse among participants was verifiable from hospital records, thus controlling for the possibility of "false" memories. One hundred twenty-nine adult women with documented histories of sexual victimization in childhood were interviewed and asked about abuse history. Seventeen years after the initial report of abuse, 62 percent of the women recalled the victimization, and 16 percent reported that at some time in the past they had forgotten the abuse.

The evidence in support of the validity of recovered memories of childhood incest in some individuals cannot be ignored. The findings are clear, irrefutable, and corroborated. Some women who have experienced sexual abuse as children appear to repress explicit recall of these memories, only to recover these memories in adulthood.

Narrative and Recovering Repressed Memories of Childhood Incest

What are social work practitioners to do? It is critical to understand and validate the signs and symptoms in women and men who have experienced incest in childhood. However, practitioners should monitor their own hypersensitivity to the issue, and avoiding interpreting every client complaint as a symptom of repressed childhood incest experiences. Proponents of the "false memory syndrome" would have us err on the side of believing little of what we hear from clients regarding childhood sexual abuse. I suggest that for social workers to be overly suspicious of a client's report of childhood incest is an invalidation of the client's emerging perceptions. It may be a perpetuation of the dynamics of the original abuse (if you tell, no one will believe you). Memories recovered during therapy provide a rich field from which to mine extremely relevant and important clinical data.

The role of the social worker trained in this area is to assist in the retrieval of implicit memories of childhood (perhaps through body work) and explicit recall of early childhood experiences. The client's task is to attach meaning to their recovered memories, as they find a voice to develop a childhood narrative.

In summary, we have considered memory encoding and retrieval, the evidence supporting the recovery of repressed memories of childhood, and touched on the importance of body work and narrative in clinical treatment. It would be unfortunate if the result of the debate was the minimization and invalidation by social workers of clients' early childhood experiences. Indeed, it would be tragic for social workers eager to avoid illusory false memories, to discourage the uncovering of valid repressed memories of incest that begin to emerge in therapy.

REFERENCES

Bass, E., & Davis, L. (1988). *The courage to heal.* New York: Harper & Row.

Briere, J., & Conte, J. (1993). Self-reported amnesia for adults molested as children. *Journal of Traumatic Stress, 6,* 21–31.

Finkelhor, D., Hotaling, G., Lewis, I., & Smith, C. (1990). Sexual abuse in the national survey of adult men and women: Prevalence, characteristics, and risk factors. *Child Abuse and Neglect, 14,* 19–28.

Frederickson, R. (1992). *Repressed memories: A journey to recovery from sexual abuse.* New York: Simon & Schuster.

Gold, S., Hughes, D., & Swingle, J. (1995, July). *Degrees of memory of sexual abuse among female survivors.* Paper presented at the 4th International Family Violence Research Conference, Durham, NH.

Herman, J., & Schatzow, E. (1987). Recovery and verification of memories of childhood sexual trauma. *Psychoanalytic Psychology, 4,* 1–14.

Sgroi, S. (1989). Stages of recovery for adult survivors of sexual abuse. In S. M. Sgroi (Ed.), *Vulnerable populations: Evaluation and treatment of sexually abused children and adult survivors* (Vol. 1, pp. 137–186). Lexington, MA: Lexington Books.

Siegel, D. (1995). Memory, trauma, and psychotherapy: A cognitive science view. *Journal of Psychotherapy Practice and Research, 4,* 92–122.

Schactel, E. (1947). On memory and childhood amnesia. *Psychiatry, 10,* 1–26.

Usher, J., & Neisser, J. (1993). Childhood amnesia and the beginnings of memory for early life events. *Journal of Experimental Psychology: General, 122,* 155–165.

Wakefield, H., & Underwager, R. (1992). Recovered memories of alleged sexual abuse: Lawsuits against parents. *Behavioral Sciences and the Law, 10,* 483–507.

Williams, L. (1994). Recall of childhood trauma: A prospective study of women's memories of child sexual abuse. *Journal of Consulting and Clinical Psychology, 62,* 1167–1176.

Williams, L. (in press). Recovered memories of abuse in women with documented child sexual victimization histories. *Journal of Traumatic Stress.*

Rejoinder to Dr. Prichard

J. TIMOTHY STOCKS

Dr. Prichard has ably and clearly presented the position of those who believe that so-called recovered memories are reliable. He has appropriately cautioned against going on "fishing expeditions" for such memories or necessarily believing "without question everything we hear from clients."

Unfortunately, he has also proceeded to contradict these self-same cautions by advocating the use of aggressive memory recovery techniques, in this instance, "body work." There are also serious problems with his arguments for the reliability of "recovered" memories.

The defense of the reliability of "recovered" memories began with a discussion of memory encoding and retrieval. Specifically, there was the assertion that childhood bodily sensations (implicit memory) could be retrieved and, through the use of "body work," brought into narrative form (explicit memory). This discussion was largely based on a literature review by Siegel (1995). However, examination of the sources (Fivush & Hudson, 1990; Nelson, 1993) from which Siegel's discussion of implicit and explicit memory is derived does not support the notion that "recovered" memories are reliable. Nelson (1993), one of the researchers cited, observed:

> The validity of any given memory is not relevant within the present theoretical framework. Although the validity of a memory may be of concern if one is interested in such issues as whether children are reliable witnesses, it is of less concern if one is interested in when they begin to retain memories in the autobiographical memory system. *Memories do not need to be true or correct to be part of that system.* (italics added, p. 8)

Siegel (1995) also noted later in the review that:

> The nature of post-event dialogue regarding an experience can influence the manner and probability of recall of an experience (p. 95), . . .[and]. . . Given the highly suggestive nature of both children and adults it is crucial that health practitioners be aware of their own biases so as not to inadvertently influence or pressure nontraumatized individuals toward believing in aspects of their histories that may not have occurred. (p. 108)

In no instance did Siegel or the source authors discuss the reliability of "body work" as a memory recovery technique. One may wonder why no information was presented in Dr. Prichard's essay on the accuracy of memory derived from "body work." The answer is simple. There is none. It is a technique with no credible empirical foundation.

The next argument was a variant on Blume's (1990) discredited "Post-Incest Syndrome" argument. It was argued that memory gaps are diagnostic of childhood sexual abuse. I have already discussed the lack of any reliable symptoms in adulthood for childhood sexual abuse. Siegel's (1995) review of the memory literature noted that many adults who experience normal development report that they do not recall details from childhood:

> Clinical implications of these findings are that therapists should not overzealously interpret lack of recall as a pathognomic indicator of "repressed" trauma. Also, an increased tendency to recall childhood in midlife may be a normal de-

velopmental event and not a sign that something in childhood is "hidden" and now is intruding on consciousness. (p. 108)

The next argument involved research about independent corroboration of "recovered" memories of sexual abuse. Two "irrefutable" studies were cited. The first (Herman & Schatzow, 1987) has already been discussed. The reader will recall that only 26 percent of the women in this study had entered with no memory of sexual abuse and later recovered a memory. The other participants were approximately equally divided between those with clear memories and those with partial memories. Furthermore, the confirmation of sexual abuse was based upon the subjects' reports that *they* had obtained confirmation. There was no indication that the authors cross-checked these reports. This is problematic because the desire to please the therapist may influence client reports (Weekes, Lynn, Green, & Brentar, 1992; Spence, 1982).

The Williams (in press) study involved a follow-up of women who were seen as children at a hospital recovery room for sexual abuse. Some of these women forgot the abuse, and some of these who forgot later remembered.

The argument that this is evidence for the reliability of "recovered memories" of sexual abuse may be stated as follows:

> **I.** If recovered memories of sexual abuse are reliable, then some adults who were abused as children will forget and later recover memories of documented sexual abuse.
> **II.** There are adults who have forgotten and later recovered memories of documented sexual abuse.

Therefore,

> **III.** Recovered memories are reliable.

This is, of course, the logical fallacy of *affirming the consequent,* which may be demonstrated by:

> **I.** If an individual is a registered voter, then he or she is over eighteen years old.
> **II.** Pat is over eighteen years old.

Therefore,

> **III.** Pat is a registered voter.

Unfortunately, not all individuals over eighteen are registered voters. Nor does it necessarily follow that all individuals who "recover" memories of sexual abuse have been sexually abused. Their memories may be confabulations.

Memory is malleable, especially within a therapeutic relationship. There is *no* way to distinguish between memories of events and memories that are confabulations. The use of aggressive memory recovery techniques has been demonstrated to have caused great harm to some clients and their families. The use of aggressive memory recovery techniques has *never* been demonstrated to help clients. The use of aggressive memory recovery techniques is *inappropriate* practice for social workers.

References

Blume, E. S. (1990). *Secret survivors: Uncovering incest and its aftereffects in women.* New York: John Wiley & Sons.
Fivush, R., & Hudson, J. A. (1990). *Knowing and remembering in young children.* New York: Cambridge University Press.
Herman, J. L., & Schatzow, E. (1987). Recovery and verification of childhood sexual trauma. *Psychoanalytic Psychology, 4,* 1–14.
Nelson, K. (1993). The psychological and social origins of autobiographical memory. *Psychological Science, 2,* 1–8.
Siegel, D. J. (1995). Memory, trauma, and psychotherapy: A cognitive science view. *Journal of Psychotherapy Practice and Research, 4,* 93–122.
Spence, D. (1992). *Narrative truth and historical truth.* New York: W. W. Norton.
Weekes, J. R., Lynn, S. J., Green, J. P., & Brentar, J. T. (1992). Pseudomemory in hypnotized and task-motivated subjects. *Journal of Abnormal Psychology, 101,* 356–360.
Williams, L. M. (in press). Recovered memories of abuse in women with documented child sexual victimization. *Journal of Traumatic Stress.*

NO

J. Timothy Stocks

Memory recovery techniques do not enhance memory and may result in the creation of memories of events that never occurred. Given the history of a hard-fought and continuing struggle for a societal concession that child sexual abuse is a real problem, it is not surprising that many clinicians and advocates have responded with hostility to the assertion that recovered memories may frequently be false memories. Many regard concerns about recovered memories as just another example of the long-standing denial or minimization of the extent of sexual abuse in our society.

Still, there are reasonable grounds for social workers to be concerned about memory work. Specifically, the concern is with the aggressive and prolonged pursuit of suspected repressed memories. This involves using memory recovery techniques such as hypnotism, dream interpretation, journaling, and guided imagery. Other problematic techniques involve having clients who do not remember abuse join incest survivors groups, telling clients who do not remember being sexually abused that they have symptoms indicative of repressed memories of sexual abuse, and disputing any client doubts about accuracy of their memories. Each of these memory retrieval techniques is unreliable. For purposes of organization, each is dealt with in turn.

Hypnosis

Hypnosis and hypnotic age regression are often used in memory recovery (Claridge, 1992; Gilligan & Kennedy, 1989; Spiegel, 1989). Although hypnosis can increase the amount of information and vividness of recall, there is a great deal of evidence that this occurs for accurate as well as for inaccurate recall. There are many examples of individuals confidently reporting hypnotically induced false memories as real (e.g., Orne, 1959, 1979; Spiegel, 1974). These and other studies (Dywan & Bowers, 1983; Perry & Laurence, 1983; Smith, 1983) demonstrating the problems and limitations of hypnosis as a memory recovery technique led the *Council on Scientific Affairs of the American Medical Association* (1985) to conduct a study of recollections obtained during hypnosis. They found that such recollections were often less reliable than nonhypnotic recall. Subsequent research has extended the finding that hypnosis is an unreliable method of memory recovery (Coons, 1988; Spanos, Quigley, Gwynn, & Glatt, 1991).

Detailed memories of so-called past lives and abduction by space aliens are a powerful example of the unreliability of hypnotic techniques of memory recovery. Research on these memories and "incidents" have demonstrated that such recall is constructive and organized in terms of current expectations and beliefs.

Dream Interpretation

Analysis of dream content has been proposed as a method for recovering abuse memories (Blume, 1990; Edward, 1987; Frederickson, 1992; Paley, 1992). According to this model, when one dreams, a conduit is opened to repressed memories. By using a dream as a focus, individuals may presumably recover memories of childhood abuse. However, research on dream content indicates no such conduit. Rather, dreams tend to incorporate material from the immediately preceding day (Nielsen & Powell, 1992). Thus, if a client is told that he or she has "symptoms" of sexual abuse or even participates in a discussion about incest, this is material that could be incorporated into a dream.

Michael Yapko (1994) probably characterized this so-called memory recovery technique best when he wrote: "Dream interpretation involves making projections about someone else's projections. Who says a dream of falling down means this, while a dream of flying means that? This area is the astrology of psychotherapy" (p. 122).

Related to dream work is the analysis of "flashbacks." Flashbacks are interpreted by memory recovery workers as being accurate, intrusive recall of a traumatic experience: "In a flashback, you reexperience the original abuse" (Bass & Davis, 1988, p. 73); "Flashbacks are the reliving of a traumatic experience, or an aspect of a trauma, as if it were happening now. Along with sensory flashes, they are a virtually universal component of Post-Incest Syndrome" (Blume, 1990, p. 100). However, Yapko (1994) has reported on an individual diagnosed as suffering from posttraumatic stress disorder as a result of POW experiences in Vietnam. The full panoply of symptoms, including "flashbacks," were displayed by this man, who ultimately committed suicide. When his wife, with the support of his therapist, attempted to have his name placed on his state's Vietnam memorial, it was discovered that he had never been to Vietnam!

Journaling

Journals or writing exercises have been proposed as a method for recovering early memories of incest. In *The Courage to Heal* (Bass & Davis, 1988), readers are advised, "If you don't remember what happened to you, write about what you do remember. Re-create the context in which the abuse happened, even if you don't remember the specifics of the abuse yet" (p. 83). In journal writing, one is to start with some pivotal point such as a feeling or notion and record in words the sensations and thoughts that arise (Frederickson, 1992). Clients are instructed to try for stream-of-consciousness writing without stopping to evaluate.

There is no empirical evidence to suggest that this technique leads to accurate memory recovery. If this technique is combined with other techniques (e.g., advising the client that she has "symptoms" of child sexual abuse, informing the client that healing may not be accomplished unless memory of abuse is recovered), the likelihood of inaccurate memories increases. Furthermore, it has been demonstrated that repeatedly thinking about a fictitious event can lead an individual to claim that they actually experienced it (Ceci, Huffman, & Smith, 1994).

Guided Imagery

The guided imagery (GI) psychodrama technique involves clients achieving a relaxed state and then picturing scenarios suggested to them by their therapists. The starting point is a hunch or misgiving from which the client and therapist presumably uncover emotionally charged early memories (Edwards, 1990).

There is no evidence that GI necessarily results in the recovery of accurate memories. Several forensic psychologists (e.g., Gudjonsson, 1985; Perry & Nogrady, 1985) have reached the conclusion that GI promotes a state similar to that of hypnosis and is an equally unreliable memory recovery method. As psychoanalyst Donald Spence (1992) has written, "The recall of the past is hostage to transference" (p. 95). A client's desire to please the therapist can be a powerful incentive to tailor memories to the therapist's pattern.

Survivors' Groups

Some memory recovery workers regard participation in incest survivors groups to be "a powerful stimulus for recovery of memory in patients with severe amnesia" (Herman & Schatzow, 1987, p. 9). As is the case with guided imagery (GI), there are no data to suggest how accurate these recovered memories are and the cautions need to be made about suggestibility (Ceci et al., 1994) and desire to please therapists (Weekes, Lynn, Green, & Brentar, 1992; Spence, 1982). Herman and Schatzow (1987) reported that thirty-nine (74 percent) of clients in their survivor groups said they were able to obtain confirmation of sexual abuse from another source. However, this group consisted of twenty women with no amnesia (38 percent), nineteen women with moderate (some recall) amnesia (36 percent), and fourteen women with severe amnesia (26 percent). At no point did the authors report on what percentage of women with severe amnesia said they were able to obtain confirmation.

Telling Clients They Have Symptoms of Sexual Abuse

Briere (1984) proposed the existence of a postsexual abuse syndrome characterized by fear, self-injurious feelings, anger problems, chronic muscle tension, and symptoms of dissociation and withdrawal. Likewise, Blume (1990) argued for the existence of a "Post-Incest Syndrome" (p. vi). Physical symptoms (e.g., arthritis, gagging, eating disorders, gynecologic disorders, headaches) have also been interpreted as manifestations of repressed memories of sexual abuse (Blume, 1990). Bass and Davis (1988) cited eating disorders, drug or alcohol addiction, suicidal feelings, and sexual problems as symptoms of sexual abuse.

In their extensive review of the sexual abuse *sequelae* literature, Beitchman et al. (1992) found evidence to suggest that sexual abuse is frequently associated with a wide array of psychological disorders in adulthood. However, they found *no evidence* for a specific postsexual abuse syndrome.

A bizarre variation on the sexual abuse symptom cluster is that of the "body memory" of sexual abuse (Bass & Davis, 1988; Blume, 1990; Courtois, 1992; Frederickson, 1992). For example:

> The body stores the memories of incest, and I have heard of dramatic uncovering and recovery of feelings and experiences through body work. This type of therapy includes massage therapy and other traditional forms of body work, as

well as newer types or adaptations specifically designed to unlock memories of such childhood traumas as incest. (Blume, 1990, p. 279)

Needless to say, there is no empirical evidence that memories are "stored" anywhere in the body besides the brain!

Disputing Client Doubts

You must believe that your client was sexually abused, even if she sometimes doubts it herself. Doubting is part of the process of coming to terms with abuse. Your client needs you to stay steady in the belief that she was abused. Joining a client in doubt would be like joining a suicidal client in her belief that suicide is the best way out. (Bass & Davis, 1988, p. 347)

However, there are numerous examples of memories of traumatic incidents that are simply not true. Perhaps the most famous example was a personal one reported by child development theorist Jean Piaget (1951/1962). When Piaget was two, his governess told his parents that she had frustrated an attempt to kidnap young Jean. Piaget *had vivid memories* of the entire incident until he was fifteen. At this time, the governess sent the parents a letter saying that she wished to make confession and return the watch she had been given as a reward. She had *made up* the entire story!

Terr (1994) has reported a therapy incident involving a thirty-two-year-old who "saw" her grandfather "standing at her feet and putting something painful into her vagina. Her therapist advised [the client] to tell her mother at once, and to consider revealing publicly what her famous grandfather had done" (p. 162). Terr asked the mother about the client's childhood medical history. An alternative explanation emerged. When the daughter was three, she underwent a painful medical procedure for treatment for "giggle bladder." The urologist was a tall, bearded, dignified man who looked almost exactly like the grandfather. Dare we consider what might have occurred had the advice of Bass and Davis (1988) been followed and alternative explanations not considered?

Conclusions

Aggressive memory recovery techniques may recover memories. The difficulty is that they recover confabulations as well as accurate memories. There is no way a therapist can distinguish between them short of external corroboration. There are no "symptoms" for reliably identifying individuals who have been sexually abused. The appropriate therapeutic response is simply to avoid the blind alley of attempting to validate what may be false memories. Rather, the worker and client should focus on helping the client to specify treatment goals and reach them. There is no evidence that clients or therapists *have* to validate a memory of abuse for there to be a successful outcome to treatment. Rather, worker and client need to help the client access resources and/or learn skills needed to reach immediate and more distant life goals.

REFERENCES

Bass, E., & Davis, L. (1988). *The courage to heal: A guide for women survivors of child sexual abuse.* New York: Harper & Row.

Beitchman, J. H., Zucker, K. J., Hood, J. E., daCosta, G. A., & Cassavia, E. (1992) A review of long-term effects of child sexual abuse. *Child Abuse and Neglect, 16,* 101–118.

Blume, E. S. (1990). *Secret survivors: Uncovering incest and its aftereffects in women.* New York: John Wiley & Sons.

Briere, J. (1984). *The effects of childhood sexual abuse on later psychological functioning: Defining a post-sexual abuse syndrome.* Paper presented at the Third National Conference on the Sexual Victimization of Children, Washington, D.C.

Brownmiller, S. (1975). *Against our will: Men, women, and rape.* New York: Simon & Schuster.

Ceci, S. J., Huffman, M. L. C., & Smith, E. (1994). Repeatedly thinking about a non-event: Source misattributions among preschoolers. Special Issue: The recovered memory/false memory debate. *Consciousness and Cognition, 3,* 388–407.

Claridge, K. (1992). Reconstructing memories of abuse: A theory-based approach. *Psychotherapy, 29,* 243–252.

Coons, P. M. (1988). Misuse of forensic hypnosis: A hypnotically elicited false confession with the apparent creation of a multiple personality. *International Journal of Clinical & Experimental Hypnosis, 36,* 1–11.

Council on Scientific Affairs. (1986). Scientific status of refreshing recollection by the use of hypnosis. *International Journal of Clinical and Experimental Hypnosis, 34,* 1–11.

Courtois, C. A. (1992). The memory retrieval process in incest survivor therapy. *Journal of Child Sexual Abuse, 1,* 15–31.

Dywan, J., & Bowers, K. S. (1983). The use of hypnosis to enhance recall. *Science, 222,* 184–185.

Edward, J. (1987). The dream as a vehicle for the recovery of childhood trauma. *Clinical Social Work Journal, 15,* 356–360.

Edwards, D. J. (1990). Cognitive therapy and the restructuring of early memories through guided imagery. *Journal of Cognitive Psychotherapy, 4,* 33–50.

Frederickson, R. (1992). *Repressed memories: A journey to recovery from sexual abuse.* New York: Simon & Schuster.

Fritz, G., Stoll, K., & Wagner, N. (1981). A comparison of males and females who were sexually molested as children. *Journal of Sex and Marital Therapy, 7,* 54–59.

Gilligan, S. G., & Kennedy, C. M. (1989). Solutions and resolutions: Eriksonian hypnotherapy with incest survivor groups. *Journal of Strategic and Systemic Therapies, 8,* 9–17.

Gold, S. N., Hawes, D., & Hohnecker, L. (1994). Degrees of repression of sexual abuse memories. *American Psychologist, 49,* 441–442.

Gudjonsson, G. H. (1985). "The use of hypnosis by the police in the investigation of crime: Is guided imagery a safe substitute?": Comment. *British Journal of Experimental and Clinical Hypnosis, 3,* 37.

Herman, J. L., & Schatzow, E. (1987). Recovery and verification of childhood sexual trauma. *Psychoanalytic Psychology, 4,* 1–14.

Nielsen, T. A., & Powell, R. A. (1992). The day-residue and dream-lag effects: A literature review and limited replication of two temporal effects in dream formation. *Dreaming, 2,* 67–77.

Olio, K. A. (1989). Memory retrieval in the treatment of adult survivors of sexual abuse. *Transactional Analysis Journal, 19,* 93–100.

Orne, M. T. (1959). The nature of hypnosis: Artifact and essence. *Journal of Abnormal Social Psychology, 58,* 277–299.

Orne, M. T. (1979). The use and misuse of hypnosis in court. *International Journal of Clinical and Experimental Hypnosis, 27,* 311–341.

Paley, K. S. (1992). Dream wars: A case study of a woman with multiple personality disorder. *Dissociation: Progress in the Dissociative Disorders, 5,* 111–116.

Perry, C., & Laurence, J. R. (1983). The enhancement of memory by hypnosis in the legal investigative situation. *Canadian Psychology, 24,* 155–167.

Perry, C., & Nogrady, H. (1985). Use of hypnosis by the police in the investigation of crime: Is guided imagery a safe substitute? *British Journal of Experimental and Clinical Hypnosis, 3,* 25–31.

Piaget, J. (1951/1962). *Play, dreams, and imitation in childhood* (Translated by C. Gattegno and F. M. Hodgson). New York: Norton.

Russell, D. E. H. (1984). *Sexual exploitation: Rape, child sexual abuse, and sexual harassment.* Beverly Hills, CA: Sage.

Smith, M. C. (1983). Hypnotic memory enhancement of witnesses: Does it work? *Psychological Bulletin, 94,* 387–407.

Spanos, N. P., Quigley, C. A., Gwynn, M. I., & Glatt, R. L. (1991). Hypnotic interrogation, pretrial preparation, and witness testimony during direct and cross-examination. *Law and Human Behavior, 15,* 639–653.

Spence, D. (1992). *Narrative truth and historical truth.* New York: W. W. Norton.

Spiegel, D. (1989). Hypnosis in the treatment of victims of sexual abuse. *Psychiatric Clinics of North America, 12,* 295–305.

Spiegel, H. (1974) The grade five syndrome: The highly hypnotizable person. *International Journal of Clinical and Experimental Hypnosis, 22,* 303–319.

Terr, L. (1994). *Unchained memories: True stories of traumatic memories, lost and found.* New York: Basic Books.

Weekes, J. R., Lynn, S. J., Green, J. P., & Brentar, J. T. (1992). Pseudomemory in hypnotized and task-motivated subjects. *Journal of Abnormal Psychology, 101,* 356–360.

Rejoinder to Dr. Stocks

DAVID C. PRICHARD

Abduction by space aliens? Past lives? To use these as examples of the use of hypnosis in the recovery of repressed memories of childhood incest presents a view of hypnosis so limited as to be of little use in the discussion. Stocks presents valid concerns with regard to extreme uses of various therapeutic techniques but presents little to refute an appropriate, monitored use of effective clinical approaches in uncovering repressed memories of childhood incest.

In his discussion on dream interpretation, Stocks implies that it is the practitioner who offers to the client an interpretation of his or her dream. This is a naive and limited approach of the use of this form of intervention. Crucial to effective dream analysis is the *client's* interpretation of the dream content. The work of the social worker is not to create a client's narrative, but rather to be with the client as he or she uncovers, discovers, interprets, and attaches meaning to her own story. Interpretation, when used effectively, belongs in the hands of the client.

Stocks dismisses the validity of flashbacks, citing only one extreme example in which a man who had never been to Vietnam claimed to experience flashbacks of his nonexistent prisoner-of-war experiences. Would Stocks have us generalize, based on this one example, that none of the flashbacks experienced by any Vietnam veteran are valid? Would he have us deny the documented trauma experienced by tens of thousands of war veterans? The evidence to the contrary is convincing, compelling, powerful, well researched and documented. The use of this as an example to make a case against the validity of flashbacks as a very real form of processing and recalling earlier memories of traumatic experience underscores the weakness of his position. If Stocks is asking us to question the validity of the trauma-induced flashbacks of tens of thousands of Vietnam war veterans, would he have us question also the trauma-induced experiences of men and women traumatized as boys and girls?

Stocks criticizes the use of journaling as an appropriate method of memory retrieval. He implies that Bass and Davis (1988) encouraged false memories of abuse, simply by encouraging clients to recall the context in which abuse could have occurred. How else is it possible to recall the presence or absence of abuse if clients do not recall its possible context? Bass and Davis (1988) do not suggest that clients invent or imagine nonexistent abuse, merely to recall as much of early childhood memories as possible. Anyone who has driven through a childhood neighborhood, not visited for years, will recollect sounds, sights, smells, names, and experiences long forgotten. Journaling merely assists clients in "visiting" the neighborhoods of their childhoods, and in recalling or triggering the valid memories of early childhood. Journaling is the written narrative of a client's life, much like talk therapy is the oral narrative.

Stocks argues that guided imagery is used by practitioners to suggest scenarios, insert memories, and assist susceptible clients to "accept false memories as accurate." Guided imagery, when used effectively, appropriately, and ethically, is a powerful means for clients to feel in control, empowered, and safe. In this approach, the therapist reflects back to the client the client's own experiences using metaphors and images that are drawn strictly from experiences and life events as previously narrated by the client. To use a musical metaphor, it is the client, not the practitioner, as implied by Stocks, who composes, conducts, and plays his or her own piece. The practitioner acts only as witness to the process and as audience. Through guided imagery, practitioners help clients find a metaphor that works for them, and, to continue the musical metaphor, to hear the whole symphonic piece, rather than one instrument, one bar at a time.

Stocks misses the point with regard to body memories. The body does indeed store memories, but it does so in the brain. A particular area of the body (often those involved in the original abuse) merely acts as a trigger for these stored memories. Who would deny that traumatized individuals do not react to environmental triggers? Body work, then, is simply an alternative method for "revisiting," perhaps triggering, long-forgotten "neighborhoods." I agree with Stocks that practitioners need to exercise reasonable caution, and I urge all practitioners keep in mind basic tenets of social work practice: begin where the client is, and validate the experiences of his or her life. It takes great courage for most clients to decide to flesh out the narrative of their early childhoods. The work is deep, intense, and time consuming. It also may be life changing and affirming. The process of uncovering repressed memories of childhood sexual abuse is a collaborative *process*. Neither the client nor the practitioner should enter into this work, nor turn away from it, lightly.

As practitioners, we must keep in mind always what it is that we seek to validate, both the actual occurrences of events, and especially the current meanings attached by clients to their perceptions of experiences that may have occurred long ago.

REFERENCE

Bass, E., & Davis, L. (1988). *The courage to heal.* New York: Harper & Row.

Should Personal Psychotherapy Be Required of Clinical Social Workers?

Marsha Wineburgh, M.S.W., maintains a private practice as a clinical social worker in New York City. She is a faculty member, supervisor, and training analyst with the Postgraduate Center for Mental Health, Adult Psychoanalytic Institute, and a doctoral student with the Wurzweiler School of Social Work.

J. Paul Gallant, Ph.D., is an assistant professor of social work with Florida International University. Dr. Gallant also offers family therapy training, supervision, and direct service to children and families in a part-time practice.

YES

MARSHA WINEBURGH

> The therapeutic situation . . . is more than just a statistical event of a doctor plus a patient. It is a **meeting** of a doctor and patient. If the doctor is rigid and insensitive to the specific requirements of the everchanging therapeutic situation, he will not be a good therapist. He might be a bully or a businessman or a dogmatist, but he is not a therapist if he refuses to be part of the on-going processes of the (psychotherapeutic) situation. (Perls, Hefferline, & Goodman, 1951, p. xi)

Although assessment, diagnosis, and treatment of mental and emotional disorders are acknowledged as fundamental characteristics of clinical social work practice, the training necessary to develop and refine the skills essential to competent practice continue to be debated within the social work profession. One of the contested areas concerns personal psychotherapy for clinical social workers. Should it be a training requirement? Perhaps another way to ask this question is: should a swimming instructor be required to know how to swim? The answer: yes, of course.

Personal psychotherapy is the traditional road to personal and professional growth. It offers access to two important worlds, each of which is important in a balanced life: the world of feelings and emotions, and the world of thoughts and ideas. To know something in its fullest sense, one needs to know intellectually as well as experientially. Since the early 1900s, psychoanalysts have been required to have their own personal psychotherapy as part of their training. Because psychoanalytic theory incorporates an artful use of the self in strategically dealing with transference and countertransference phenomena, the working alliance as well as the real relationship, a training analysis has been required historically to ensure that the "complexes of the practitioner" would not interfere with the treatment (Hughes, 1989, p. 8). Those clinical social workers whose practice skills are informed by models derived from psychodynamic theories, for instance, drive theory, British or American object relations theory, self theory, and ego psychology, should also be required to include personal psychotherapy as part of their training inasmuch as therapist self-knowledge is an essential tool in the therapeutic process.

As for other practice models, both the building and the strategic use of the relationship between client and practitioner and the conscious use of one's professional self within the relationship are essential ingredients of the treatment process (Goldstein, 1984). Each of these areas benefits from practitioner self-awareness and personal maturity, which can be enhanced by personal therapy.

The Therapeutic Alliance

Social work has always advocated the importance of relationship skills to direct practice (Biestek, 1957; Perlman, 1979; Richmond, 1917), recognizing the client–therapist relationship as providing the context for all treatment processes.

Empirical evidence suggests that the therapeutic alliance or working relationship is the best predictor of psychotherapy outcome (Safran, McMain, Crocker & Murray, 1990). Studies have consistently demonstrated that, although there are no predictable outcome differences among various therapies, relationship factors have much greater predictive power with regard to outcome than do technical factors (Beutler, Crago & Arizmendi, 1986; Lampert, Shapiro, & Bergin, 1986). Although much of the research on the effect of the therapeutic alliance has come from the arena of psychodynamic individual treatment, behavior therapists are beginning to show interest in examining the interaction between behavioral techniques and relationship variables (Marziali & Alexander, 1991).

Practitioner contributions to the working relationship include warmth, interest, positive emotional involvement, and lack of negative attitudes (Luborsky,

McLellan, Woody, O'Brien, & Auerbach, 1985). Carl Rogers (1957) asserted that effective practitioners must offer conditions of empathy, warmth, and genuineness, the bases of a therapeutic relationship. Empathy, authenticity, engagement, and collaboration skills are essential to managing the treatment situation.

The Professional Self

To be effective, a practitioner must be able to use an empathetic, collaborative mind-set, use one's professional self differentially, attend to relationship issues, tolerate pleasant and unpleasant affects in oneself and know the difference between self-disclosure behavior and narcissistic gratification. Goldstein (1990) suggests that "effective practice is less a technical enterprise than it is a creative, reflective and, to a considerable extent, an artistic and dramatic event" (p. 38). It requires an ability to identify and work with elusive defenses such as denial, projection, and projective identification as well as erotic attachments and subtle narcissistic transferences. What does a practitioner do with feelings of boredom, frustration, or therapeutic zeal? Difficult patients who use passive–aggressive or hostile–dependent defenses have the capacity to stir up powerful, or at the very least uncomfortable, affects in the clinician. Personal therapy offers a model for how to contend with one's reactions to strong, unpleasant feelings and, further, how to intervene in a helpful strategic way rather than rejecting the client's behavior. Personal therapy helps the practitioner identify areas in which his or her own problems may distort his or her judgment. Personal conflicts of the therapist must be controlled to see the client's issues more clearly.

Research data suggest that many, if not most, mental health practitioners enter psychotherapy at some point in their careers. Although most of this research is in the psychology literature, data indicate that psychodynamic psychotherapists who do individual treatment primarily receive "the greatest amount of personal individual psychotherapy both before and after entering the profession" (Guy, Stark, & Polestra, 1988, p. 475). Surveys of clinical psychologists have shown that those who have had therapy, regardless of its duration, value it as a critical component of their practice. MacDevitt (1987) found that practitioners reported that personal therapy provides insights and awareness of countertransference that enhance their psychotherapeutic skills.

A significant number of social workers were included in Norcross, Strausser-Kirtland, and Missar's study (1988) of mental health practitioners. When asked to identify how personal treatment shaped their values with regard to therapy, most respondents referred to the critical role of nonspecific factors such as empathy, warmth, patience, and acceptance as well as understanding transference and countertransference dynamics.

In their seminal contribution to social work research, Mackey and Mackey (1994) explored the relationship between personal therapy of clinical social workers and the development of the professional self. Based on personal interviews with fifteen experienced clinicians, five aspects of personal therapy were found to relate to the development of the professional self: the therapist as model, understanding the therapeutic process, enhancement of empathy, self-awareness, and personal/professional development. They concluded that therapy appeared to nurture the development of personal qualities essential to effective clinical practice: a caring, respectful, and acceptable use of self with clients. Therapy also enhanced the development of empathy and professional skill, "including an integration of the cognitive and affective dimensions in relationships characterized by balancing connectedness with separateness" (p. 497).

Ultimately, the issue of **requiring** personal psychotherapy must be addressed in terms of the underlying issues of competency and ethical behavior. Returning to the example of the swimming instructor, the student swimmer (client) has an explicit or implicit trust that the instructor (practitioner) will not let any harm come to him during the swimming lesson. Not only must the instructor be knowledgeable about the mechanics of swimming, and be able to communicate this to each student, taking into consideration the intensity of individual anxiety, but the instructor also must be able to save the student from drowning should a problem arise. Likewise, the practitioner, by virtue of a similar trust, should have the fullest possible preparation for practice which would include maximizing those personal qualities which promote empathy and the capacity to use one's self in a mature professional manner. This would mandate personal psychotherapy.

REFERENCES

Beutler, L. E., Crago, M., & Arizmendi, T. G. (1986). Therapist variables in psychotherapy process and outcome. In S. L. Garfield & A. E. Bergin (Eds.), *Handbook of psychotherapy and behavior change* (3rd ed., pp. 257–301). New York: John Wiley.

Biestek, E. (1957). *The casework relationship.* Chicago, IL: Loyola University Press.

Goldstein, E. (1984). *Ego psychology and social work practice.* New York: The Free Press.

Goldstein, E. (1990). The knowledge base of social work practice. *Families in Society, 71,* 32–43.

Guy, J. D., Stark, M. J. & Polestra, P. L. (1988). Personal psychotherapy for psychotherapists before and after entering professional practice. *Professional Psychology: Research and Practice, 19,* 474–476.

Hughes, J. M. (1989). *Reshaping the psychoanalytic domain.* Berkeley, CA: The University of California Press.

Lampert, M. J., Shapiro, D. A., & Bergin, A. E. (1986). The effectiveness of psychotherapy. In S. L. Garfield & A. E. Bergin (Eds.), *Handbook of psychotherapy and behavioral change* (3rd ed., pp. 157–211). New York: John Wiley.

Luborsky, L., McLellan, A. T., Woody, G. E., O'Brien, C. P., & Auerbach, A. (1985). Therapist success and its determinants. *Archives of General Psychiatry, 42,* 602–611.

MacDevitt, J. (1987). Therapists' personal therapy and professional awareness. *Psychotherapy, 24,* 693–703.

Mackey, R. A., & Mackey, E. F. (1994). Personal psychotherapy and the development of a professional self. *Families in Society, 75,* 490–498.

Marziali, E., & Alexander, L. (1991). The power of the therapeutic relationship. *American Journal of Orthopsychiatry, 61,* 383–391.

Norcross, J. C., Strausser-Kirtland, D., & Missar, C. D. (1988). The processes and outcomes of psychotherapists' personal treatment experiences. *Psychotherapy, 25,* 36–43.

Perlman, H. H. (1979). *Relationship: The heart of helping people.* Chicago: University of Chicago Press.

Perls, F., Hefferline, R., & Goodman, P. (1951). *Gestalt therapy: Excitement and growth in the human personality.* New York: Julian Press.

Richmond, M. (1917). *Social diagnosis.* New York: Russell Sage Foundation.

Rogers, C. R. (1957). The necessary and sufficient conditions of therapeutic personality change. *Journal of Consulting Psychology, 21,* 95–103.

Safran, J. D., McMain, S., Crocker, P., & Murray, P. (1990). Therapeutic rupture as a therapy event for empirical investigation. *Psychotherapy, 27,* 154–165.

Rejoinder to Ms. Wineburgh
J. Paul Gallant

With great interest I read Marsha Wineburgh's argument in favor of required personal psychotherapy for clinical social workers. I believe I would have been swayed by her well-written piece to accept the argument in the affirmative were it not for two compelling conditions. First, she offers a quite acceptable argument for the benefits of personal therapy to professional and personal growth. However, she does not speak to the requirement aspect of personal therapy for social workers. This imperative is the cornerstone piece of this debate, and it is unfortunate that it was not addressed. Second, Ms. Wineburgh exposes her bias for a very specific form of personal therapy, that is, therapy that is informed by psychodynamic theories. It is my observation that social work education programs are increasingly changing their curriculum to offer clinical theories more consistent with developments in the practice world and are moving away from the traditional influence of psychoanalytic and psychodynamic theories.

Ms. Wineburgh begins with the implied suggestion that personal psychotherapy be viewed as a training requirement for clinical social workers. By not referring to the actual training that takes place in graduate clinical social work programs, one could understand her to suggest that personal therapy is the one exclusive training method for effective practice. She finds support for this argument in her assertion that personal psychotherapy has been the traditional road to personal and professional growth and cites the requirement of personal therapy for psychoanalysts in training.

Readers of this debate should identify strongly with Ms. Wineburgh's argument if they also find themselves embracing the following ideas: (1) a preference for clinical social work practice informed by psychoanalytic or psychodynamic theory. This should keep you strongly attached to traditional ideas but quite removed from more modern and postmodern theories and practices more closely attuned with an ecological/person-in-environment perspective; (2) a belief that one can actually be neutral in the therapeutic situation, at least the belief that one can avoid the interference of one's "complexes" in treatment. In my opinion, maintaining the illusion of neutrality serves the purpose of blinding one's own awareness of his or her effect on the therapeutic process, which is unavoidable; (3) believing the only way to therapist self-knowledge is through personal therapy. That is one of the assumptions in Ms. Wineburgh's argument; (4) a belief that one's learning and experience in graduate social work education including, hopefully, a sound field internship, is insufficient preparation for effective practice. Ms. Wineburgh argues for required personal therapy but does not provide a rationale for necessarily adding on to one's graduate experience; (5) a belief that all personal therapy is a positive and useful experience. This is a clear assumption in her argument. Ms. Wineburgh cites rudimentary research to support her implied assertion that *all* personal therapy offers a therapist a model, enhanced empathy, and other contributions to personal growth.

Ms. Wineburgh opens and closes her piece using the analogy of the swimming instructor and the importance of the swimming instructor knowing how to swim. Applying her analogy to her argument, I am left with the very clear message that the practitioner should learn to swim only in the murky waters of the psychoanalytic/psychodynamic pool and no other, even though in the neighboring pools the instructors are learning more effectively and more quickly and having more fun.

NO

J. Paul Gallant

Practitioners in various professional fields have advocated personal therapy as a useful method in the training of psychotherapists. Influenced by Freud and the psychoanalytic tradition, many advance the view that personal psychotherapy should be a prerequisite for the practitioner to have an intimate knowledge of herself or himself so as to avoid the negative influence of one's personality on psychotherapeutic work with clients. Yet, for decades much argument has occurred about the value of a personal therapy experience. Through a review of the existing research findings on the subject and a discussion of the relevance of personal therapy for one's clinical expertise, I argue against such a requirement.

The Research

I was delighted to find a recently published review (Garfield, 1995) of the existing available data on the relative importance of the practitioner's personal therapy as a variable in psychotherapy. The author finds that no hard and fast conclusions can be drawn from this research but does state:

> However, what data exist do not appear to lend any strong support to the widely held view concerning the importance of personal psychotherapy for effectively conducting psychotherapy." (Garfield, 1995, p. 70)

Garfield cites several studies, two of which conclude that it has not been empirically demonstrated that personal therapy is beneficial to client outcome (Beutler, Machado, & Neufeldt, 1994; Clark, 1986). In the latter study, the author concludes, "What does seem to be related to client outcome is the experience of the therapist" (Clark, 1986, p. 542). The amount of experience a clinical social worker possesses may be a more influential factor in determining effective practice than one's history of personal psychotherapy. Katz, Lorr, and Rubenstein (1958) found similar results in their review of therapy cases at thirteen Veterans' Administration mental health clinics; there was no relation between patient improvement and whether the therapist did or did not experience personal therapy. These authors did find that patient improvement was positively related to the length of the therapist's professional experience.

Other studies have focused on personal therapy and its relevance to client outcome. The influence of therapist personal psychotherapy on the likelihood that their clients would prematurely terminate treatment was examined by McNair, Lorr, and Callahan (1963). Premature terminators were defined as patients who discontinued therapy without the consent of their clinicians less than sixteen weeks after they began treatment. Clinicians with personal therapy did not differ significantly from therapists with no personal therapy in the extent to which patients prematurely terminated their therapy. In a related study, McNair, Lorr, Young, Roth, and Boyd (1964) conducted a three-year follow-up of male psychiatric outpatients who had been in individual psychotherapy for at least four months. Although therapists with more personal therapy kept their patients in treatment longer, the authors found no significant relationship between the therapist's having had personal psychotherapy and their patient's final status.

An earlier study (Garfield & Bergin, 1971) examined the value of personal therapy for psychotherapists on client outcome. The clients of those psychotherapists who had *not* undergone personal therapy consistently demonstrated the *greatest* amount of change, and the clients of the therapists who had 175 hours or less of therapy showed more change on two of the three measures of change than did the clients of therapists who experienced the larger amounts of personal therapy. Garfield and Bergin concluded that in the case of student therapists, some therapy is more harmful than none, and a lot can be even worse. The authors suggested that therapists undergoing personal psychotherapy may be too distracted with their own issues to attend effectively to the problems of others.

Before concluding this review of the relevant research, some findings relating to the "law of thirds" is worth mentioning. The "law of thirds" suggests something like the following: one-third of personal therapy is helpful, one-third is neither helpful nor unhelpful, and one-third is more harmful than helpful. Henry, Sims, & Spray (1971) found that 29 percent of the psychoanalysts, 46 percent of the psychiatrists and 35 percent of the psychologists indicated that they were not satisfied with their personal therapy. These results address personal satisfaction with therapy and not directly the value of such personal therapy on one's effectiveness as a psychotherapist. However, these findings do invite us to consider the possible deleterious effects of mandatory personal therapy on clinical social workers.

To summarize this review of the empirical data, I return to the recent survey work of Garfield (1995), who states:

Unfortunately, we have little objective evidence on which to base any firm conclusions as to whether or not personal therapy makes a person a better therapist. In the final analysis, one would want to appraise the therapeutic outcomes of therapists who had received personal therapy with a comparable group of therapists who had not. (p. 68)

Imposing *More* Requirements on Clinical Social Workers?

What are the possible assumptions that support the view that mandatory personal psychotherapy for clinical social workers will help them to be more effective in their professional practice? Let us examine the underlying assumptions of this perspective. One is the view that forcing change on someone is a preferred practice. Anyone who has experience in direct practice with individuals, families, groups, organizations, or communities will most likely argue against the idea that forcing change on someone is the most effective method to employ. Making personal therapy a prerequisite for clinical social work practice is tantamount to employing the principle of forced change. Needless to state, forced change is in direct conflict with the principle of client self-determination, one of the basic values of the profession.

A second assumption is that psychotherapy is a preferred method of change in social work. One might give validity to this assumption if clinical social work were composed solely of psychotherapists. One of the unique features of our profession is its broad base of theoretical models and fields of practice. Making personal psychotherapy a requirement implies that such individual therapy is privileged over other opportunities for gaining self-awareness and self-understanding, such as working "in communitas," that being the personal growth that emanates from immersing oneself in the community of others, in coalition building, and other social work practices involving one's relationships with clients and colleagues. Also, many clinical social workers do not practice psychotherapy per se, such as individuals serving in medical or school settings.

Third, it is assumed that M.S.W. education is automatically inadequate in developing students' self-awareness and personal growth. The supervised field practicum with its hundreds of hours of practice experience is an integral part of the curriculum in social work education. The objective of the practicum is to produce a professionally reflective, self-evaluating, knowledgeable, and developing social worker. In the field, with the supportive supervision of an experienced field instructor, the student examines one's own values, behaviors, and skills in problem solving. Hopefully, this occurs in a safe and nurturing environment.

In addition to the practicum experience with the field instructor serving in a mentoring role, there is the extensive coursework with opportunity for the student to gain knowledge that includes self-knowledge of one's ability at interviewing, relationship building, assessing, intervening, and evaluating one's practice. The infusion of ethics and values throughout the curriculum is characterized by a range of learning opportunities, assignments, case and class presentations, and readings that direct explicit attention to these vital dimensions of social work practice. Supposedly, professional education and socialization involves an attempt to instill in students the values that will prepare them for responsible, critical, reflective social work practice as they are confronted with ethical dilemmas inherent in the day-to-day work. I argue that the classroom setting can also provide opportunity for students to grow in self-knowledge and self-awareness that in many respects can be, effectively though unintentionally, a therapeutic experience.

There are many professional schools that require students to undertake personal psychotherapy before or during the course of their respective programs. A colleague and professor in one such program sent me the requirements as outlined in their program's practicum manual. It states that students are required to be in personal psychotherapy at their own expense while in the training program. The manual indicates that this is consistent with the accreditation body's requirement that applicants have had sufficient therapy to protect their clients from the students' issues and that it is also essential in learning how to do psychotherapy. Students should consult their supervisor in choosing a therapist. The therapist should be someone whose therapeutic approach is congruent with that of the training program, that is, psychoanalytically oriented psychotherapy.

Integrating such a requirement into the preparation of clinical social workers would appear to bring forth numerous ethical, practical, and bureaucratic dilemmas to say the least. What sort of personal therapy? Behavior therapy? What models of practice would be approved? Solution-focused? Task-centered? Which are more consistent with social work's emphasis on the person-in-environment or ecological perspective? What about liability? Who could be exempt from this requirement? What about confidentiality? Dual relationships? Cost? What are the time limits? The questions appear endless.

In closing, I refer to the visionary statement of a prominent social work practitioner and educator who stated the following twenty-five years ago:

> Surely we can all think of a particular therapist whose work has appeared to have benefited from treatment; and we can think of another whose work has not. But even if it were established that the performance of some therapists does improve as a result of personal treatment, this of itself does not justify an inflexible requirement for all. In the future—as in the present—we can expect that most trainees who can benefit from treatment will continue to seek and obtain it voluntarily. And as we learn how to improve our selection of candidates and our methods of training, I think it likely that the issue of treatment as a part of training will become less important. Moreover, this trend will continue as different forms of treatment, such as family therapy and group therapy, gain in prestige and prevalence in relation to the status of analysis, as they seem to be doing. (Leader, 1971, p. 239)

REFERENCES

Beutler, L., Machado, P., & Neufeldt, S. (1994). Therapist variables. In A. E. Bergin & S. L. Garfield (Eds.), *Handbook of psychotherapy and behavior change* (pp. 229–269). New York: Wiley.

Clark, M. (1986). Personal therapy: A review of empirical research. *Professional Psychology: Research and Practice, 17,* 541–543.

Garfield, S. (1995). *Psychotherapy: An eclectic-integrative approach.* New York: Wiley.

Garfield, S., & Bergin, A. (1971). Personal therapy, outcome and some therapist variables. *Psychotherapy: Theory, Research and Practice, 8,* 251–253.

Henry, W. E., Sims, J. H., & Spray, S. L. (1971). *The fifth profession.* San Francisco, CA: Jossey-Bass

Katz, M., Lorr, M., & Rubenstein, E. (1958). Remainer patient attributes and their relation to subsequent improvement in psychotherapy. *Journal of Consulting Psychology, 22,* 411–413.

Leader, A. (1971). The argument against required personal analysis in training for psychotherapy. In R. Holt (Ed.), *New horizons for psychotherapy* (pp. 231–240). New York: International Universities Press, Inc.

McNair, D., Lorr, M., & Callahan, D. (1963). Patient and therapist influences on quitting psychotherapy. *Journal of Consulting Psychology, 27,* 10–17.

McNair, D., Lorr, M., Young, H., Roth, I., & Boyd, R. (1964). A three-year follow-up of psychotherapy patients. *Journal of Clinical Psychology, 20,* 258–264.

Rejoinder to Dr. Gallant Marsha Wineburgh

Controversy at its best stimulates clarification of ideas and better definitions for further research. Dr. Paul Gallant's well-written argument against required personal psychotherapy for clinical social workers identifies several issues for further discussion. Because of space limitations, only two are addressed: imposing requirements for training in clinical social work, and the nature of research on psychotherapy.

Imposing Requirements for Training

The definition of clinical social work practice has expanded from its traditional psychiatric roots to encompass virtually any area of direct practice. I agree with Dr. Gallant that clinical social work currently embraces many aspects of practice that have little to do with treating the mentally ill. However, if we restrict our discussion to just those practitioners who are *offering* psychotherapy, supervision, or the teaching of treatment a strong case can be made for personal psychotherapy as a part of professional education. Clinicians use themselves as instruments in the complex negotiation of change. It is hard to imagine that exposure to an experience that can enhance self-awareness and personal growth, as one's personal therapy does, would not be an essential ingredient of training.

As Dr. Gallant noted, the idea of forcing someone into treatment is highly problematic. Not only is it poor practice to force change on someone, but change that is the result of compliance is not really change at all. However, anyone who elects to enter the specialty area of psychotherapy in effect self-selects to expose themselves to all of the training tools of the trade, and that should include personal psychotherapy.

When I attended my M.S.W. program in the 1960s, psychotherapy was considered a form of punishment for those students who were having difficulty or who were seriously disturbed. The recommendation for personal treatment has less of a stigma today, but a student's desire to become a psychotherapist is still frowned on by many in the social work educational community. As the curricula in MSW programs shift to more generic interventions at the expense of courses on the theory and technique, social work education can, at best, offer only an introduction to self-awareness and the possibilities of personal growth. One must learn to separate feelings from ideas and to separate thinking and feeling from action. To the extent that defenses developed in childhood affect feelings, thoughts, and attitudes, classroom and personal advisement by social work faculty can be only partially successful in attaining these goals. Personal psychotherapy offers a unique and comprehensive opportunity to explore and understand one's self in relation to the world.

The Nature of Research in Psychotherapy

It is interesting to note that there is no overlap in the reference list accompanying each of the essays. Why not? Perhaps it says something about the nature of research in psychotherapy. Since the 1950s, a distinction has been made between process and outcome research, with the former dealing with *how* changes occur, and the latter with *what* changes occur. Methodological issues have led to a decline in process research; however, good studies appropriately address not only the outcomes but also what happened between the beginning and the end of treatment. Perhaps this dichotomy between process and outcome accounts, in part, for the lack of overlap in our references. Most of the studies cited by Dr. Gallant are outcome research, whereas my references are from process studies which address issues concerning the relationship between the practitioner and the client and the development of the professional self.

Psychotherapy is a complicated process. Intervening variables such as the type of therapy, diagnosis, presenting problem, third-party influences, and personality fit between practitioner and client must be accounted for in any investigation. Thus the attempt to find a correlation between the personal therapy of the clinical social worker and the outcomes of treatment is a highly complex endeavor that we have only begun to have the ability to measure.

Should Clinical Social Workers Seek Psychotropic Medication Prescription Privileges?

Sophia F. Dziegielewski, Ph.D., received her M.S.W. and Ph.D. in social work from Florida State University. Currently she is an Associate Professor in the School of Social Work at The University of Alabama. Before that, she spent seven years training physicians, medical students, and residents at Meharry Medical College and in the United States Army.

Kia J. Bentley, Ph.D., is an Associate Professor with the School of Social Work at Virginia Commonwealth University, and co-author (with Joe Walsh) of *The Social Worker, & Psychotropic Medication* (1996, Brooks/Cole). She has also published articles on the right to refuse medication, medication adherence, and curriculum issues in social work and psychopharmacology.

YES

SOPHIA F. DZIEGIELEWSKI

Social workers actively work with psychiatrists and other health professionals and are involved in most aspects of psychiatric treatment, including the monitoring or dispensing of psychotropic medications (Cohen, 1988). Generally, these social work services have been provided under the auspice of a medical model (Berg & Wallace, 1987). Although the role that social workers perform can vary, it generally entails encouraging medication compliance, monitoring side effects, and working with families with regard to mediation use and compliance (Gerhart & Brooks, 1983). In a survey conducted by Miller, Wiedeman, and Linn (1980),

90 percent of the student social workers surveyed had clients who used medications as part of treatment, and several of the student social workers questioned reported that they actually filled out the prescription blanks for the psychiatrist to sign. It remains clear that over the years, the role of social workers in the management and psychoeducation of medication use with the mentally ill has expanded (Bentley & Reeves, 1992).

Social workers are often called on to assist in reporting medication dosage reactions and side effects, and how these symptoms are impairing or supporting conjunct verbal therapy. In a recent study of sixty social workers, it was found that 93 percent of social workers agreed that psychotropics were necessary in treating the mentally ill, and 88 percent believed that the use of medications helped clients to improve (Berg & Wallace, 1987). It remains apparent that the issue of competent social work involvement with medications in the mental health practice arena is and remains a practice reality.

There is sparse debate among social work professionals regarding whether they should pursue the ability to prescribe medications. Actually, in an extensive search of the social work literature, nothing could be found that related directly to advocation for prescription privileges. This makes my position a very difficult one to assume, because on the surface social workers appear content to be merely "gatekeepers" at the medications door. Because medications are a routine part of mental health practice in social work, this lack of interest in pursuing the right to prescribe psychotropic medications disturbs me.

As a workshop leader teaching social work practitioners about the use of medications, I often ask the question, "why not us?" The response from the audience is initially one of disbelief and genuine surprise. I often receive statements such as "we could never do that," or "we don't have the training." My response to this is, "why not us; the other professionals also need additional training and are making plans to get it; why not have the option to choose with them?" I believe that in not trying to make this "option" available, we close a door to an inevitable part of our therapeutic practice—present and future.

Whether we agree or not, medications are a part of our mental health practice reality, and we have to be able to monitor and use their effects to better help our clients. It has been my experience that once the mystique surrounding the use of medications has been addressed through formal pharmacological education (that is social work friendly), the opinions of social work professionals seem to change. Groups of social workers taking my workshops become more open to the possibility—and "yes," they begin to understand the necessity for the option to prescribe to be made available.

In understanding the lack of interest by our field, the question of "why are social workers so leery of opening up this avenue as a practice possibility?" needs to be explored. To address this, the following reasons (given by social work professionals at medication training workshops) are explicated: (1) they fear they might not practice competently or responsibly; (2) they believe that the medical field is so tightly united that they do not have a chance of entering this area; and (3) they fear they do not have enough training to embark on this area. In this essay, each of these responses is addressed.

Competent and Responsible Practice

Today, a wide range of nonphysician health care providers are able to prescribe medications and are doing so in a competent and professional manner (DeLeon, Fox & Graham, 1991; Mahoney, 1992a). Nonphysician specialties that possess prescription privileges include: dentists and podiatrists (in all states), optometrists (in thirty-one states), nurse practitioners (in forty states), physician assistants (in thirty-two states), clinical pharmacists (in five states), and midwives (Department of Defense, 1995; Deleon, 1994; Mahoney, 1992a). Actually, psychologists in the Indian Health Service can and do prescribe psychoactive medications subject to minimal physician supervision; and, in times of need, the Navy has granted prescriptive authority to psychologists deployed aboard Naval hospital ships (Department of Defense, 1995). Research supports the competence of these professionals and in many cases the actual decrease of written prescriptions by these providers.

Physicians throughout history have generally been considered the "legitimate" profession for prescription privileges. Actually, physicians did become licensed years before all other health care professionals. This allowed them to claim words like "diagnosing," "treating," and "prescribing" as their own, and to claim medication prescription as their exclusive domain of practice (Pearson, 1994, p. 13). Pearson (1994) argues that nurses were "too intimidated and poor to admit that they too were diagnosing and treating and prescribing for their patients (Pearson, 1994, p. 13). As social workers, have we not been doing the same thing (Miller et al., 1980)? Does this argument not also apply to us?

One issue that should not be overlooked and that differentiates us from all of the other professionals seeking prescription privileges is what makes social workers special contributors in the pharmacological scheme. This differentiation is based primarily on the inclusion of the "person in situation" stance that has long since been our heritage. May & Belsky (1992) argue against prescription privileges for fellow psychologists and see as the new frontier of psychology commitment to include the social context and thus community influence to decrease human suffering. Is this not what social workers have been doing since the onset of our profession? Because we have this perspective already, would we not be well served to use it to broaden our current horizon and incorporate it into pharmacological usage?

Many times social workers spend the most "clinical" time with their clients and often are used to assist other professionals in understanding the social dynamics that surround medication use and abuse. For example, we frequently suggest simple dosing regimens such as time-sustaining injection as opposed to having to take pills for the resistant client. Prescription privileges would allow social work professionals to fill a much-needed "one-stop-shop approach" in the mental health arena. Is "one stop" really so bad compared with what presently exists? Currently, the course of most mental health treatment that involves social work professionals generally follows this path. First, the social worker is seen by the client as the primary source of counseling and assistance. Second, the social worker must meet with the psychiatrist to advise him or her of how the client is responding to treatment. And lastly, the client is forced to wait to see the psychiatrist who actually writes the prescription and makes a medication adjustment or continuance based on what he or she has been told by the social worker. By allowing social workers to take ultimate responsibility, for what most are doing anyway, credible and responsible practice could be enhanced.

Opposition by Medical Doctors

A second major concern voiced by social work professionals is that of being able to overcome the power and resistance that would be encountered from physicians. It is true that the ability to gain prescription privileges by other nonphysicians has been and remains a slow evolutionary process (DeLeon, 1994; Burns, DeLeon, Chemtob, Welch, & Samuels, 1988), particularly in the case of master's-level nurse practitioners, who have had limited prescription privileges since 1965. Resistance to this trend remains in spite of numerous research studies that have validated the competency and effectiveness of those that fill this new role (Mahoney, 1992a; 1992b; 1992c).

The supremacy of the physician as prescriber remains strong because many of us in this society still believe that physicians have "superior omnipotent knowledge" (Pearson, 1994, p. 12). Therefore, the evolution of medicine is often presented as an incredible journey of medical interventions based on solid scientific evidence. However, research scientists from McMaster University concurred that, out of thousands of articles researched in the biomedical journals, fewer than 1 percent were supported by solid scientific evidence (cited in Pearson, 1994). To further this myth to the general public, many times prescription advertisements openly state that "only your physician can prescribe" or "see your physician for a prescription." Advertising such as this is simply not true, because other disciplines can and do prescribe the same medication(s). In examining the issue of opposition by physicians, the following remain as obstacles to be addressed: physicians have a strong social and political hold on the prescription market and this hold will not be an easy one to break; and the fight that social workers will have to undertake will equal, if not exceed, that of the other disciplines requesting this privilege.

Lack of Professional Training in Psychopharmacology

The argument is made that social workers are not receiving adequate training in psychopharmacology in schools of social work; however, all of the other disciplines seeking prescription privileges also must address the same shortfall. Psychologists are actively pursuing the acquisition of prescription privileges and designing criteria and courses to support this movement (Callan, 1994; Department of Defense, 1995; Sleek, 1994a; Sleek, 1994b); while nurse practitioners remain active in providing preliminary courses and continuing education to their master's-level practitioners (Fullerton & Pickwell, 1993). It is important to remember that classes in advanced pharmacological training and education are possible to achieve and are currently available through the other disciplines seeking prescription privileges.

Although social work education has made some attempt to address the need for training in medication use in current social work curriculum (Bentley & Reeves, 1992) this area remains sorely lacking. A foundation course in pharmacology for social workers remains essential. In addition, evidence of introductory courses in anatomy and physiology and chemistry would also be helpful. On completion of these requirements and receiving advanced clinical status in the profession (social work clinical licensure), a two-year fellowship training program could be made available, in which the use of medications in the mental health setting could be clearly addressed. Fellowship models such as those used in psychology would afford the social work professional equal opportunity to gain access and learn the needed pharmacological and related medical aspects.

One of the biggest fears social workers express is that they will not be able to know enough about all the aspects of different medications and interactions. To address this fear, I (over the last seven years) have helped to train numerous primary care physicians (who often prescribe neuroleptic medications) and can honestly say that most physicians only know and use twenty-five or thirty medications on a regular basis, and when they are in doubt they also refer or seek advice. With additional help, support and formal training social workers can also do this. They do not have to know everything about every medication. It is not that hard to learn—once you have been trained. Most mental health social workers have not been formally trained and still continue to provide excellent "gatekeeping" services. Imagine what we could do and provide for our patients if we had the responsibility and ability to provide total mental health treatment for which medications remain an integral part.

Future Directions

In closing, my task has been a difficult one based on the fact that few if any have taken this stance before. Our profession needs to grow and change with the environmental times. If you disagree, I hope you will not just shoot the messenger but rather explore this "option" as an important and progressive one for our profession's future viability. We need to make this path an "option" for those advanced clinicians interested in it.

If this essay has stimulated interest in the pursuit of prescriptive authority for social workers, the following steps need to be addressed to start the process. First, we must educate all social work professionals on the importance of prescriptive authority; and we as a profession need to join together to support all advanced-level social workers who are interested in gaining (limited) prescription privileges. Second, we must organize and support the development of a subspecialty group to help provide education, information, and reference for prescription privileges (Faucher, 1992). This group needs to be introduced and affiliated with the National Association of Social Workers and other substantive social work groups, particularly those with national membership. The prescription privileging group would further be responsible for contacting, establishing, and gaining access to state legislative groups.

Third, social work must then look toward "building coalitions" with other groups that are entertaining similar struggles. One such group with the closest affiliation would be that of the clinical psychologists; however, the importance of an allegiance with nursing, physicians' assistants, podiatrists, optometrists, clinical pharmacists, and midwives should also be considered.

It will be important in building these coalitions to note both the positive and negative aspects of the needs of each group. However, the strength gained in numbers will be a positive addition for all. Furthermore, social work can learn from these other professions because the struggles that social work would entail would be similar to those of these other professions. To highlight this concept, a recent article written to encourage and support prescribing authority for nurse–midwives provided a historical review of the struggle to legalize the profession (Fennell, 1991). The struggle that midwifery has had to become a profession has been a profound one, yet they have now gained limited prescription privileges in several states. For the profession of social work, these steps constitute a beginning. This will not be an easy task for social work professionals, and the road toward gaining prescription privileges will be a long and arduous one. However, we have to start somewhere. As a profession we have been taught to advocate for our clients. Now we must advocate for ourselves, and in turn we will be able to better serve and advocate for our clients as well. The right to prescribe, and the additional education it will require, will not be of interest to all social workers. However, for those who are interested, we should not close the door; rather we should support our colleagues to help provide competent and professional social work prescription privileging.

REFERENCES

Bentley, K. J., & Reeves, J. (1992). Integrating psychopharmacology into social work curriculum: Suggested content and resources. *Journal of Teaching in Social Work, 6,* 41–58.

Berg, W. E., & Wallace, M. (1987). Effect of treatment setting on social workers' knowledge of psychotropic drugs. *Health and Social Work, 12,* 144–151.

Burns, S. M., DeLeon, P. H., Chemtob, C. M., Welch, B. L. & Samuels, R. M. (1988). Psychotropic medicine: A new technique for psychology? *Psychotherapy: Theory, Research, Practice and Training, 25,* 508–515.

Cohen, D. (1988). Social work and psychotropic drug treatments. *Social Service Review, 62,* 577–599.

DeLeon, P. H., Fox, R. F., & Graham, S. R. (1991). Prescription privileges: Psychologies next frontier? *American Psychologist, 46,* 384–393.

DeLeon, P. H. (1994). Should non-physician mental health professionals be allowed to prescribe medicine? In S. A. Kirk & S. D. Einbinder (Eds.), *Controversial Issues in Mental Health* (pp. 177–187). Boston, MA: Allyn and Bacon.

Department of Defense. (1995, February). Psychopharmacology demonstration project: Training military psychologists to prescribe. *Government Relations, Practice Directorate.* Washington, DC: Author.

Fennell, K. S. (1991). Prescriptive authority for nurse midwives: A historical review. *Nursing Clinics of North America, 26,* 511–522.

Faucher, M. A. (1992). Prescriptive authority for advanced nurse practitioners: A blue print for action. *Journal of Pediatric Health Care, 6,* 25–31.

Fullerton J. T., & Pickwell, S. (1993). Pharmacology education and the acquisition of prescriptive authority. *Journal of American Academy of Nurse Practitioners, 5*(2), 62–66.

Gerhart, U. C., & Brooks, A. D. (1983). The social work practitioner and antipsychotic medications. *Social Work, 28,* 454.

Mahoney, D. F. (1992a). Appropriateness of geriatric prescribing decisions made by nurse practitioners and physicians. *Health Policy in Action, 26,* 41–46.

Mahoney, D. F. (1992b). Nurse practitioners as prescribers: Past research trends and future study needs. *Health Care Issues, 17,* 44–76.

Mahoney, D. F. (1992c). A comparative analysis of nurse practitioners with and without prescriptive authority. *Journal of the American Academy of Nurse Practitioners, 4*(2), 71–76.

May, W. T., & Belsky, J. (1992). Response to prescription privileges: Psychology's next call? or the siren call: Should psychologists medicate? *American Psychologist, 47,* 427.

Miller, R. S., Wiedeman, G. H., & Linn, L. (1980). Prescribing psychotropic drugs: Whose responsibility? *Social Work in Health Care, 6,* 51–61.

Pearson, L. J. (1994). Annual update of how each state stands on legislative issues affecting advanced nursing practice. *Nurse Practitioner, 19,* 11–53.

Sleek, S. (1994a, September). Prescription privileges efforts gain momentum. *APA Monitor, 25*(9), 21.

Sleek, S. (1994b, February). Panel develops training model for prescriptions. *APA Monitor, 25*(2), 35.

Rejoinder to Dr. Dziegielewski

Kia J. Bentley

Dr. Dziegielewski correctly points out the importance of social workers in collaborating with physicians, clients, and families to help monitor and manage prescribed psychotropic medication regimens. She also notes the expansion of prescription writing privileges in related professions and urges us to consider "why not us" too. She challenges us to consider more fully why social workers should not at least have the option of pursuing prescription writing privileges, possibly through completion of a two-year fellowship program. She argues that we could be just as competent and responsible as other professionals in this task. She admits we would have quite a battle in front of us, but presumably it would all be worth it in the end.

None of these arguments surprised me. The only real surprise I had in reviewing her manuscript was the lack of discussion on how being able to write prescriptions would actually help social workers better serve clients or how it would explicitly advance the profession. At one point, she briefly mentions how obtaining prescription privileges might increase the possibilities of "one-stop" shopping for clients. You could say it is probably a good thing that she was so honest and did not use veiled rationalizations and portray this as some professional act of altruism. However, it is a bit disappointing. I would have liked a lot more on how the privilege might improve our responsiveness to clients. Is this Dr. Dziegielewski's admission, that her arguments really do not relate to clients at all, but only to the presumed best interests of the profession, or to a subset of clinically trained M.S.W. social workers? This somehow seems to be the heart of her argument, although no where does she explicitly state how getting prescription privileges might move the profession forward.

I would agree with Dr. Dziegielewski, however, that the profession needs to be vigilant to insure that we never sell ourselves short. We should never fail to explore new avenues of service out of some historical inferiority complex or sexist notions of appropriate roles and activities of our female-dominated profession. At the same time, I have argued for disciplinary realism and humility and greater interdisciplinary respect and collaboration. Although the mental health services of the twenty-first century may indeed be delivered in a one-stop shop, high-quality comprehensive care is very unlikely to be delivered by a single professional.

NO

Kia J. Bentley

There is unmistakable movement toward expanding prescription writing privileges among non-M.D.s, including clinical psychologists, doctoral level pharmacists (Pharm.D.s), and clinical nurse specialists and practitioners. Two major arguments touted in support of this trend are that increased prescription-writing privileges will presumably allow other mental health professionals to provide more comprehensive treatment to clients, as well as increase client's access to quality psychopharmacological services (DeLeon & Pies, 1994; Wiggins, 1994). Because between 50 and 70 percent of psychotropic drug prescriptions are currently written by general physicians (Olfson & Klerman, 1993) without substantial training in psychopharmacology, the thinking is that other professionals, *with* specialized or advanced training, could dramatically increase the availability of psychopharmacological services, especially in those rural or other areas where there are not enough M.D.s to go around. In private moments with other mental health professionals, some have also pointed to the increased earnings potential of nonmedical mental health providers in the event of prescription privilege expansion. I have yet to see that argument elaborated on in print, however. All in all, these are compelling arguments. But it is important to consider their relevance to social work. We are a profession, like nursing and others, that seeks to provide "holistic" care, a profession, like psychiatry, that claims to rest on a biopsychosocial understanding of human behavior. Indeed, my colleague, Joe Walsh, and I just completed a text that calls for social workers to *expand* their roles in medication management in mental health. We call for increased training in schools of social work in psychopharmacology. We plead with social workers to use the clinical, educational, case management, research, and advocacy skills that they have to be more active in, and responsive to, the medication-related dilemmas of their clients (Bentley & Walsh, 1996). Is it not logical then to suggest that we jump on the bandwagon and support prescription writing privileges for social workers, the number one providers of mental health care in the country?

Yes, I suppose it does make sense. In fact, after reading an early draft of our book while in Richmond for a family visit, Joe's father-in-law, a retired engineer, said he thought we should take that pro-prescription position. He said he had been quite surprised to read in our last chapter that we come down on the conservative side of the debate, especially given our basic premise of the need for increased social work involvement in psychopharmacology. So what is holding me back? What makes me a little nervous?

Simply put, one of the things I worry about is professional (should I say it?) arrogance. I worry that we too often portray ourselves as if we are the only profession that *really* cares about the client, who *really* has a full picture of what's going on, who is *really* in the best position professionally to respond to ALL of the client's needs and perform the range of intervention tasks. I see too often social workers subtly denigrate other professions to highlight our own uniquenesses and contributions. In the past, I have been guilty of this myself. Interestingly, the one article to appear in a social work journal that *does* advocate that social workers work toward prescription-writing privileges does so only after saying "psychiatry is unnecessarily burdened with irrelevant traditions" and "clinical psychology has never been able to get its own house in order" (Abroms & Greenfield, 1973, p. 133). (Does anyone else see those comments as ironic?).

Instead I would argue for what could be called disciplinary humility by social workers, and indeed all mental health professionals. What does that look like? I think it is a much fuller and richer appreciation of the roles and contributions of sibling professionals in psychology, nursing, psychiatry, pharmacy, occupational therapy, and pastoral counseling, to name just a few. I believe if we all had greater knowledge of the mutual and respective philosophical perspectives, theories, professional roles, and functions of others, the client would be more likely to benefit from the great potential of *real* interdisciplinary collaboration, unencumbered by substantial role confusion, role conflict, and disciplinary power plays. I have argued that it is only when each of the disciplines has a deep understanding of the legitimacy of other disciplines and professionals that we will be understood and embraced as a full partner in the helping professional arena. I am talking, admittedly idealistically, about what it will take to rise above turf battles and guild politics in an era in which the battle for the mental health dollar has never been more fierce.

So how does this relate to prescription writing? It suggests that, as I see it right now, the type of interdisciplinary respect and collaboration that I am speaking of can probably best develop when professions admit their boundaries of expertise. We have so longed for other professions to acknowledge their limits and recognize *our* expertise in the area of psychosocial assessment and intervention. It seems natural that we should then accept the admitted expertise of others in psychopharmacology and spend our time building on, complementing, enriching, and expanding the work of others. Yes, the profession is rightfully paying more attention to the impact of biology on human behavior and on our role as helpers. Likewise, some physicians are beginning to pay more attention to the social and emotional influences on health. That does not mean anyone would suggest that in 1996 physicians should start personally doing psychosocial assessments, insight-oriented counseling, social skills training, or organizational restructuring. Rather it suggests a heightened mandate for interdisciplinary communication and collaboration. Specifically, we would hope that a physician would work *with* a social worker around his or her "patient's" psychosocial and emotional issues. Ideally this social worker would be sharing office space with the physician.

Not surprisingly, in psychology, those opposed to expanded prescription-writing privileges have expressed concerns similar to those above; specifically, that such a move would hurt the credibility of their field and confuse their distinctiveness (Boswell & Litwin, 1992). In spite of such objections, it seems that in the coming years the debate in our sibling professions may not be so much about *whether* to seek prescription-writing privileges but *under what conditions* it should be allowed. For example, although certain nursing professionals (clinical specialists and practitioners) have various levels of privileges in most states, there are always limits to the type of medications that can be prescribed. In a pilot prescription program in California, Pharm.D.s allowed to prescribe clozapine were closely supervised by psychiatric residents (Dishman, Ellenor, Lacro, & Lohr,

1994). Thus, questions remain about what kind of limits will be placed on the settings, the type of medication, dosages, or level of independent decision making allowed even among those professionals where expansion is expected in the next few years. I have found no one yet that is suggesting that psychologists, nurses, and pharmacists have unlimited prescription-writing privileges with absolutely no medical oversight. For social workers, this may give us a hint into the kind of professional battles we might be fighting in the next decade if we were to successfully advocate for prescription-writing privileges. Can you see NASW organizing a national effort to increase the types of drugs its members can prescribe, or Political Action for Candidate Election (PACE) backing only those candidates who support "social work prescription laws" in their state?

Although there would be nothing at all wrong with either of those efforts, the much more basic and important question is about opportunity costs. *Are these the battles we as a profession want to fight?* It seems a bit ironic having only recently caught our breath from intensive national efforts at gaining licensure, and having pretty much buried the notion of having psychiatrists "sign off" on our work, that we would seek the right to engage in some activity that is highly likely to resurrect strikingly similar practices. Would such an effort cause us to repeat past mistakes with respect to our professional functioning, roles, and focus? For example, will Kutchins and Kirk uncover widespread reliance on certain medications by prescribing social workers based purely on the limitations of our legal authority rather than client symptoms or need, just as they discovered the relationship between diagnosis and reimbursement (Kirk & Kutchins, 1992). Will we again become so caught up in more self-serving professional causes that we have no time, money, or energy left to advocate for our client's *expressed* priorities, such as access to decent independent housing, meaningful employment, affordable transportation and health care, and opportunities for recreation and fulfilling relationships? On a slightly different but equally important note, would we aggressively seek data that answer questions about whether prescription-writing privileges among social workers helps our clients and improves the quality of *their* lives? I am afraid our own history may not speak well for us there.

I have managed thus far to avoid the most obvious reason why this is not a good time for social workers to seek prescription-writing privileges. Or at least I have not yet directly stated it. That is that we are not educationally prepared to offer that service. It seems that the curriculum crunch in social work education is simply too severe now to allow for significant addition of content. Many already find it almost humorous that in our two-year M.S.W. programs we pretend to teach everything there is to know about human behavior in all its diversity; about all the skills, techniques, strategies, programs, and such that can change it; *and* about the historical, sociopolitical, cultural, and organizational context of all human service delivery! Although one could argue for postgraduate institutes as an avenue for preparing social workers for new roles in prescribing psychotropic medication, arguments questioning the profession's proper focus and use of resources would again emerge. Would we end up with a further tiered profession: B.S.W., M.S.W., M.S.W. +2, M.S.W. +5, L.C.S.W. with or without psychotropic medication certification, Board Certified Diplomat (BCD) with or without medication certification.... Or perhaps this will be the twenty-first century's version of the clinical doctorate?

I have not used the strong language of Elliot and Kintzler (1973), who side with me in opposition to this question when they exclaim that obtaining the privilege would be "at the expense of corrupting our training programs and abandoning our own areas of expertise" (p. 136). I have also not pointed to potentially serious ethical and legal concerns that might emerge if social workers are placed in the position of acting beyond their expertise (see Miller, Wiedeman & Linn, 1980). But I have clearly gotten carried away with "what ifs" and hypotheticals and that may not be fair, especially because realism is on my side in this debate. I *do* want to get back to Joe's father-in-law, because he has helped me to frame the "bottom line" issues in this debate. He says, for example, that it is irrelevant if social work education is currently adequate to prepare social workers to prescribe psychotropic medication. If the profession decides to move in that direction, social work education will have to creatively respond. And I agree. He also says that social work should *not* get hung up on what other professions do or do not do, or what they will sanction us doing or not sanction. And I agree that no other profession should define us. Finally, the retired engineer says the way he sees it, there are really only two things to ask: would it be best for clients?, and would it be best for our profession? And maybe this is the whole thing. I am just not yet convinced that it is best for either.

REFERENCES

Abroms, G., & Greenfield, N. (1973). Drug-prescribing and the non-medical therapist. *Clinical Social Work Journal, 1,* 132–134.

Bentley, K. J., & Walsh, J. (1996). *The social worker & psychotropic medication.* Pacific Grove, CA: Brooks/Cole.

Boswell, D. L., & Litwin, W. J. (1992). Limited prescription privileges for psychologists: A one year follow-up. *Professional Psychology, 23,* 108–113.

DeLeon, P. H., & Pies, R. W. (1994). Should non-physician mental health professionals be allowed to prescribe medicine? In S. Kirk & S. D. Einbinder (Eds.), *Controversial issues in mental health* (pp. 177–188). Boston: Allyn & Bacon.

Dishman, B. R., Ellenor, G. L., Lacro, J. P., & Lohr, J. B. (1994). Pharmacists' role in clozapine therapy at a Veterans Affairs Medical Center. *American Journal of Hospital Pharmacy, 51,* 899–901.

Elliot, C., & Kintzler, C. (1973). No prescription pads for social workers. *Clinical Social Work Journal, 1,* 134–136.

Kirk, S., & Kutchins, H. (1992). *The selling of DSM: The rhetoric of science in psychiatry.* New York: Aldine de Gruyter.

Miller, R., Wiedeman, G. & Linn, G., (1980). Prescribing psychotropic drugs: Whose responsibility? *Social Work in Health Care, 6*(1), 51–61.

Olfson, M., & Klerman, O. (1993). Trends in the prescription of psychotropic medications: The role of physician specialty. *Medical Care, 31,* 559–564.

Wiggins, J. G. (1994). Would you want your child to be a psychologist? *American Psychologist, 49,* 485–492.

AUTHOR'S NOTE

The author thanks Joe Walsh and his father-in-law for their respective contributions to this chapter.

Rejoinder to Dr. Bentley
SOPHIA F. DZIEGIELEWSKI

In response, much to my surprise, Dr. Bentley and I generally agreed on the future of prescription privileging for social workers. I would like, however, to clarify and expound on several issues. First, Dr. Bentley and I agree that in general we are finally spending time on the "impact of biology on human behavior," and physicians are beginning to pay more attention to the social and emotional influences on health. She exemplifies this point with the statement "that does not mean anyone would suggest that in 1996 physicians should start personally doing psychosocial assessments, insight-oriented training, social skills training, or organizational restructuring." She uses this argument to reinforce the point that we need an interdisciplinary approach to address client-centered care, and social workers should remain as gatekeepers.

It is here that I suggest a different interpretation of this trend. Specialty physicians (e.g., surgeons, neurologists, etc.) are finding themselves in a tight and limited market. Therefore, many specialty physicians are seeking retraining in the primary care field (family medicine, internal medicine, and general pediatrics, etc.). In these retraining programs, an emphasis on individually doing psychosocial assessments, for example, is exactly what is happening, and what I have been teaching for the last seven years. Social workers are an integral part of most primary care medicine residency programs because of this very reason. Physicians are expected to do more today that just address biological needs. They must understand the implications of social factors in all aspects of the medical care they provide. It is this continued recognition and understanding that help to decrease medication and general treatment noncompliance. Therefore, Dr. Bentley and I agree that interdisciplinary teamwork will remain a practice reality. However, if physicians plan to remain as the "Captain" of the team, they must be aware of not only what the other team members are doing but how to help and advise them in this area. The mystique of medication knowledge no longer is in their realm alone; therefore, they have been forced to realize (and be trained in) the importance of understanding the entire person–environment stance.

Several other points we agree on include: (1) the need for additional training beyond what is offered in schools of social work; (2) that social workers should not get overly concerned with what other professions sanction as acceptable for us to do; (3) if we decide to fight this battle, it will not be an easy one; and, (4) our field (particularly the need to acquire the necessary education) will "creatively respond" if we as a profession choose to move in this direction.

Dr. Bentley further exemplifies the need to choose our battles wisely and questions whether fighting this difficult battle would subtract from our energy to help our clients. Again we agree that we always need to advocate for our clients. To take this further, however, we must never forget that we must also advocate for ourselves and our profession. This is a door that needs to be made available, which in turn can make our profession more responsive to our clients' needs. Medication use is and will remain a practice reality. In general, social workers were born fighting, and thank goodness that most of us feel strongly enough about our clients and our profession that we simply will not run out of energy.

In closing, I would like to end with the words of my friend Dr. Bentley " In spite of such objections . . . the debate within our sibling professions may not be so much about *whether* to seek prescription writing privileges but *under what conditions* it should be allowed." Again we agree, as today this era of managed care is creating a whole new practice revolution for which prescription medication remains an integral component. Specialty physicians are scared, and the need for holistic medical practice with a focus on wellness and prevention is burgeoning. To Dr. Bentley and all of my other colleagues, it is clear that the revolution has started. Now social workers must decide whether we want to take an active part in this fight or whether we just want to sit at the "gate" and make sure the other medical specialties get through. If we decide to fight for the **option** to prescribe medication, and I hope we will, we will benefit our clients and ourselves as a profession. If we decide not to, in our position of hesitancy and apathy, I hope someone tells the other professions (including Joe Walsh and his father-in-law) to remember to relieve us from our "watchpost"—so we can help celebrate their victory.

Should Public Sector Clinical Social Workers Be Required to Be Licensed?

Peggy H. Cleveland, Ph.D., is the Director of the Division of Social Work, Valdosta State University, Valdosta, Georgia. Dr. Cleveland earned her M.S.W. in 1975 and her Ph.D. in 1987 from the University of Georgia. Her practice experience includes both micro and macro levels, and she is licensed in Georgia as a clinical social worker and as a marriage and family therapist.

Jan Ligon, M.S.W., is the former Crisis Services Director for the DeKalb Community Service Board, a large public sector provider of mental health, substance abuse, mental retardation, and crisis services in the Atlanta, Georgia, area. He received an M.S.W. degree from the University of Georgia in 1989, where he is currently pursuing his Ph.D. in social work.

YES

PEGGY CLEVELAND

After more than twenty years of efforts, fifty states and jurisdictions have some form of legal regulation of social work practice (Hardcastle, 1987). The task of obtaining licensing for social workers has been difficult and fraught with ambivalence, not only for legislatures but also for professional social workers and academics. In descriptions of the efforts of specific disciplines to obtain licensing (counseling [Brooks & Gerstein, 1990], psychology [Cummings, 1990], school psychology [Prywansky, 1993], and social work [Garcia, 1990]), authors report a lack of unity in the pursuit of licensing, particularly between those in academia and those who are in practice. It is interesting that although some social workers have pursued the establishment of posteducation credentials for approximately twenty years (Garcia, 1990), the issue of the desirability of licensing is still being debated. The reasons given for the opinions for or against licensing are so far largely philosophical and not empirical.

For the historical perspective of social workers' pursuit of licensing, please see Garcia, 1990; Thyer & Biggerstaff, 1989; and Hardcastle, 1987. The purpose of this essay is to speak for the desirability of licensing for social workers in general and specifically for those in the public sector. The assumption is that social workers in public agencies should be subject to the same credentialing process as social workers in other sectors.

Gandy and Raymond (1979) provided one of the first discussions on the desirability of licensing and stated that reasons in support of legal regulation included the provision for a legal definition of the profession, the protection of clients, raising standards of practice, the establishment of accountability, and to provide a basis for further development of the profession. How can this rationale have relevance only to those in the private sector?

In Georgia as in many other states, there have been those in positions in agency practice designated as a social work positions who called themselves social workers although they have no degree in social work. Licensing prohibits this practice. In Georgia, the title protection act in 1985 and recent practice protection law in 1994 have for the first time in this State defined social work practice and, therefore, make it mandatory that those who call themselves social workers and do the work of social workers actually be social workers. Is this desirable? I believe so. What other profession agrees that those without a degree can define themselves as part of that profession and practice that discipline? Do people without proper credentials call themselves nurses, physicians, attorneys, teachers, psychologists? Those who say that practitioners without social work education can be good social workers are defining professional practice in terms of a few tasks that some people can perform. Can one with a calming voice who can draw blood, give injections, take blood pressures, and leave good notes for a physician, be a nurse? No! For the same reason, those with only good hearts, natural empathy, and a natural bent for case management cannot be social workers.

A profession is distinguished by a body of knowledge and a code of ethics. A license is one of the indications that the body of knowledge has been acquired and that a code of ethics provides a basic standard of practice. Why should those social workers who are employed in the public sector be excluded from the requirement of professional status or of the benefits that licensing might afford them and their clients?

Surely the mastery or at least passing of the requirements of an accredited program indicates to some degree the acquisition of a body of knowledge. However, the degree cannot assure that the profession is regulating itself after the degree is awarded. A recent newspaper story reminds us of the importance of this regulation. A practitioner of another discipline was charged with sexual misconduct and surrendered his license to practice (White, 1995). This kind of blatant abuse of clients is fortunately rare among professional people, but licensing provides a way of terminating the practice of those who might violate the terms of the fiduciary relationship that social workers have with their clients.

Kutchins (1991) declares that there are three important aspects of fiduciary relations existing between social workers and their clients:

1. Special duties that arise because of the trust or confidence in the fiduciary.
2. The powers of the fiduciary to dominate and influence the client because of the nature of the relationship.
3. Because of the relationship, the fiduciary must act in the best interest of the client. (p. 107)

Why should social workers in the public sector be exempt from these parameters of the relationship with their clients?

There is little in social work education that helps professional helpers to deal with the issues of intensity and intimacy with their clients. This lack leaves professional helpers to deal with these issues without much support or direction. Consequently, both professionals and their clients are very vulnerable. Licensing with a requirement of continuing education in ethics and a process of accountability reduce this vulnerability for clients and increase the likelihood of retribution for practitioners when violations occur.

Thyer and Biggerstaff (1989) assert:

Public-sector agencies establish controls over professional practice through their bureaucratic structure which hierarchically arranges practitioners to provide a system of checks and balances. As long as the large majority of social work services are offered through public employment of social workers, legal regulation is not deemed necessary by social workers or lawmakers. (p. 22)

This statement seems to indicate that the monitoring of practice by supervision is greater in the public sector. However, there are no studies available that tell us exactly what kind of supervision is available in public agencies. One unpublished survey (Cleveland & Ligon, 1995) gives some preliminary data that are of interest. A survey of 126 social workers in Georgia shows that ninety-three (73.8 percent) of these work in the public sector. Twenty-three (18.3 percent) social workers stated that they receive no supervision in their jobs. Of the 101 (80.2 percent) of those who have supervision, sixty-one (48.4 percent) of these had task supervision only, with no content on practice issues. Sixty-eight (54 percent) reported that supervision that would meet the requirements for clinical licensing was not available in their agencies. These results in this small sample may indicate to us the need to determine if the monitoring in public agencies is in fact occurring.

Another story (Gerth, 1995) reports a chilling episode in which four social workers are charged with complicity to commit murder. In these two articles, employees in the Department of Social Services were accused of faulty investigation and inaccurate record keeping, which resulted in a child's death. At best this disproves the belief that those in public agencies have enough supervision to warrant exclusion from licensing requirements. I wonder if any other discipline is subject to this rationale. For instance, should nurses in public health be exempt from licensing because the bureaucratic hierarchy monitors practice well enough to assure good practice? Ask a nurse!

A social worker reports (Dougherty, 1995) an example of decentralizing the social work unit in a hospital. The hospital reorganized out of existence the social work unit and assigned social workers in various units of the hospital to do counseling, discharge planning, and resource brokering. In these situations, the social workers are working with various disciplines and are always subject to another disciplines' definition of their practice. Without a thorough professional grounding, the unique perspectives of social workers (many of whom are B.S.W.s in this specific situation) may begin to diminish in the merging of ideas about what the tasks are and how they should be done.

Clark and Abeles (1994), in an excellent article on ethical issues in mental health organizations, declared that

> The manager ensures quality of patient care.... The manager assures the quality of his or her staff by making it a policy to monitor whether clinicians update their skills and knowledge, provide competent and consistent care, understand the privilege of confidentiality and other client rights, keep adequate records, and observe personal morality.... Managers are responsible for educating staff and support personnel about ethical practices. (p. 9)

This contention sounds great, but I wonder how often it really happens in any agency. In the absence of this kind of management, regulation is very important. If managers were licensed and subject to continuing education requirements, management styles might be positively affected.

Another consideration is that those who work in the public arena have a job description that is completely determined by the agency. Public policy making is a political process that includes assigning the implementation of these policies to administrators in bureaucracies, who in turn oversee the actual execution of the policies by those frontline workers who may have no professional identity except that of agency worker. Often the assurance of client's rights becomes an issue of law and not of values. This, in itself, will significantly affect the kind of practice that takes place in the agency. This is not to generalize that all people who do social services without an M.S.W. have no training or professional values; nor is it to say that all professionals with social work degrees are superior practitioners. It is to say that this particular way of assigning job descriptions requires caution. These definitions of social work practice may not be congruent with professional standards and may be challenged by those who are well trained professionally and have ongoing continuing education. Social workers in all agencies need good professional grounding so that they do not get caught up in the bureaucracy or get lost among the diverse professional groups. The professional viewpoint often goes beyond the agency definition of the job. This viewpoint should be heard. This challenge may be upsetting to agencies who prefer to define social work practice on their own terms, but it may be beneficial to the consumers of their services in the long run.

Munson (1983) stated that since the 1960s social workers have become more specialized in the methods of working with people, and those in direct practice are expected to know how to function as effective workers with individuals, peer groups, and families. All three of these methods are to be practiced with diverse populations of people of all age-groups and in varied settings. This expectation along with the functional changes that are taking place in social work have required an extraordinary increase in the body of knowledge of social workers. No M.S.W. program, no matter how good, can provide this kind of knowledge. A good program of continuing education can begin to keep practicing social workers informed of new and developing theories and models. In the survey noted (Cleveland & Ligon, 1995), participants were asked to rate their agreement with the statement, "Licensing assures that professionals continue to learn." Ninety (71.4 percent) agreed strongly. Only twenty (15.9 percent) were undecided. Although all states that legally regulate the practice of social work do not require continuing education, licensing usually requires some kind of continuing education that may not take place if practitioners did not need to renew their licenses periodically.

Another important consideration in the question of whether social workers in the public sector should be licensed is the fact that public and private are no longer as disparate as they once were. Purchasing social services, or privatization, has become a dominant method in the delivery of services by public agencies. Terrell (1987, p. 436) reports that "contracting is a primary means of delivering these services, although the balance between public and private provision varies with state and local circumstances."

This method of purchasing services is enhancing flexibility in service delivery and access to services. Medicaid and Medicare finance private vendors to provide a wide range of services, and these are used to provide a diversity of programs in services to aging, in mental health, public health services, social services, and probation and juvenile services (Terrell, 1987). The funding sources and others, such as health maintenance organizations, are requiring licensed practitioners of all disciplines to deliver these services. Social workers who are not licensed must relinquish these jobs to professional counselors, psychologists, and marriage and family therapists. The postulate that the "real" social workers are in public agencies and those who are not as dedicated are in private agencies may be time worn and irrelevant in light of the many changes in health care and social service delivery. There are growing options for social workers, especially in rural areas, who have the requisite training and experience to take advantage of them.

Economics is no doubt an important factor in public agencies hiring uncredentialed people. Many times I have heard, and experienced myself, the philosophy of "hire them cheap, burn them up, and let them go." No profession should succumb to this kind of disrespect. Agencies who respect their workers and provide an atmosphere of growth are likely to keep them and also to provide good services for their consumers.

We all know that in many areas of the country there is a shortage of social workers, and requiring all social workers to be licensed causes a hardship on agencies who deliver social services. This is an irrefutable fact, but there must be better solutions to this problem than exempting social workers in the public sector from licensing requirements. Such shortages have served to enhance other professions and may enhance ours if we take advantage of a great opportunity for academia and the practice community to work together in some very creative ways to provide the kind of educational experiences that the social service providers need to be credentialed. This seems to be a much better use of our time than fighting licensing requirements that are beneficial to social workers.

REFERENCES

Brooks, D., & Gerstein, L. (1990). Counselor credentialing and interprofessional collaboration. *Journal of Counseling & Development, 68,* 477–484.

Clark, B., & Abeles, N. (1994). Ethical issues and dilemmas in the mental health organization. *Administration and Policy on Mental Health, 22,* 7–17.

Cleveland, P., & Ligon, J. (1995). *Attitudes towards licensure and supervision: Results of a study of urban and rural social workers.* Unpublished manuscript.

Cummings, N. (1990). The credentialing of professional psychologists and its implication for the other mental health disciplines. *Journal of Counseling & Development, 68,* 485–490.

Dougherty, B. (1995). President, Knightingale Home Health Agency, Grand Forks, ND: Personal Communication, June 26.

Gandy, J. T., & Raymond, F. B. (1979). A study of strategies used in the pursuit of legal regulation of social work. *Journal of Sociology and Social Welfare, 6,* 464–476.

Garcia, A. (1990). An examination of the social work profession's efforts to achieve legal regulation. *Journal of Counseling & Development, 68,* 491–497.

Gerth, J. (1995, June 24). Social worker relates steps she took to protect adorable, precious child. *The Courier-Journal,* p. 1.

Gerth, J. (1995, June 25). Social worker said she took the therapist's word that the boy wasn't abused. *The Courier-Journal,* p. 1.

Hardcastle, D. (1987). Legal regulation of social work. In A. Minahan, (Ed.). *Encyclopedia of Social Work* (18th ed., vol. 2, pp. 203–217). Silver Spring, MD: National Association of Social Workers.

Kutchins, H. (1991). The fiduciary relationship: The legal basis for social workers' responsibilities to clients. *Social Work, 36,* 106–113.

Munson, C. E. (1983). *An introduction to clinical social work supervision.* New York: Haworth.

Pryzwansky, W. (1993). The regulation of school psychology: A historical perspective on certification, licensure, and accreditation. *Journal of School Psychology, 31,* 219–235.

Terrell, P. (1987). Purchasing social services in mental health. In A. Minahan (Ed.). *Encyclopedia of social work* (pp. 434–442). Silver Spring, MD: National Association of Social Workers.

Thyer, B., & Biggerstaff, M. (1989). *Professional social work credentialing and legal regulation.* Springfield, IL: Charles C. Thomas.

White, J. (1995). State board plugs loophole on licensing psychologists. *The Macon Telegraph,* June 1, 1B.

Rejoinder to Dr. Cleveland

JAN LIGON

Dr. Cleveland underscores a number of important reasons for social work licensure and then asks why public sector workers should be "excluded from the requirement of professional status or the benefits that licensing might afford them and their clients." Dr. Cleveland argues that, without licensure, professionals and consumers would be excluded from its benefits, whereas my position remains that mandated licensure inordinately raises the stakes in the public sector at the expense of those who are the most in need of help and who are usually without any other alternative for services.

As further stated by Dr. Cleveland, "funding sources and others, such as health maintenance organizations, are requiring licensed practitioners of all disciplines to deliver these services." As a billable resource to the private sector, it is not surprising that many licensed workers who are currently employed in the public sector are being lured by private providers with offers of higher salaries and better working conditions. As these private providers increase their demand for the licensed worker, the value of the license increases and shortages may result. Although Dr. Cleveland asserts that "such shortages have served to enhance other professions and may enhance ours," I contend that such enhancements are at the expense of our consumers as the public provider finds that recruiting and retaining professionals becomes increasingly difficult to accomplish.

A shortage of social workers increases the demand for the degree and leads to schools of social work escalating such arbitrary and discriminatory barriers as minimum entrance examination scores as a way to screen out applicants. Although I agree with Dr. Cleveland's statement that "there are growing options for social workers, especially in rural areas," increases in demand for the social work degree could adversely affect those in rural areas who must compete with their urban counterparts for a finite number of available admission slots. In addition, opportunities for practicum experiences in the public sector could be reduced by further losses of licensed workers and a lack of available supervision for both rural and urban students.

Although I agree with Dr. Cleveland that "public and private are no longer as disparate as they once were," I must reinforce that gaps still exist. The public sector simply cannot adapt as quickly as the private sector relative to the pace of change that is occurring. For example, we are committed to reducing our dependence on taxpayer funding of public programs, but we do not deny services to those who are unable to pay. Private providers simply do not encounter this dilemma.

Nursing, which Dr. Cleveland uses as a comparative discipline, may offer our profession an alternative licensure approach for consideration. My agency employs four different levels of licensed nurses, who offer a range of both skills and salary costs. Although the highest-level nurse is compensated at three times the level of the lowest, the availability of multiple levels of skills enables us to afford to provide services that are congruent to client needs. I believe that it would be beneficial to social workers to increase the availability of licensure to baccalaureate level workers for several reasons. First, there are many jobs that can be accomplished very effectively by the B.S.W. social worker, whereas others require the M.S.W. Second, because there are more B.S.W. than M.S.W. programs, the degree is simply more accessible to students. Finally, B.S.W. licensure would support all of the benefits identified by Dr. Cleveland to both the profession and the consumer of services.

Although I fully agree with Dr. Cleveland's support of title protection, I believe that we can learn from nursing by broadening our definition of the social worker. I agree with Dr. Cleveland that "social workers who are not licensed must relinquish these jobs to professional counselors, psychologists, and marriage and family therapists." However, Dr. Cleveland expresses further concern that when "a hospital reorganized out of existence the social work unit," there would be a diminishing of "the unique perspectives of social workers." To mandate only the licensure of the master's-level clinical public sector social worker would be detrimental at this time. I believe we need to take a broadened perspective of the profession and consider other alternatives, such as additional levels of licensure, that will enhance the overall profession as opposed to only the master's-level licensed clinician.

NO

Jan Ligon

As a Licensed Clinical Social Worker who is employed in the public sector, I am both supportive of licensure and an advocate for social workers to pursue careers in the public domain (Ligon, 1995). However, to *require* all clinical (master's-level) public workers to be licensed could adversely affect public sector services. For this reason, I do not support such a mandate. Although the history of licensure is available elsewhere (Thyer & Biggerstaff, 1989), literature about its impact on the profession is limited (Cassidy & Bullard, 1961; Garcia, 1990; Gray, 1990; Iverson, 1987; Land, 1987; Strom, 1992).

Licensure's Effect on Social Work Values

In the early 1960s, Cassidy and Bullard (1961) expressed concern that "insufficient attention has been given to the research aspects—the fact-gathering possibilities—inherent in mandatory licensing" (p. 63). By 1989, forty-eight states had passed licensure laws, which included a mandatory statute in some states (Garcia, 1990). However, concerns about its impact continued, with Gray (1990) stating that "little empirical research has been conducted into licensure's influence on the profession" (p. 53). Although Land (1987) acknowledged that these laws offered such potential benefits as consumer protection, she also observed a change in student motivation to choose social work as a career. With licensure came an increased opportunity for private practice through third-party payments and a corresponding shift in student career goals from helping the underserved to wanting "a relatively quick license to become a shrink" (Land, 1987, p. 75).

Regarding women and minorities, Iversen (1987) states that, although licensure "may improve the status of women" (p. 232), there is also the risk of "the perpetuation of a paternalistic, authoritarian structure" (p. 232) by licensure boards, which could be composed of predominantly male or racial majority members. She also observed that "the potentially exclusionary effect of extended graduate education as a requirement for licensure" (p. 232) could adversely affect women and minorities. Because many states have only one master's degree program in social work, increases in demand for the degree can force schools to use barriers, such as minimum scores on entrance examinations, which also may be discriminatory. Reimbursement shifts to third-party providers and the trend toward managed care also may conflict with more traditional social work values, according to Strom (1992).

Licensure and the Rural Social Worker

These earlier publications focused on concerns that licensure and reimbursement would "siphon off competent workers from agency jobs into private practice" that would lead to a possible "reduction in services to the poor" (Iverson, 1987, p. 232). A survey of 126 social workers concerning licensure and supervision (Cleveland & Ligon, 1995) indicated differences between urban (41.4 percent) and rural (58.6 percent) respondents. Though 80 percent of those licensed at the clinical level were urban workers, only 20 percent of the licensed workers were from rural areas. Rural workers may experience barriers to such licensure requirements as clinical supervision and continuing education. Although 52 percent of the urban respondents reported receiving supervision through their employers, only 31 percent of the rural workers were provided clinical supervision. Approved continuing education is also a common requirement to maintain licensed status. Although 85 percent of respondents reported obtaining continuing education each year, rural workers may not have access to training in their locale. Unlike their urban counterparts, rural workers may be forced to incur additional expenses, including travel and workshop fees, to obtain the required continuing education. To mandate the licensure of public sector clinical social workers could be an additional hardship on workers in rural areas, where public services are often the only ones available.

Licensure's Impact on the Public Sector

The lack of parity between the public and private sectors is most recently evidenced by the advent of managed care. As Strom (1992) states, "some social work professionals have been uneasy with the prospect of privately delivered services" and further reports that "the advent of vendorship has done nothing to diminish these concerns" (1992, pp. 399). Reimbursement contingent on licensure has a significant influence on the recruitment, retention, compensation, and ultimate career goals of many master's-level social workers. Although the public sector may provide suitable employment for an initial period of post-master's practice, once the clinical license is acquired, many workers move to the private sector, where compensation and working conditions are usually more attractive. Others may begin a part-time private practice with the goal of a full-time endeavor. In addition, there is the risk that losses of experienced workers in the public sector could adversely affect the opportunity for students to experience public sector internships because of the lack of qualified field supervisors.

It can be very difficult for the public sector to compete with the private market with respect to compensation and working conditions. The move to managed care and other projected shifts in the provider system have alerted the public sector to the need for licensed workers and to accredit public systems. However, legislative and governing entities, public benefits programs, and other funding resources are slow to change when compared with the private sector.

Unfortunately, this disparity has resulted in the employment of many workers in the public arena who have neither a social work education nor a license. Though a significant need exists for social workers in the public sector, recruiters in many states find great difficulty in hiring social workers for available positions (Ligon, 1995). Based on survey comments (Cleveland & Ligon, 1995), public sector social workers may not perceive the value of a license in the same fashion as those in the private sector. Although one urban worker stated, "I think licensure is essential," and another reported that "it makes the profession," a public sector worker stated, "I believe that licensure is not relevant for public/government social workers and is, in fact, a detriment to advocacy and credibility." Public sector respondents may relate the license's value to job requirements or compensation. As one respondent reported, "I do not live where licensure is available, but it is both costly and time-consuming and is not required on my job. From my observations, licensure, or lack thereof, is no guarantee of a quality professional." It is difficult to mandate licensure in the public sector when the employer may be unable to acknowledge its value to the employee, primarily through suitable compensation.

Conclusion and Recommendations

Although there is hope that gaps between the public and private systems will close over time, earlier fears that the underserved would be adversely affected by licensure (Iverson, 1987; Land, 1987) may have merit, whereas concerns around a lack of research (Cassidy & Bullard, 1961; Gray, 1990) remain essentially unresolved. Though it is impossible to speculate about what events will transpire as these systems evolve, it will behoove each of us to learn more about our fellow social workers, the needs of our consumers and their families, and the efficacy of our interventions. For example, when states mail licensure renewals, an instrument could be included to obtain valuable data that could be used to shape and improve our profession.

Before we mandate licensure in the public sector, we should not only consider both the advantages and disadvantages, but we should compare the efficacy of this policy in states already having such a requirement with those that do not. It would seem that this information is essential before making such a critical decision. Furthermore, some states currently license at both the master's and baccalaureate levels, and there is a risk that to mandate the former could devalue the latter. Once again, comparative research on the efficacy of workers at different educational levels would provide valuable information to use in making decisions concerning licensure policy.

Public sector social workers help many of our most vulnerable citizens who often have nowhere else to turn. They are served by systems that are struggling to adapt to massive political, societal, and systemic changes. A thorough consideration of the pros and cons of a licensure mandate is essential so that we do not jeopardize services to those who are at the greatest risk of being adversely affected by mandating clinical licensure in the public sector.

REFERENCES

Cassidy, E. S., & Bullard, M. M. (1961). The California story. *Social Work, 6,* 56–65.

Cleveland, P. H., & Ligon, J. (1995). *Attitudes towards licensure and supervision: Results of a study of urban and rural social workers.* Manuscript in preparation.

Garcia, A. (1990). An examination of the social work profession's efforts to achieve legal regulation. *Journal of Counseling and Development, 68,* 491–497.

Gray, S. (1990). The interplay of social work licensure and supervision: An exploratory study. *The Clinical Supervisor, 8,* 53–65.

Iverson, R. R. (1987). Licensure: Help or hindrance to women social workers. *Social Casework, 68,* 229–233.

Land, H. (1987). The effects of licensure on student motivation and career choice, *Social Work, 32,* 75–77.

Ligon, J. (1995). Myths of the public sector. *The New Social Worker, 2*(1), 19.

Strom, K. (1992). Reimbursement demands and treatment decisions: A growing dilemma for social workers. *Social Work, 37,* 398–403.

Thyer, B. A., & Biggerstaff, M A. (1989). *Professional social work credentialing and legal regulation.* Springfield, IL: Charles C. Thomas.

Rejoinder to Mr. Ligon
PEGGY CLEVELAND

Mr. Ligon's answer to whether public sector social workers should be licensed is basically a question about whether licensing is "worth it" given all the inconveniences and probabilities. This perspective is certainly worth consideration but at the same time seems to be presenting specious arguments.

It is true that we are making decisions largely on philosophical arguments. Those cited by Mr. Ligon continue that trend. For instance, Land (1987) gives four quotes from students who express the goal of being in the private practice of psychotherapy. In the entire article, the author never tells us how many students she has talked to or what other students besides these four said about their goals. This article may represent more of the author's bias toward clinical work than the goals and values of social work students. Overall, it is not helpful in determining the value of licensing.

Similarly, the argument that licensing may be discriminatory in some way toward women and minorities and the suggestion that licensure and reimbursement would "siphon off competent workers from agency jobs into private practice" and would lead to a possible "reduction in services to the poor" are all philosophical. These questions do not relate to the essential question of whether public sector practitioners should be licensed. They do relate to possible impacts of licensing in general and are, therefore, important issues for study.

The barriers to continuing education and supervision are very real problems for those in rural areas particularly, but are still not questions about the value of licensing. These concerns are about convenience, not accountability in practice. Sure, it is harder for those who live a long way from Schools of Social Work to get their degrees. Sure, it is harder for those who live farther away from continuing education programs to get to these sessions. Are those real reasons why social workers in the public sector do not need to be licensed? I think not. There are many ways to resolve those issues that honor the initiative and ingenuity of social workers and social work educators without perpetuating the idea that credentialing in rural areas should not be tried because it is too difficult to accomplish.

Licensing and clinical are not synonymous! Our profession and agencies can be and should be more attentive to distinguishing between the competencies of professionals at varying levels of education. Licensing can also occur at different levels. If licensing is indeed an effort to protect consumers and to hold practitioners accountable for responsible practice, then all social workers should be licensed. If we choose to define clinical work as a specialty within the profession that has a different status or different requirements, then additional licensing should be required for that specialty. That difference, however, does not negate the need for accountability for all professionals who deliver services to vulnerable people. All social workers deliver services to vulnerable people, whether they function as administrators or in the private practice of psychotherapy.

The assumption that private practice represents a deviation from the goals of the social work profession may or may not be true. It is true, however, that licensing presents a way for social workers to be engaged in the private practice of psychotherapy. Keeping licensing from all social workers because a few may go in to private practice is not a reasonable alternative.

There are social workers who are engaged in the paid private practice of macro skills and models, such as consultation, grant writing, supervision, and evaluation. Are the goals of these people at variance with those of the social work profession? If they are, how is that related to the licensing of social workers in the public sector?

We have a false dichotomy in the assumption that poor people get help in the public sector and rich people get help in the private sector. Both poor and rich and those in between get help in schools, in health care delivery systems, in mental health facilities, in employee assistance programs, in forensic programs, in family service agencies, in child and adult protective services, and in religion-related service agencies. All of these agencies have the same need for skilled and accountable practitioners. It is indeed difficult for administrators to employ licensed social workers when they are not available. That is a dilemma that will take the combined efforts of professional organizations, professional practitioners, and social work educators to resolve.

This discussion surely points out the need for more attention to be given to the issue of licensing of social workers. There are implications for research, for social work education, and for professional association of career social workers. My hope is that we can begin to do the systematic, unbiased study that will enable us to make the decisions that we need to make about this important issue.

REFERENCE

Land, H. (1987). The effects of licensure on student motivation and career choice. *Social Work 32*, 75–77

Should Social Workers Participate in Assisted Suicide?

David (Pat) Boyle, Ph.D., is an Assistant Professor of Social Work with the University of Georgia. He earned his Ph.D. in social work from the UGA in 1994, after pastoring for sixteen years as an Ordained Minister with a small Appalachian congregation. His eighteen years of mental health practice experience have largely been in rural settings with elderly clients.

Kelly Canady, M.S.W., is District Office Manager of the Dublin office of the Hospice of Central Georgia. He has been involved in serving as a social worker for terminally ill patients since receiving his M.S.W. from the University of Georgia in 1989. Mr. Canady has had the experience of being diagnosed with a terminal illness, and is now considered cured.

YES

David P. Boyle

The question is very relevant because many social workers are now employed in settings dealing with severely ill persons, such as acute-care hospitals, nursing homes, hospices, home health agencies, acquired immune deficiency syndrome (AIDS) services, Alzheimer's chapters, and many others. One modern industrial state has allowed the practice of physician-assisted suicide (the Netherlands), and one state, Oregon, has passed a law, Measure 16 (now being appealed), which allows physician-assisted suicide (Solomon, 1995). Social workers are employed in many of the same agencies in which physicians may, at some point, be allowed to participate in assisted suicide and could potentially be involved in decisions involving patients that they serve.

179

First, for purposes of this discussion, I will use the dictionary definition of suicide: "the intentional taking of one's life" (Flexner, 1987). I will use the term *assisted* to mean with the help of another human being. Suicide itself is not illegal in the United States if one acts alone (Quill, 1993). At this point in history in the United States, most medical ethicists make a clear distinction between active and passive roles by the physician in helping a patient to die. It is currently acceptable to help a patient die by stopping a life-sustaining treatment, when requested to do so by the patient or in the event that the treatment becomes medically useless. It is not yet acceptable for a doctor to help a patient to die in an active way even if the amount of suffering is just as great, so long as the patient is not receiving a life-sustaining treatment that can be stopped. Those who are dependent on a life-sustaining treatment, therefore, are the only ones who currently receive the medical right to choose death. However, patients who have the courage, strength, and means to act alone can still release themselves through suicide. Most, however, who are suffering from painful and terminal diseases find themselves trapped in terrible suffering until death comes in some more passive way (Quill, 1993). For purposes of this discussion, the term *assisted suicide* will mean situations in which a patient desires active means of ending life, not simply passive assistance by withdrawal of treatment. In an assisted suicide, a patient is still carrying out his or her own act even though he or she is indirectly aided by an assistant. Some thinkers are beginning to support an ethical position favoring assisted suicide. When the assistant has a motivation of compassion for an incurably ill person who clearly and repeatedly requests help, the act can be both ethical and moral, if not legal (Quill, 1993).

Secondly, the word *should* implies a moralistic or ethical position. Social workers come from many different backgrounds, but most probably come from or are familiar with traditional religions which promote codes of behavior as guides for actions. These codes are rule governed or deontological in terms of the discipline of ethics. According to such codes, the right thing to do is to submit to a higher will (Baier, 1980), which is usually revealed through some inspired scripture or tradition of wisdom, such as the Bible. For persons subscribing to traditional religion as the basis for moral governance, the presence or absence of a rule or tradition in that religion would be the source of the *should*. However, in spite of the presence of a clear tradition in Judeo-Christian thinking that proscribes suicide, the scriptures say little specifically against it. Probably such a thought rarely occurred to the ancient Jews who gave us their sacred writings.

In any case, the modern quandary of the prospect of ending life painlessly or of sustaining it artificially, sometimes with great pain involved, through the use of technology, had not arisen and is still a relatively new situation for the human race. Neither did persons in earlier days have access to the knowledge of what was likely to happen in view of specific diagnoses, such as Alzheimer's disease or AIDS. Thus, the prospect of a certain, but slow and painful death did not arise, because of both the lack of knowledge and the lack of medical interventions to sustain or prolong life when diseases struck.

Even today, there are many persons of various religious persuasions who would argue that there is never any occasion for a caring professional to assist in arranging or supporting the taking of life. However, a quick look at most religious positions will find that there are almost always exceptions—abortion when the mother's life is in danger, capital punishment for heinous crimes, discontinuance of exotic treatments for a comatose, frail patient; killing in a "just" war, or in personal self-defense.

One branch of moral philosophy derives its *should* from the principle that moral actions should be judged on their results or consequences. The most popular of these consequentialist theories, utilitarianism, would aim to maximize the good for the most people (Baier, 1980). A specific type of utilitarianism that is widely discussed today is situation ethics. Situation ethics (Fletcher, 1966) very simply is the idea that "moral" acts have the intention to accomplish the most loving outcome or the greatest human well-being in any given situation. Because of the concern for human well-being, the decisionally flexible method, and concern for the greatest good realizable, rather than an adherence to moral norms, situationism seems to attract many, if not most, social workers (Reamer, 1990). Thus, many social workers derive their *should* from some type of situationalist thinking.

It is my contention that social workers have a professional obligation (an additional source of the "should") to be available, when they are employed in caring for the terminally ill, to assist persons who are deemed competent to make decisions about their own lives and treatment, to assist these persons in reaching a decision to terminate their own life when there is a terminal condition for which there is no known treatment likely to result in recovery, and that involves intense suffering for the individual. That is, the client is enabled to decide to mitigate suffering only for himself or herself, which is the basis for the decision. A desire to spare suffering to family and friends who might have to watch the client's suffering may be admirable in its concern for others, but crosses the line of self-determination and begins to involve the will and welfare of others for whom the client is not entitled to speak. This position is based on the National Association of Social Workers' Code of Ethics (COE) (1993), for which the preamble states: "...the fundamental values of the social work profession...include the worth, dignity, and uniqueness of all persons as well as their rights and opportunities" (p. v). The Preamble to the COE additionally states that the social worker is expected to take into consideration all of the principles in this code that have a bearing on any situation in which ethical judgment is to be exercised and professional intervention or conduct is planned.

Several sections of the COE bear on the discussion of assisted suicide. For example: Section I Article C 2 states that "The social worker should act to prevent practices that are inhumane or discriminatory against any person or group of persons" (p. 4). A case can be made that forcing the terminally ill AIDS or cancer patient to live out the deteriorating phases of disease is both inhumane in that it forces the client to endure extreme suffering and discriminatory in that it deprives such persons of the option to choose to end life that physically healthy people maintain by their ability to obtain the means to end their lives on their own at any time.

Section II Article F 6 of the COE states: "The social worker should provide clients with accurate and complete information regarding the extent and nature of the services available to them" (p. 5). In cases of terminal illness, one of the options in some countries, the Netherlands, by law, (Solomon, 1995) and many others, by professional practice, is assisted suicide. If a client wants to consider this option, the social worker is bound to discuss the possibilities and resources, according to this interpretation of the code of ethics.

Section II Article G 3 of the COE states: "The social worker should not engage in any action that violates or diminishes the civil or legal rights of clients" (p. 6). This section seems to imply that social workers should work to see that impaired persons, even the terminally ill, are not deprived of rights available to others because of their limiting conditions.

Section VI Article P 2 of the COE states: "The social worker should act to ensure that all persons have access to the resources, services, and opportunities which they require" (p. 10). This section seems to encourage social workers to make the linkages for impaired persons to the resources that they believe they need. In cases of terminal illness in which the client wants information, it would seem ethically necessary for the social worker to provide such information.

Section V O 2 of the COE states: "The social worker should critically examine, and keep current with, emerging knowledge relevant to social work" (p. 8). This section seems to require that social workers should become knowledgeable of critical issues. For social workers dealing with terminal patients, this section would seem to imply that they must participate at least in the discussion about assisted suicide, if not in actual implementation of the process.

Finally, the term *participate* requires definition. I would suggest that there are degrees of involvement in any social work interaction or intervention. In terms of participation in assisted suicide, the following range of degrees of participation would all qualify as interventions. Some workers might be comfortable with the lesser degrees and some with full participation, depending on their value bases and extent of involvement with the client and service system.

Referral for Counseling

If a client indicates that he or she is struggling with a decision about suicide and the client clearly does not meet the criteria for major depression and does not have a history of suicidal thinking, the worker may refer to a counseling agency for counseling about the issue, as well as for additional screening for possible mental health problems.

Providing Specific Information on Methods of Suicide

If a client has been through a counseling process and has reached a decision that assisted suicide is a real option, the social worker could refer the client to agencies that provide counseling and information (Hemlock Society, The Euthanasia Research & Guidance Organization, Choice in Dying, The Euthanasia Education Fund) or to a source of information on methods of assisted suicide (Gentles, 1995; Humphry, 1991; Quill, 1993).

Counseling toward a Decision

If a social worker works in an agency that provides counseling services and receives a referral with the specific question of possible assisted suicide, the worker could choose to provide counseling for that person in reaching a decision about whether to choose assisted suicide. Ethically, the social worker must be comfortable with the possible choices of the client and knowledgeable about the issues and options.

Participation in a Team That Implements Decisions

With the real possibility that Oregon may legalize assisted suicide, a social worker could conceivably be called to serve in several capacities. It is likely that ethics review boards will be set up in settings serving patients who choose assisted suicide. Likely, social workers will be asked to serve on such boards because of the profession's expertise in mental health, family systems, and in viewing clients holistically from an ecological perspective. This role would be mostly advisory or consultative to medical professionals. A more intensive team involvement could evolve in settings that implement the assisted suicide plan. For example, a team consisting of a physician, nurse, chaplain, and social worker could be designated to stay with a client through the total process, including working with survivors through the burial and grief experiences. It is likely that the social worker would often be chosen by the client to be present during the actual death because of the ability of the social worker to build relationships with persons in distress and their families. Social workers in hospices are now often asked by patients and families to be present and to stay in touch through the death, burial, and grief processes when there has been significant involvement with the patient. The major difference would be the manner of death. A social worker in such a setting would have to have very clear values about the termination of life and the conditions under which it is ethical for that worker to participate.

Summary

Given that there are suffering persons in need of services around their possible assisted suicides, I believe that social workers should not rule out participation in this critical and increasingly relevant area. Medical technology has made it possible to sustain what is technically called life beyond all natural processes. Natural processes would have brought merciful death to intensely suffering persons in previous generations. Social technology through social work skills—study, analysis, critical thinking, counseling, family work, networking, team building, resource development, research, and more—must keep pace by participating in the ethical discussions and final resolutions that our society demands.

REFERENCES

Baier, K. (1980). Deontological theories. In K. Baier (Ed.), *The Encyclopedia of medical ethics* (pp. 130–135). New York: Plenum Press.

Fletcher, J. (1966). *Situation ethics.* Philadelphia, PA: Westminster Press.

Flexner, S. B. (Ed.). (1987). *The Random House dictionary of the English language.* New York: Random House.

Gentles, I. (1995). *Euthanasia and assisted suicide.* Dawn Mills, Ontario: General Publishing Company.

Humphry, D. (1991). *Final exit.* Seacaucus, NJ: Carol Publishing.

National Association of Social Workers. (1993). *Code of ethics.* Washington, DC: Author.

Quill, T. E. (1991). Death and dignity: A case of individualized decision making. *New England Journal of Medicine, 324,* 691–694.

Reamer, J. (1990). *Ethical dilemmas in social service.* (2nd ed.) New York: Columbia University Press.

Solomon, A. (1995). A death of one's own. *The New Yorker, 71*(13), 54–69.

Rejoinder to Dr. Boyle
KELLY CANADY

Dr. Boyle has done a fine job of expressing the views of the traditional utilitarian. However, I find the justification for deciding the value of life based on its utility to be horrifying. I am sure that Dr. Boyle speaks honestly from his own experiences, but I am led to conclude that he has not been fully informed of changes that have taken place in the medical and social community that weaken his arguments in favor of assisted suicide. His statement that individuals who are dependent on a life-sustaining treatment as being the only ones who currently receive the medical right to choose death is incorrect. In hospice care, for example, any individual with a life expectancy of less than six months is eligible for full palliative care, regardless of his or her previous medical treatment history. This includes persons with human immunodeficiency virus (HIV) disease, Alzheimer's, and other chronic illnesses. Likewise, his statement that *most* individuals with terminal illnesses find themselves *trapped* in terrible suffering is overgeneralized. My experience is that *most* hospice patients are not trapped in suffering, because pain management is the primary focus of care. I think Dr. Boyle should rethink his views with regard to the above issues.

Dr. Boyle's attempt to link the lack of clear direction on suicides in the early Judeo-Christian days on the notion that slow and painful deaths did not arise because of a lack of knowledge and medical interventions to sustain or prolong life is preposterous. It is more logical to assume that the reason for such short life expectancies was because of various diseases that were nontreatable. One such disease that comes to mind is leprosy, which not only left the person in a state of slow deterioration but resulted in great social rejection. Even our most common diseases (dysentery, tetanus, pneumonia) often led to death in earlier centuries.

Dr. Boyle's use of the NASW Code of Ethics is a creative use of this elastic document, but we must keep in mind that a basic principle of our practice is that of nonmaleficence, or to do no harm. The utilitarian view would serve the identified patient and disregard the emotional needs of the extended relationships. In assisted suicide, the goodness of the act does not rule out the fact that one act sets a precedent for future consequences that, in my opinion, would be detrimental to our society at large. Dr. Boyle's use of the Netherlands and of the state of Oregon as support for the use of assisted suicide is hardly compelling. The Netherlands, in its many years of practicing euthanasia, has done little to draw its close liberal neighboring counties into similar practices.

We have come to a deep awareness as a profession and as a nation of the importance of a person's right to self-determination. If we want to learn how to restore quality of life and worth to the terminally ill, we could begin by learning how other cultures integrate dying and death into a natural part of the life process. I maintain that the consideration of assisted suicide as an option for social work to support is a symptom of a greater problem in our society. I think for the social work profession to endorse assisted suicide legislation and its implementation would be a giant step backwards.

NO

KELLY CANADY

I am very pleased to take the "no" position on social workers participating in assisted suicides. I hope to point out some practical, moral, and ethical issues in support of my stand.

I am reminded of how, in my first quarter of social work school, I learned that the social worker's goal is to assist clients in achieving their maximum social and emotional potential through interventions supported by an array of community resources. The social worker's responsibility is to protect the personal rights of the individual, so that the highest level of self-realization is obtained. Throughout literature that defines the role of a social worker in a client relationship, it is clearly explained that these goals are our primary focus, unless they would lead to dysfunctional or self-destructive behavior. The social worker's challenge is to assist clients to see beyond their inherent adversities. It is within our professional skills to help others to see their capability to learn new behaviors and to experience interpersonal growth. It is disturbing for me to think that a profession that exalts its ability to improve the quality of one's life across the life span would entertain the idea of participating in assisted suicide.

As a hospice social worker, I am often asked about our agency's position on assisted suicide. Our answer is that we neither hasten nor prolong the dying process but provide palliative or comfort care for the rest of the patient's life. The questions that I am asked show that many people are very confused on the distinctions among palliative care, assisted suicide, active and passive euthanasia, and so forth. Definitions of the boundaries of these distinctly different medical interventions are so blurred that it causes me concern about how they are used almost interchangeably.

I strongly believe that the culture of our "death-denying" society is again being influenced by the philosophies of groups such as the Hemlock Society and individuals such as Dr. Jack Kervorkian, to accept the idea that there is a way to paint a pretty face on the process of dying and death. Though the hospice movement is still in its infancy, it has made great progress in bringing the experience of dying and death into the mainstream of society and gradually reshaping our public response to this ultimate phase of the life cycle. It is encouraging to see how courses on all levels of our educational system are beginning to reintroduce the subject of death in such a way as to hopefully remove the stigmas and myths associated with the dying process. Though progress has been made, it has not kept pace with the growing movement of the assisted suicide proponents.

It has been my frustration to hear comments on how various terminal illnesses are labeled as being "unmanageable" when it comes to pain control, and thereby, hopeless with respect to improved quality of life. What I think social workers need to do is speak honestly about the misleading information that is being presented to our public. Credit needs to be given to the medical profession and supportive services that have worked diligently to research alternative means of treating protracted or terminal illnesses. I believe that this is clearly seen in the work of hospice personnel who monitor patient's pain management needs in such a way as to promote the highest level of pain control with the fewest possible side effects.

Through the hundreds of patients that I have had the opportunity to counsel through their dying experience, I have yet to see an appreciable number of patients that could not get the necessary level of medications to control their pain. I do admit that my experiences may not accurately represent the full spectrum of persons with terminal illnesses and their associated social consequences, but I doubt that any laws or policies necessary to regulate assisted suicides would represent the full spectrum either.

My training has taught me that the two most frequently mentioned concerns of a terminally ill person are, "Am I going to be in pain?" and "Am I going to be alone?" As someone who has personally experienced a so-called terminal illness, I can speak knowledgeably about such concerns. I believe that these fears are born from a society that has largely relegated the responsibilities of caring for the dying to sterile institutions, and, as a result, has left us with a generation who do not have the skills to cope with the realities of death. It is time that the myths about the dying process be set right, and a very integral part of our life experience, that of dying, be given back to the family unit. My fear is that any lesser directive would create an irreversible backlash, which would result in a devaluing of life itself. To condone assisted suicide would definitely be moving in the opposite direction from where we need to be headed as a society.

I can only believe that a person's choice for assisted suicide is based in a pathological condition that social workers are trained to alleviate. Would not we attempt to dissuade a client who expressed thoughts of suicide? It is our ethical responsibility to protect these individuals from harming themselves, even to the extent of committing them to a psychiatric facility. Why would we treat a person with a terminal illness any differently? Is it our own ineptness at dealing with the issue of dying and death that leads us into believing that assisted suicide would be the appropriate alternative? Certainly, we are capable of identifying, measuring, and treating a person for such potential motivators as depression, overwhelming anxiety, guilt, and obsessive, fatalistic thinking. The list could go on, but the point needs to be clear that resources are available to relieve terminally ill persons from such psychological stressors that could cloud their decision-making ability. For a social worker to walk away from such a challenge, and label it as hopeless, flies directly into the face of our professional foundation.

I speak personally for those persons who have been the recipients of a diagnosis of a terminal illness and have lived beyond our projected "death date," to live full, productive lives. I can speak for the emotions associated with living with such an illness, the fears of a long, painful dying process, the guilt of being a financial and emotional burden on family and friends, the active fear of losing one's self-identity, independence, and physical abilities, and the social rejection from some who did not have the skills to cope with my terminal illness. What if assisted suicide laws were in place at the time of my prognosis? I realize that this is only a hypothetical question, but is not the issue of assisted suicide based on such hypotheticals? Where are the "facts" when it comes to the questions of "What is quality of life?" and "Who should decide when quality exists no more?" The primary assumption is that all terminal illnesses are going to lead to physical, mental, spiritual, and emotional agony. I dread the thought of how I may have elected the "easy way out" (i.e., assisted suicide) after receiving my prognosis, based on my emotional state at that time. The best hope that I was given was through daily chemotherapy treatments and a prognosis of "We will have to wait and see what happens." The research literature of that time gave me little chance of living beyond six to twelve months. Though that was more than ten years ago, I cannot look at that experience without seeing the personal growth that I, my family, and friends experienced during the most critical months of my illness. I am thankful that there were sources of hope beyond my vision and wisdom.

There are several problems that I see in implementing assisted suicide as an acceptable practice. First, what defines a "terminal illness"? Certainly, this should be a medical decision, made by a physician familiar with that type of illness. The difficulty is that all physicians are not alike, nor do they subscribe to the same philosophies of medicine. How do we define "quality of life"? My experience has been that it is virtually impossible to achieve a consensus on terms such as "terminal illness," much less "intolerable suffering and pain." Even if these terms could be defined to fit categories of the population, where does it stop? What about persons with mental disorders such as chronic schizophrenia or depression? Is their life any different from the terminally ill when it comes to hope for a cure or improved quality of life? This brings to mind the "slippery slope" theory, that once the door is opened for certain categories of illnesses, the practice will spread to other similar situations. I am sure that proponents of assisted suicide would argue that adequate safeguards would be in place to prevent such abuses. We should not overlook the driving force that economics tend to play in these cases.

In my opinion, the initial successes of the hospice movement were based on its economic attractiveness and not so much on the alternative of being able to care for someone at home. With the introduction of diagnostic-related groups, hospitals have seen the hospice as a referral source. Insurance companies have seen hospices as a cost-saving alternative to potentially expensive, high-tech hospitalizations. The secondary gain for our society has been to see how dying and death can be treated with dignity. But, what we need to realize is the possibility that we may be more "diligent" in providing the option of assisted suicide to the elderly and poorer segments of our society. Assisted suicide may even come to be seen as an expectation of some individuals.

I see assisted suicide as a convenience-based solution to an inevitable event, and as treating the symptom of a larger problem—the devaluing of life. I believe this is a reflection of how distant our society has gotten from the aging, dying, and death process. Because of medical advances, it is not uncommon for persons to be in their forties or fifties before they experience the loss of a significant person in their life. By living longer, by often being geographically removed, and by using residential institutional facilities, we have been able to distance ourselves from the emotional impact of dealing with the deaths of our loved ones.

In our "no deposit–no return, drive-thru-window" culture, it is easy to see that we have grown into a society that has very little ritual around the dying and death event. Funerals have almost become a textbook process, with very little personal effect for the deceased. We just let the funeral home take care of the details and pay the bill later. The anxiety that I see in working with dying patients and their caregivers comes from their not knowing what to do or what to expect when it comes to dying, especially in a home setting. It has been my personal reward to play an active role in teaching families what are appropriate behaviors for the patient and the caregivers. Most of their fears are relieved when they know that someone is going to be there with them to "walk them through" the process.

To say that assisted suicide is acceptable is to say that there is no benefit in staying alive through the dying process. I must disagree. There are several aspects of the dying process that are beneficial to both the patient and the caregivers. First, I must base this belief on the premise that no one dies truly alone. There is always a ripple effect. Whether we recognize it or not, it touches our life in some way. It may be negative, as in devaluing of life, or it may be positive, as found in the person who has maintained as much control as possible, until death. I see patients who are given compassionate care by loved ones, in an environment that is familiar to them, where they are encouraged to live life as fully as possible, where hope is defined in what they can still do, such as planning when to eat, when to sleep, or to spend time doing favorite activities, or even to plan their own funeral. I see the opportunity to resolve painful experiences from their past, to express thoughts and feelings about special events and people, and to put closure to their life. On the other side, I see caregivers who are given a chance to spend quality time with their loved one, time that would be missed if the patient had chosen assisted suicide. I see an opportunity for caregivers to begin their grieving process long before the death of the loved one, which I believe makes their bereavement less traumatic. These people tend to emotionally heal sooner because they were firsthand in seeing the death coming. I see younger members of the family participating in the caregiving responsibilities, and learning that dying deserves the honor and respect that it is given. I cannot help but believe that these younger members are saying to themselves, "When I am dying, someone will be there to care for me, too." This promotes the value of life, and takes the fear out of dying. Being able to be directly involved with the dying process seems to displace most of the physical and emotional drain on the caregivers. I have too often heard the caregivers say, after the death of the loved one, "I would do it all over again, if I had to." My concern is that assisted suicide could deny the caregivers the normal anticipatory grief process that is so important in formulating a healthy view of a future life.

In a society that has already pushed the fears of aging and chronic illnesses to the limit, we do not need to be tagging any more fears onto the inevitables of life. There will always be such circumstances to contend with. It is our challenge as social workers, and as a society, to find ways to blend these natural events into our lifestyles. It is our responsibility to redefine hope in seemingly hopeless situations. We have to keep in mind that hopelessness for a cure does not mean hopelessness for quality of life.

Successful efforts have been made in recent years to improve the rights of patients, to have greater control over medical interventions, for instance, with the Living Will and the Durable Power of Attorney for Health Care. I believe that these give adequate representation to the choices of most situations, if only more people would use them. We have to give up the idea that we can have an answer for every situation. I think that we have to believe that assisted suicide is little more than suicide, itself, and that ending the life of an individual would be counterproductive to our training as health care professionals. I believe the solution to this debate lies in education. As social workers, we need to educate the public on resources available to them that can assist in lessening the strife of chronic or terminal illnesses. We need to become more informed on the dynamics of working with persons with such illnesses. We need to advocate for community services in areas that offer little or no services to meet the special needs of this population. We need to be aggressive in moving forward with the focus of reshaping our culture by supporting the fact that death is a natural part of the life cycle. Until we accept this view, we will never fully understand the true meaning of life.

Rejoinder to Mr. Canady   DAVID BOYLE

I am appreciative of Mr. Canady's thoughtful statement of the "no" position on the question. He presents a reasoned and sensitive discussion of the issue. His personal and professional life experiences certainly give him credibility in the discussion. The difference in our positions is attributable to the polarity of tension between two social work values, self-determination and client well-being. Fortunately for our clients, there is currently considerable discussion in the field about these and other ethical concerns in relation to suicide and terminal illness (Callahan, 1994).

However, I differ with a number of assertions. "The social worker's challenge is to assist clients to see beyond their inherent adversities." As a veteran of eighteen years of experience in public mental health, I would see the challenge more in the area of helping a person with a terminal illness to find meaning in the current situation and to maximize personal choice and feelings of dignity and self-worth.

Having worked as a consultant with a hospice staff for several years, I agree that hospice personnel "monitor the patient's pain management to promote the highest level of pain control with the fewest possible side effects." However, as anyone who deals with dying persons will also attest, pain is a very subjective process, and pain management still has a long way to go (Fintzy, 1993). For some conditions, "the highest level of pain control" is not very good. By what right does our society consign a competent, knowledgeable human being to go through the often lengthy process of dying with the likelihood of much pain when there is another alternative?

Mr. Canady astutely identifies some problems our society has with dying. It should be a "part of our life experience" and should "be given back to the family." My proposals for participation in assisted suicide also promote this process. Persons who have participated in assisted suicide testify that they indeed became more aware of the preciousness of life and of the life of their loved one (Solomon, 1995).

The issue of quality of life is precisely the area under debate. I maintain that only the dying person has the right to decide whether he or she should continue life when life has lost enough quality for the dying person to reach a decision to end it. Such a decision is not an "easy way out," and it is likely that relatively few persons would choose assisted suicide even if it were available with many supports and safeguards. In my many years' experience as a social worker and a minister, I have not found that even the intensely suffering terminally ill are just dying to die.

Finally, I agree that issues of economics and human rights deserve careful attention in the discussion. Most persons who are participating in the discussion and the few who have publicly acknowledged their plans for assisted suicide are overwhelmingly white and high income (Solomon, 1995). Thus, once again, generally only if you are white and have money is it possible to reach and carry out a personal decision that protects one's dignity, autonomy, and perceived quality of life.

REFERENCES

Callahan, J. (1994). The ethics of assisted suicide. *Health and Social Work, 19,* 237–244.

Fintzy, R. T., (1993). Letter to the editor in response to the article, The dangers of legalizing physician-assisted suicide. *American Journal of Psychiatry* (1993), *150,* 143–145. In *American Journal of Psychiatry* (1993), *150,* 1901.

Solomon, A. (1995). A death of one's own. *New Yorker, 71*(13), 54–69.

Is the Diagnosis of "Multiple Personality Disorder" (Dissociative Identity Disorder) Valid?

Cynthia Newbern, M.S.W., was recently commissioned as a Captain in the United States Air Force. She is stationed at Keesler Air Force Base in Biloxi, Mississippi, serving as a clinical social worker in the second largest hospital in the Air Force. Captain Newbern is also working on her Ph.D. in social work at the University of Georgia.

Elizabeth Randall, Ph.D., has had extensive experience, both with her own caseload and as a treatment team member, in working with persons meeting the DSM criteria for multiple personality disorder (dissociative identity disorder). Dr. Randall is currently an Assistant Professor of social work at West Virginia University, where she teaches in the direct practice track.

YES

CYNTHIA NEWBERN

Dissociative identity disorder (DID) relabels multiple personality disorder in the new DSM-IV (American Psychiatric Association, 1994). Diagnostic criteria include (1) the presence of two or more personality states that can (2) take control of one's behavior, accompanied by (3) an inability to recall ... too extensive to be explained by ordinary forgetfulness (American Psychiatric Association, 1994). The validity of this diagnosis has been hotly debated in many professional fields in the past several years. Four major questions have emerged in the literature: (1) How does a clinician make the diagnosis of DID? (2) Can more than one per-

sonality exist in one body? (3) If so, how can the person with DID be accountable for all of his or her actions? (4) What is the best model of treatment?

A threefold argument answers the four disturbing questions. Beahrs (1994), van Praag (1993), and Ross (1995) provide arguments that shed new light on the diagnosis. Essentially, the subjective experience of identity of the client must be understood by anyone who is working with someone with DID. To better understand the subjective disorder of identity, one may compare it with body image disturbance, which is one of the diagnostic criteria of anorexia nervosa in the DSM-IV.

The threefold argument consists of the following: (1) The subjective experience of the patient, in addition to objective information obtained from valid and reliable tests, should be used to diagnose the DID patient (van Praag, 1993; Ross 1995); (2) The patient with dissociative identity disorder is held legally accountable for his or her actions (This assumes an underlying competency in the defendant with DID [Beahrs, 1994]); and (3) Treatment approaches to the DID patient should include validation of underlying competency in long-term cognitive therapy.

The Use of Subjective Experience in Diagnosis

What do "alter personality," "entity," and "personality state" mean, anyway? Piper (1994) argues that the criteria for the dissociative identity disorder diagnosis includes an "open concept" for the diagnostician. If another personality is observed, the diagnosis can be made. However, the diagnosis can also be made if no other personality is observed. Skeptics argue that this method is not scientific. A patient must exhibit a cluster of measurable, observable behaviors before a DSM-IV diagnosis can be made with any certainty. Relying on valid and reliable tests is important (see, for example, studies on the validity and reliability of the Dissociative Experience Scale by Ross [1995]). But our love affair with outcome measures has caused us to neglect important information that can be gained by gathering information from the patient about his or her subjective experience of his or her identity. Can a clinician prove that a patient has another personality? Can the patient prove it? The answer is no. To argue whether more than one personality exists in one body is moot. The point to prove is whether the patient has a subjective identity disorder with dissociative pathology. Indeed, the name change of the diagnosis from multiple personality disorder to dissociative identity disorder in the DSM-IV redefines the diagnosis such that the DID patient is assessed as one person who has disordered personal identity accompanied with dissociative pathology. The patient is seen as one who has a global impairment of identity, not as a body that contains more than one person. Viewing the patient as one person who has a subjective impairment makes sense of the anomalies that exist in the legal and clinical fields. These anomalies, which have been incorrectly used to argue against the existence of the diagnosis, are discussed in detail after a comparison is made with assessment of a patient who suffers from body image disturbance.

Consider the patient who suffers from anorexia nervosa. One of the DSM-IV criteria for the diagnosis is body image disturbance. The definition of body image disturbance is "disturbance in the way in which one's body weight or shape is experienced; undue influence of body weight or shape on self-evaluation, or denial of the seriousness of current low body weight" (American Psychiatric Association, 1994, p. 545). Let us focus on the first part of the criteria for the sake of argument, "disturbance in the way in which one's body weight or shape is experienced." Imagine that a patient who has been suffering from anorexia nervosa weighs only eighty pounds. Part of the reason that she will not eat is because in her mind she sees herself as weighing well over two hundred pounds. This disturbed body image is real to her, and it influences her behavior to such an extent that it is life threatening. Do we argue about the existence of the disturbed body image of the patient? Extensive research on body image disturbance has been conducted by Thompson (1990). Objective measures of this subjective disturbance have been developed. However, the patient's report of the image she has of her body is also very important information in diagnosis and treatment of the disorder. We should afford the patient with dissociative identity disorder the same respect.

Van Praag (1993) argues that subjective pathology is neglected in the current method of diagnosis and treatment and that the state-of-the-art diagnostic procedures have concealed loyalties to a largely behavioral viewpoint. The logical positivist psychiatric vernacular of the diagnostic and statistical manuals has enhanced our ability to diagnose and treat patients. However, the potential dangers of objectification are: a preoccupation with the obvious; a disregard for the subjective constituents of the psychopathological spectrum; a system of diagnosing mainly grounded on symptoms and detached from cause, particularly from determinants of a psychological nature; and oversimplification (van Praag, 1993). The reductionistic nature of the current methods of diagnosis equates "subjective" with "vague" or "undefined." If we consider the patient with body image disturbance who has starved herself nearly to death to become thin, we can appreciate her view of herself as being obese as neither vague or undefined. This is not to argue that objective measurements should not be used to explore other symptoms, but these measurements should be used in concert with the patient's report of her subjective experience.

The Legal Accountability of the DID Defendant

Beahrs (1994) brilliantly illuminates the arguments for and against the existence of DID by answering the question: do we view the dissociated aspects of selfhood as autonomous entities that exist in substantive reality, or do we view them as a useful heuristic? If we literally believe that more than one person exists in a single body, then anomalies exist in the legal and clinical fields. The legal question is addressed first.

Beahrs suggests that two fundamental issues underlie the decision courts make in holding multiple personalities responsible. First, for practical reasons, it is only meaningful to deal with a single body. It is not possible to imprison one part-self while granting pardon or commendation to another. Second, it is not one's global mental state that determines culpability, but one's state in relationship to the offense committed, at the time of the offense. "An offender is culpable *who knew what he or she was doing at that time, and that others would disapprove.* Only this is the *mens rea* that makes a crime a crime. In DID the fact that competent awareness and intentionality remain intact even when concealed is fundamental to the nature of the disorder" (Beahrs, 1994, p. 227).

Beahrs further explains that the legal debate exists because there is a tacit assumption that DID implies "not guilty" and the reverse. This is simply not true. Even when the diagnosis is affirmed, appellate case law holds patients with DID accountable. This applies to pleas based on impaired consciousness (amnesia), nonvolition (alters taking control), and external victimization (coercion). Courts conclude that even if global impairment of functioning exists in any defendant, "the law adjudges criminal liability of the person according to the person's state of mind at the time of the act; we will not begin to parcel criminal accountability out among various inhabitants of the mind (Beahrs, 1994, p. 227).

At the heart of holding DID patients accountable for their crimes is a belief that the defendant is one person in a single body who has impaired subjective identity with dissociative pathology. That he or she cannot remember the crime is not the issue. People who commit vehicular homicide during an alcohol-induced blackout are also held accountable for their actions.

Treatment Approaches

Successful treatment approaches to DID include reinforcing and validating the impressive autonomous strengths that DID patients have but disclaim. Iatrogenic regression may occur if excessively nurturant countertransference is used in therapy (Fine, 1989). According to Halleck (1990), failing to hold patients responsible for their actions is a primary factor leading to regression in treatment rather than improvement. The autonomous coping mechanisms that are hidden will never surface in the patient if the therapist fosters a dependent relationship with the client.

According to Beahrs, this same "hidden competency" that holds DID patients responsible in case law is the underlying competency that needs to be validated and reified in therapy. Consider the patient with body image disturbance again. In treatment, does the therapist validate the image of an obese body by suggesting that the patient purchase size 22 clothing? Because the patient sees herself as overweight, does the therapist reify this disturbed image by encouraging the patient to lose weight? Obviously, the answer is no. Likewise, the therapist who is working with the DID patient does not reify the patient's alter personalities by failing to hold the patient responsible for his or her actions. The alter personalities should be seen as schemas that need to be corrected by using long-term cognitive therapy with the patient. Patients must learn to redefine their sense of personal identity. During the course of treatment, patients should enhance their coping skills in all aspects of their daily living.

Conclusion

The diagnosis of dissociative identity disorder helps us to understand a complicated disorder of identity with dissociated features. It is a useful heuristic that will help the mental health field to successfully treat the patient. The subjective report of the patient's identity disorder with accompanying dissociative pathology needs to weigh as heavily in diagnosis as do conclusions from valid and reliable outcome measures. In the legal and clinical fields, the underlying competency of the DID patient must be affirmed.

REFERENCES

American Psychiatric Association. (1994). *Diagnostic and statistical manual of mental disorders (4th ed.).* Washington DC: Author.

Beahrs, J. O. (1994). Dissociative identity disorder: Adaptive deception of self and others. *Bulletin of the American Academy of Psychiatry and the Law, 22,* 223–233.

Fine, C. G. (1989). Treatment errors and iatrogenesis across therapeutic modalities in MPD and allied dissociative disorders. *Dissociation, 2,* 77–82.

Halleck, S. L. (1990). Dissociative phenomenon and the question of responsibility. *International Journal of Clinical and Experimental Hypnosis, 38,* 298–314.

Piper, A. P. (1994). Multiple personality disorder. *British Journal of Psychiatry, 164,* 600–612.

Ross, C. (1995). Diagnosis of dissociative identity disorder. In L. M. Cohen, J. N. Berzoff, & M. R. Elin (Eds.), *Dissociative identity disorder: theoretical and treatment controversies* (pp. 261–284). Northvale, NJ: Aronson.

Thompson, J. (1990). *Body image disturbance: Assessment and treatment.* New York: Pergamon.

van Praag, H. M. (1993). *"Make-believes" in psychiatry or the perils of progress.* New York: Brunner and Mazel.

Rejoinder to Ms. Newbern   ELIZABETH J. RANDALL

The central premise of Newbern's defense of the validity of the construct "multiple personality disorder" appears to be that one need only accept this phenomenon as valid within the subjective experience of the patient, and all remaining diagnostic, legal, and logical difficulties will be happily resolved. The deal, apparently, is this: one encounters a multiple; treats him or her *as if* he or she is a multiple because he or she (they?) feel 'multiplish' this year (or month); and one provides treatment *as if* this were indeed the case.

Before proceeding with my complaints against this notion, I will say one thing in its defense: I do think it is best, when working with a self-proclaimed multiple, initially to accept his or her self-label without debate, in the interests both of humanitarian concern and of allowing a working alliance to develop. However, this is also a good rule of thumb in working with patients who present *as if* they were targets of an elaborate plot by space invaders, or other florid delusions. I knew a psychiatrist whose patient was convinced she was carrying a viable pregnancy in her left buttock. "Congratulations, when is the baby due?" was his response, and thus he began to soothe her into cooperating (in due course) with an antipsychotic treatment plan, for which she was later very thankful. This does *not* mean that the professional is obligated to reify the patient's self-description, buy into it, and enter it onto his or her record as a scientifically satisfactory explanation of the problem! The diagnostic implications of this suggestion are mind boggling. If one were obliged to code every sort of subjective reality patients think up, one would soon run out of numbers. Many patients are convinced, when they present for treatment, that their essential problem is that they are "unlucky." "Some people are just lucky," they sigh, "but not me." Shall we propose a new diagnostic category for study, *418.22, Unlucky, chronic undifferentiated?*

Newbern's case in defense of multiple personality is also, in my opinion, too heavily dependent on comparisons with another diagnostic category, that of anorexia nervosa and its accompanying symptoms of body image distortion or disturbance. Her arguments that, in such cases, the subjective reality experienced by the patient must be taken into account and understood, are sensitive and reasonable (I would argue that this is a universal truism in clinical practice). However, this does *not* mean writing a treatment plan that includes helping the patient stick to a reducing diet, or encouraging him or her to work out or exercise more. Newbern is far too kind and lenient with the DID treatment industry by failing to acknowledge that practices such as these are very closely analogous to the kind of mining for symptoms, and wallowing in multiplicity as a way of life, that goes on all too often among DID true believers, in a complicated collusion involving both the treatment providers and patients.

Newbern's comparison between anorectics and alleged multiples is made repeatedly, but lacking justification, remains one of apples and oranges. Both patient categories are primarily female, but what else do they have in common? The psychosocial issues; prototypical family dynamics; and commonly seen style or pattern of interpersonal relatedness are all more disparate than similar. If one is going by gender dominance alone, why not create analogies between multiples and patients with depression? Conversely, some interesting parallels might legitimately be drawn among the clinical and psychosocial characteristics of alleged multiples and those with borderline personality. Yet these potential comparisons are sidestepped by Newbern. Why is this? Could it be that these comparisons bring one too close to the possibility that a great many multiples might be understood with more clinical utility as borderlines in multiple clothing?

In summary, I applaud Newbern's client-centeredness, which recommends that we agree to label patients multiple if they call themselves so. At least this is better than actively promoting multiplicity in patients who did not realize they had it, until they fell into the hands of a captain of the DID industry. Yet these values of respect and acceptance need to extend both ways, and we need to show a little respect for ourselves, too, and not feel guilty or presumptuous in thinking our training and judgment count for something. In clinical practice, it is not a virtue, but an abdication of professional responsibility, to take at face value everything one hears.

NO

ELIZABETH J. RANDALL

Dissociative identity disorder (DID), although relatively unimportant as a psychiatric disorder, is currently enjoying great celebrity as a *cause*. Work by Csikszentmihaly (1993) on evolutionary epistemology has fascinating implications for the recent growth in the DID treatment industry, as more and more people take up this cause. He speaks of mimesis, the force by which "memes," or discrete units of culturally relative truth, take on a life of their own and proliferate, once articulated. Understood as a meme, then, the spread of DID may be seen as an example of mimetic proliferation. However, Csikszentmihaly warns: "Although we might initially adopt memes because they are useful, it is often the case that after a certain point they begin to affect our actions and thoughts in ways that are at best ambiguous and at worst definitely not in our best interest" (1993, p. 123). Social workers must be especially alert for these forces because of professional socialization favoring strong positions of advocacy, and must strive to maintain objectivity and balance.

The fervor with which the cause of DID is currently being embraced is directly related to a powerful consensus among true believers that a patient with DID must necessarily have been the victim of prolonged and horrific abuse during childhood, most often within families. It is the *cause* of doing battle with evil in this guise that is being played out again and again in the particular metaphorical expression known as the treatment of dissociative identity disorder. For the purposes of the current debate, I am going to argue that the incidence of DID has been vastly overestimated in recent years, because of misinterpretations concerning its traumatic pathogenesis. Furthermore, I cite literature suggesting that the disorder itself may not be a naturally occurring neuropsychiatric response to trauma, even when trauma has been present.

The Link to Extreme Childhood Trauma

According to Ross, a well-known proponent of DID treatment, "To understand the reality of DID is to understand the reality of childhood trauma and its effects" (1995b, p. 68). Gelinas (1995) goes on to develop parallels between those benighted persons who cannot accept "the trauma paradigm," and skeptics from earlier centuries who persecuted Copernicus and Galileo. Many authors in the thick of the current DID fracas agree that acceptance or nonacceptance of this "trauma paradigm" is very close to the heart of the DID debate (Merskey, 1992; North, Ryall, Ricci, & Wetzel, 1993; Simpson, 1995).

Few reasonably informed citizens, let alone clinicians (who hear so much) continue to deny the existence of child abuse today. This is the reason child protective service agencies are now commonplace (and very busy, as reports pour in). What remains a subject of hot debate, however, is the peculiar combination of intense emotional malignancy, sadism, hierarchical organization, and uncanny skill at avoiding detection so often attributed to the perpetrators of the abuse leading to DID (Gelinas, 1995; Greaves, 1993). Anecdotal reports abound of intergenerational traditions of ritualized abuse; satanic elements; bestial elements; and marvelous technologies of mind control and deception, for which no forensic evidence can be found (North et al., 1993). There would have to be millions of abusers of this uncommonly competent ilk, many doubtless members of ritual organizations, to support Ross's claim (1991) of a true prevalence rate of 1 percent for DID (or MPD, as it was designated then) in the general population. Unquestionably, there are many deeply disturbed people in the world who are capable of heinous acts. But credibility itself is abused, and dies, when we are asked to accept the ethological (and epidemiological) implications of estimates of this magnitude.

Recently we have been reminded in a gripping way by Sagan and Druyan (1993) that we must own the raw, atavistic side of our nature, and that we are indeed capable of, and able to relish, great violence under certain circumstances. Yet they also remind us that we are indelibly programmed at a genetic level to want our own bloodlines to survive and reproduce. Similarly, Csikszentmihaly (1993, p. 65) stresses that "the individual person, as far as the genes are concerned, is only a vehicle for their own reproduction and further dissemination." Clinical experience shows that perpetrators of abuse continue to feel these forces no less powerfully than healthier persons, although their motives (and skills) become warped and conflicted in various ways, and to various degrees, by their own pain or unmet need.

The huge majority of the interpersonal violence that has been committed during history has been directed against culturally different others, not one's own bloodlines (Sakheim, 1995). In view of this knowledge, how are we to reconcile a faith in the existence of millions of furtive, barely human beings who reproduce solely to crystallize preternatural powers, and who are exempt from such genetic imperatives? And how are we to suppose they possess the supremely willful and robotic ability to disavow such naturalistic urges as attachment, affiliation, and other forces of human socialization as we understand them? Unfortunately, the illogic of this is insufficiently troubling to true believers in DID, who are equally comfortable with attributing startlingly improbable mental capacities to the patients themselves. Yet superstitious beliefs such as these contribute to the implacably judgmental attitude that persons who commit child abuse can only be understood in terms of a core being of occult fiendishness; that is, as monsters, rather than as human beings gone developmentally awry, and in pain of their own. In my opinion, these beliefs are not only fundamentally incorrect, but also harmfully divisive, and antithetical to social work values.

The Case against DID

In the tradition of the DID debate, I will share my own pet peeve concerning DID lore. I think of this as the "he-raped-me-too" syndrome. The histories of DID patients are replete with accounts of their vain attempts over time to seek assistance and safety, only to discover that the would-be rescuer, whether law enforcement officer, psychiatrist, clergyman, or other, has transmogrified into yet another rapist (bogeyman). There is no doubt that abuses of power and influence of this sort can and do happen. Yet to accept these accounts every time they are produced leads to their absurd statistical proliferation (Ross, 1995a), with potentially tragic consequences for both patients and society.

Other highlights of the case against DID are as follows:

• It has been demonstrated that claims of symptoms consistent with DID can readily be produced under laboratory conditions by experimental demand characteristics (Spanos, Weekes, & Menary, 1986). Spanos (1994) has also recently constructed a more comprehensive and compelling case that multiplicity is a "context-bound, goal-directed social behavior geared to the expectations of others, and its characteristics have changed over time to meet changing expectations" (p. 143).

• It has been shown that studies of differences of galvanic skin response, visual acuity, and other measures of organismic response to stimuli, which have been used as purported evidence of different physiological responsiveness among alter identities in a DID patient, have yielded no scientifically meaningful results, because they fail to rule out such rival explanations as normal variability, and the effects of arousal and mood state, rather than personality or identity state (Simpson, 1995).

• It has been demonstrated that DID is seen in large numbers only among North American middle-class women, from the late teens to the late forties, most with excellent health insurance benefits. Practically all have comorbid psychiatric conditions that predate their revelations of multiplicity (Merskey, 1992). Most cases are also diagnosed by a small minority of clinicians. These findings seriously challenge beliefs that this is a naturalistically occurring disorder (Spanos, 1994) but support the case of artifactual generation of symptoms among believers in *the cause* rather well.

• Even DID advocates are increasingly bothered by growing disclosures of false-positive diagnoses; retraction of reports claiming symptoms; iatrogenic worsening of patients' conditions once the diagnosis is made; and demonstrable similarities between the psychological profiles of persons known to be facile with dissembling and misstatement and those of DID patients (Kluft, 1995).

Many other relevant and fascinating aspects of the ongoing debate could be reviewed, but space will not permit.

Conclusion

Thigpen and Cleckley (1957, 1984), who presented *The Three Faces of Eve* to the world, later wrote that they never saw another true case after working with Eve, despite receiving thousands of referrals. I have never seen a true case either, despite eleven years of experience and plenty of exposure, both inpatient and outpatient. Like many others, I have treated DID patients successfully using mainly supportive and cognitive techniques, including lots of work on responsibility, choice, and increased intentionality of lifestyle. This included weaning patients away from reinforcement of DID descriptors and mythology. In my favorite case, this plan resulted in wellness; success in the world of work; success in partner choice and marriage; and termination of treatment with remission of all but intermittent mild dysphoria.

To me, the meme of DID is the most pathologizing notion in all of human services. DID true believers seem to have cathected the term "overwhelming," as in, "it [DID] is a developmentally protective illusion that actually functions to buffer the organism from the *overwhelming* impact of unmodulated trauma" (Ross, 1995b, p. 67). In DID lore, dissociation is the only defense, whereas other forms of coping and resiliency are unheard of. Yet the power, ingenuity, and malice attributed to abusers, who are seen as relentlessly devoted to inventing new ways of inflicting misery, pain, and humiliation, are as limitless as the imagination. It is hard to understand how clinical methods or other social services based on an urgent necessity of accepting this world view can essentially be healing.

202 Debate 15

Csikszentmihaly, M. (1993). *The evolving self: A psychology for the third millennium.* New York: HarperCollins.

Gelinas, D. J. (1995). Dissociative identity and the trauma paradigm. In L. M. Cohen, J. N. Berzoff, & M. R. Elin (Eds.), *Dissociative identity disorder: Theoretical and treatment controversies* (pp. 175–222). Northvale, NJ: Jason Aronson.

Greaves, (1993). A history of multiple personality disorder. In R. P. Kluft & C. G. Fine (Eds.), *Clinical perspectives on multiple personality disorder* (pp. 355–380). Washington, DC: American Psychiatric Press.

Kluft, R. P. (1995). Current controversies surrounding dissociative identity disorder. In L. M. Cohen, J. N. Berzoff, & M. R. Elin (Eds.), *Dissociative identity disorder: Theoretical and treatment controversies* (pp. 347–378). Northvale, NJ: Jason Aronson.

Merskey, H. (1992). The manufacture of personalities: The production of multiple personality disorder. *British Journal of Psychiatry, 160,* 327–340.

North, C. S., Ryall, J. M., Ricci, D. A., & Wetzel, R. D. (1993). *Multiple personalities, multiple disorders: Psychiatric classification and media influence.* New York: Oxford University Press.

Ross, C. A. (1991). Epidemiology of multiple personality disorder and dissociation. *Psychiatric Clinics of North America, 14,* 503–517.

Ross, C. A. (1995a). Diagnosis of dissociative identity disorder. In L. M. Cohen, J. N. Berzoff, & M. R. Elin (Eds.), *Dissociative identity disorder: Theoretical and treatment controversies* (pp. 261–284). Northvale, NJ: Jason Aronson.

Ross, C. A. (1995b). The validity and reliability of dissociative identity disorder. In L. M. Cohen, J. N. Berzoff, & M. R. Elin (Eds.), *Dissociative identity disorder: Theoretical and treatment controversies* (pp. 65–86). Northvale, NJ: Jason Aronson.

Sagan, C., & Druyan, A. (1993). *Shadows of forgotten ancestors: A search for who we are.* New York: Ballantine.

Sakheim, D. K. (1995). Allegations of ritual abuse. In L. M. Cohen, J. N. Berzoff, & M. R. Elin (Eds.), *Dissociative identity disorder: Theoretical and treatment controversies* (pp. 327–346). Northvale, NJ: Jason Aronson.

Simpson, M. A. (1995). Gullible's travels, or the importance of being multiple. In L. M. Cohen, J. N. Berzoff, and M. R. Elin (Eds.), *Dissociative identity disorder: Theoretical and treatment controversies* (pp. 87–134). Northvale, NJ: Jason Aronson.

Spanos, N. P. (1994). Multiple identity enactments and multiple personality disorder: A sociocognitive perspective. *Psychological Bulletin, 116,* 143–165.

Spanos, N. P., Weekes, J. R., & Menary, E. (1986). Hypnotic interview and age regression procedures in the elicitation of multiple personality symptoms: A simulation study. *Psychiatry, 49,* 298–311.

Thigpen, C. H., & Cleckley, H. M. (1957). *The three faces of Eve.* New York: McGraw Hill.

Thigpen, C. H., & Cleckley, H. M. (1984). On the incidence of multiple personality disorder: A brief communication. *International Journal of Clinical and Experimental Hypnosis, 32,* 63–66.

Rejoinder to Dr. Randall CYNTHIA NEWBERN

Do we agree more than disagree? Cognitive therapy is the treatment of choice for the DID patients treated by this clinician and by Dr. Randall, in addition to supportive therapy. This is the one point on which we both agree. The paths that we have taken to reach this end vary on five important points. First, cognitive therapy reduces the risk of iatrogenic artifact; second, childhood trauma history is not included in the criteria for diagnosis; third, the memes argument could also be applied to schizophrenia, and panic disorder; fourth, signs and symptoms of the illness have been documented for centuries in many countries; and fifth, brainwashing patients to create additional personalities in the therapeutic relationship is impossible.

First, increasing the underlying competencies of the patient is one of the goals of cognitive therapy with a DID patient. According to Beahrs (1994), a noted forensic psychiatrist, the focus on the client's competencies in treatment minimizes the regressive dependency and the iatrogenic artifact that so many clinicians fear will happen if the therapist fosters a dependent relationship with the patient. I wholeheartedly agree with Dr. Randall's suggestion that the focus of treatment should be on responsibility, choice, and increased intentionality of lifestyle in therapy. A competent therapist would not encourage an enmeshed relationship with a patient, particularly a DID patient.

Secondly, a central theme of many disbelievers is the notion that severe childhood sexual trauma must exist to diagnose a patient with DID. One only has to read the items listed for diagnosis of DID to see that such trauma is not a criterion for diagnosis. This begs the question, "Can one have DID with no history of childhood sexual trauma?" The answer is yes. For decades we have examined the cause of schizophrenia, a complex disorder that is believed to have many biopsychosocial dimensions. Must we question its existence as a disorder as we search for its cause? No. We should afford the same respect to the DID diagnosis as we conduct research to determine its cause.

This leads us to the third argument, that DID is a memes that has taken on a life of its own, propelled by overprotective therapists who are fighting the bogeyman. As stated above, DID may be caused by other factors that have not yet been discovered. Additionally, are we that cynical about our own profession that we would accuse hundreds, even thousands of clinicians as being unethical in diagnosis and treatment of a disorder just to obtain insurance payments? Consider what happened in the early part of this century when schizophrenia and panic disorder were created as diagnoses (Ross, 1995). Clinicians began using the diagnoses to attach meaning to clusters of symptoms presented to them by patients. Did either of these diagnoses become memes? How is DID different, and why has it come under such fire? I argue that the creation of the DID diagnosis decades ago helped clinicians make sense of a cluster of symptoms presented by patients who previously received improper treatment because of prior misdiagnoses.

Fourth, Ross (1995) argues that cultures all over the world have reported similar symptom clusters as those found in DID patients. The labels may be different, but they all describe a kind of amnesia experienced by someone who appears to be possessed by another entity or spirit. What is the cause of such disorders? Without giving credibility to the subjective reports of patients who suffer with DID, and to clinicians and researchers who are dedicating their careers to answer this question, we may never know.

Finally, Ross (1995) also presents a historical picture of the notion that additional personalities can be created by a therapist. This is simply not true. He concludes that it is very difficult to create secure amnesia barriers and dissociated personality states. His conclusion is based on extensive mind control research funded by military intelligence agencies and by the CIA. In one case in which an amnesic barrier was created, several electro-convulsive treatments were used. Again, do we have so little faith in our colleagues that we actually believe that there are multiple personality mills that exist in therapeutic offices?

Dissociative identity disorder is one of the most misunderstood diagnoses of the twentieth century. Understanding the notion that one person suffers a subjective disorder of identity is critical. Viewing the patient as someone who has an underlying competence and focusing on his or her strengths in therapy will help patients, clinicians, and the courts.

REFERENCES

Beahrs, J. O. (1994). Dissociative identity disorder: Adaptive deception of self and others. *Bulletin of the American Academy of Psychiatry and the Law, 2,* 223–233.

Ross, C. (1995). Dissociative identity disorder. In L. M. Cohen, J. N. Berzoff, & M. R. Elin (Eds.), *Dissociative identity disorder.* Northvale, NJ: Aronson.

Should Social Workers Participate in Social Service Eligibility Determinations That May Lead to the Identification of Illegal Immigrants?

Alicia R. Isaac, D.P.A., received her M.S.W. from the University of Georgia in 1978, and her D.P.A., also from the University of Georgia, in 1995. Formerly Director of Admissions, she is now an Assistant Professor of Social Work with the University of Georgia.

Larry Nackerud, Ph.D., earned his M.S.W. from Tulane University in 1977, and his Ph.D. in Human Service Studies from Cornell University in 1991. He taught for two years as an Assistant Professor with the Department of Social Work at Western New Mexico University, and is currently an Assistant Professor of Social Work with the University of Georgia.

YES

Alicia R. Isaac

The problem of service provision to illegal aliens in the United States is a very complex one for social work practice. Social workers are often on the front lines, being responsible for establishing the eligibility of these immigrants for welfare programs and benefits. Participating in eligibility determinations may place social workers in the uncomfortable position of identifying illegal aliens. Though detection of illegal aliens may result in the deportation of individuals and sometimes entire families, and the creation of conflict for human service providers, social workers must be engaged in fair, standard, and consistent practices that determine the eligibility of any client for services.

According to recent estimates, there are approximately three to four million illegal aliens in this country (Rosenberg, 1991). Because many illegal aliens do not present themselves for services or educate their children in the public school systems, it is believed that their numbers are higher. Although the Immigration Reform and Control Act of 1986 and the Immigration Act of 1990 amended immigration policy in this country, vast numbers of men and now women and children still come to the United States without formal sanction. Because the United States is such an ethnically diverse country, illegal aliens are not often identified unless they present themselves for social services, which places social workers in the role of policing agents.

The dilemma for social workers who participate in determining the service eligibility of illegal aliens, and as a result may be responsible for their deportation, is not an easy one. As one considers the dilemma, first, there is the struggle between a global sense of social justice and human rights, versus justice and equity for American citizens and taxpayers. Second, there is the impact on public policy and social conditions if social workers do not actively advocate for human rights and social change. Third, administrative and system efficiency may be greatly affected by establishing a series of policies and operating procedures that allow social workers to disregard certain factual information about clients. Discretionary decision making found throughout bureaucratic behavior is often a "two-edged sword." The ability to turn one's head in one situation affords the same opportunity to exercise bias and discrimination in other situations. Though discretionary latitude can be used to benefit clients, it also can be used to exclude specific groups from receiving services. This discretion then strips bureaucracy and individual social workers of certain checks and balances that ensure accountability and equity. Fourth, there is a legal standard that must be respected. Finally, by not participating in eligibility-establishing processes that may identify illegal aliens, social workers may potentially jeopardize the well-being of these immigrants as well as the well-being of the general public.

The mood of this country toward immigrants, human rights, and social justice is constantly shifting. There have been several periods in our history when immigrants seeking freedom, dignity, and escape from oppression were welcomed, particularly if they were European and brought certain skills and values with them. However, immigrants from the Caribbean, Mexico, and various third-world countries have not been so readily welcomed, even when they have come to this country for the very same reasons. Iatridis (1994, p. 62) defines social justice as "relationships among people and the distribution of society's resources on the basis of valid claims (distributive justice)." Distributive justice is then the *valid* distribution of benefits and their costs throughout society.

This is where the dilemma becomes more poignant for social workers. How does one with a belief in human rights and social justice turn his or her back on persons who have come to this country seeking asylum and a better way of life? How does one then balance this against the claims that illegal aliens are depleting the resources and opportunities of American citizens? Where is the happy medium?

A discussion of whether social workers should be involved in these processes must begin with the statement that social workers should not be obligated to expose illegal aliens because they are taking resources and jobs away from Americans. It is a much broader issue than that. Contrary to popular opinion, illegal aliens do not usually take jobs from poor Americans. Most of them work in jobs that are readily available, are hard labor, are low in pay, and are not typically sought after by American workers (Weintraub, 1984). Also, many illegal aliens pay social security and federal taxes, which they never make claims against for fear of being detected. Although some illegal aliens may use public education and health services, they are rarely the recipients of Aid to Families with Dependent Children (AFDC) and food stamps (Lander, Caldwell, & Siegel, 1993). It is important from the onset that we reject as a viable argument for participating in eligibility processes that exposing illegal aliens protects the American poor, and that we focus on the greater societal benefit of why this is a necessary evil.

If we can reasonably remove the element of competing for existing resources in this country as a social justice concern for the American citizenry from the discussion, we are left with the larger human rights problem. If social workers opt to handle human rights issues and seek distributive justice by turning their heads to the intrinsic problems of human rights policies, we never move to a salient, articulated ideology about who we are in the world and the importance of our relationship with others. Social work practice has the responsibility of helping to shape global and national human rights philosophy, a mission that somewhat irresponsibly we have long allowed statespersons and politicians to take the credit for. Granted, we cannot just participate in processes that expose illegal aliens and assume in time that all wrongs will be made right. Social work practice must use this as a means to bring human rights inequities to the forefront and actively advocate for the development and implementation of a global and national human rights ideology.

Service provision is continually affected by how well we implement public policy. Public policy is reactionary and continually impacted by our success or failure in providing services. Social change in the form of adjusted policies and new or expanded programs rarely occurs without some upheaval in the consciousness of the American public. Based on most analyses, even after the federal immigration legislation in 1986 and 1990, there is still no comprehensive national policy to deal with immigrants and illegal aliens (Rosenberg, 1991). Without a "wake-up call" to the American public about the struggle of state and local agencies to provide assistance during the largest immigration wave in this country in seventy years, chances of innovative, proactive policies and programs emerging are slim. Even as early as 1979, it was evident that state and local community agencies were bearing the brunt of providing health and social services to alien families (Young, Hall, & Collins, 1979). Without public support, we increase the odds of seeing a myriad of fragmented, reactive services that resemble our efforts to alleviate other social ills such as unemployment. In this country, we do not feel compelled to take care of certain problems until we are absolutely pushed to the edge; problems such as child abuse, domestic violence, teenage pregnancy, and chronic mental illness. Our track record indicates that we may not deal with the challenges of illegal immigration until they end up in our middle-class living rooms.

As in the construction of a human rights ideology, social workers have an obligation to the development and implementation of public policy for social change (Jansson, 1994). This obligation will require getting the facts and making a "wake-up call" to the American public. Critics to this approach may argue that social change should not be accomplished on the backs of or at the expense of other human beings. Unfortunately though, social change does not occur in a vacuum. As Frederick Douglas stated, "without struggle, there is no progress." The struggles of the Civil Rights Movement of the 1950s and 1960s are classic examples of the price that must be paid for eventual freedom.

If we are to create policies and programs in this country for how we will treat immigrating world citizens that is commensurate with a respectable human rights ideology, social workers must participate in established processes that expose the truth. Without exposure, we are certain to have no change. The benefits of a collective civil rights movement that exposed and attempted to deal with the ugly horrors of oppression in this country were successful in liberating many more people than the Underground Railroad ever could have.

Within each bureaucratic structure and the implementation of standard operating procedures, there is inherent discretionary decision-making authority. If we give social workers the choice not to participate in a process that exposes illegal aliens, the result may well benefit this particular client group. However, what is to prevent social workers from using those same powers to discriminate against individuals or other select groups that they find less favorable? Will we turn our heads or "plead the fifth" in other instances in which clients run the risk of being disadvantaged by our efforts? How do we draw the line? Do we not participate in activities that might reveal the mother who has left her children alone at home again after repeated warnings? Should we turn our heads to the teenager involved in shoplifting because we know that if he gets expelled from school again, he will never graduate? How do we know what is justified to turn our heads to? Who gets helped and who gets hurt?

The legality of our actions is also at question here. Whether we like the law or not, the law is our standard of judgment that guides our practices and behaviors. No matter how tragic or difficult the situation that prompted their flight to this country, illegal aliens have broken the law by being here without sanction. Social work practice cannot maintain its credibility in the professional community if it openly condones breaking the law.

Finally, social workers have the responsibility to provide the most effective service possible. By not participating in processes that may expose illegal aliens, our judgments and assessments lack the facts that would promote efficient, effective service provision that is in the best interest of all. For example, there have been numerous cases in which families here illegally had to be identified and risk deportation to save the life of a child. These may be hard choices, but they are also realities. The bottom line is that we cannot make sound decisions and take care of clients' needs with limited information.

Without a doubt, the issue of social workers participating in eligibility processes that may identify illegal aliens is a complex and conflicted one. However, from a human rights, social policy, social change, legal, and value-to-society perspective, the risks of not participating in eligibility requirements that may expose illegal aliens are too great. Social workers have no choice but to take a stand and create the environment for lasting change in immigration policy.

References

Iatridis, D. (1994). *Social policy: Institutional context of social development and human services.* Pacific Grove, CA: Brooks/Cole.

Jansson, B. (1994). *Social policy: From theory to policy practice.* Pacific Grove, CA: Brooks/Cole.

Lander, A., Caldwell, B., & Siegel, M. (1993). *Immigration and illegal aliens.* Wylie, TX: Information Plus.

Morales, A., & Sheafor, B. (1995). *Social work: A profession of many faces.* Boston, MA: Allyn and Bacon.

Rosenberg, D. (1991). Serving America's newcomers. *Public Welfare, 1,* 28–37.

Weintraub, S. (1984). Illegal immigrants in Texas: Impact on social services and other considerations. *International Migration Review, 8,* 733–747.

Young, C., Hall, W., & Collins, J. (1979). Providing health and social services to illegal alien families: A dilemma for Community Agencies. *Social Work in Health Care, 4,* 309–318.

Rejoinder to Dr. Isaac
LARRY NACKERUD

Dr. Isaac elucidates well the points of conflict in the stated question. I concur with her assessment that a mixing of the public policy arenas of social service provision and illegal immigration creates a dilemma for social workers. I do, however, take particular issue with an implicit assumption in her description of the nature of that dilemma. I also find her overall advice to social workers to be quite contradictory.

Dr. Isaac mistakenly assumes that the dilemma arises for social workers when the detection of illegal immigrants seeking social services results in deportation back to their home country. This is a sanitized version of the reality faced by illegal immigrants in need of social services and social workers given the responsibility of determining their eligibility. In fact, if detection by a social worker resulted in deportation, then the dilemma would no longer exist. The dilemma is *not* that persons in the United States seeking social services will be deported. The dilemma is that people in the United States without sanction and denied social services will remain in the country.

For example, although persons from Mexico represent a sizeable portion of the persons who are in the United States without sanction, they, in fact, are seldom ever deported. When detected and apprehended by immigration officials, more than 90 percent of Mexicans in the United States without sanction choose to take advantage of their legal right to voluntary departure (Reimers, 1992). The right to voluntary departure allows these Mexicans to leave the United States without participation in a deportation hearing. Although it temporarily eases their legal burden, the right to choose voluntary departure also allows Mexicans in the United States without sanction to repeatedly enter and leave, seemingly without penalty. This is just one example of how the dilemma of social service provision and illegal immigrants does not simply just go away.

Dr. Isaac's overall advice to social workers is also quite contradictory. Concerning illegal immigrants and the question of their eligibility for social services, social workers are encouraged to "advocate for change, expose the truth, and work to establish innovative, proactive policies and programs." Social workers are exhorted to "take a stand and create the environment for lasting change in immigration policy." Frederick Douglas is even quoted in this regard.

This call to action has a hollow ring to it. According to Dr. Isaac, social workers are to first consider the inequities of refusing to provide social services to illegal immigrants, second, to advocate for changes in immigration policy on a national and global level, and finally, to just follow the rules on a local level. This is a unique twist on that popular bumper sticker that reads "Think Globally, Act Locally." Dr. Isaac's recommended course of action for social workers seems to be "Think Globally about Change, But Locally Just Follow the Rules."

I believe that most social workers today and, indeed, the profession as a whole, are much too eager to advocate for change on a national or global level, all the while just following the rules on a local level. I do not argue that the rules of an agency or bureaucracy are to be completely ignored, but at the same time I believe social workers are wrong to hold those rules in the highest regard. Neither positive shifts in global social relations nor meaningful social change on a local level will ever be achieved by absolute complicity with stated sets of rules (Guba & Lincoln, 1989).

Social workers, both as individuals and as a distinct professional group, should refuse to participate in social service eligibility determinations that are intended to identify illegal immigrants. The provision or receipt of social services should not be based on citizenship, but rather merely on the presence of a person or their child in the United States. This is what is meant by equal protection under the law. Equal protection means that a Salvadoran woman who is in the country without sanction and has been raped can be provided a social service by a social worker. Equal protection under the law means that a Mexican child who is in the country without sanction and has been physically abused can receive protective services provided by a social worker. Social workers should advocate for the provision of social services to anyone who is in the country and in need.

REFERENCES

Guba, E. G., & Lincoln, Y. S. (1989). *Fourth generation evaluation.* Newbury Park: Sage.

Reimers, D. M. (1992). *Still the golden door: The third world comes to America* (2nd ed.). New York: Columbia University Press.

NO

LARRY NACKERUD

I answer the stated question with a resounding "no." All members of the social work community should do the same. Although there are a multitude of reasons why social workers should take such a position, I discuss here only the most prominent. At the conclusion of this brief discussion, I offer examples of alternative strategies by which social workers can address problematic issues related to the presence of illegal immigrants (more graciously referred to as undocumented persons) in the United States.

Plyler v. Doe

Eligibility determinations leading to the identification of illegal immigrants, or their children, and the subsequent denial of social services should be viewed as legally suspect. In the past, when individual states have attempted to deny the receipt of social services on the basis of citizenship, the U.S. Supreme Court has ruled their efforts to be in violation of the equal protection clause of the fourteenth amendment of the Constitution (Spiro, 1994).

In 1975, Section 21.031 of the Texas Education Code was amended with the clear intent to limit tuition-free basic education to "citizens of the United States or legally admitted aliens (Hull, 1981, p. 43)." Children of illegal immigrants were thus denied access to the fundamental social service of public education. The resultant lawsuit was entitled Plyler *v.* Doe and decided in 1982 by the U.S. Supreme Court. Texas and other states were constrained from denying equal access to public education on the basis of an illegal immigrant status. Stressed in the federal court review process was the innocence of the children involved and the pervasive negative effects of the illiteracy that would result from such a denial (Spiro, 1994). The reasoning of the justices in Plyler *v.* Doe should give reason to pause for all social workers before participating in eligibility determinations aimed at the denial of social services to illegal immigrants.

California's mean-spirited Proposition 187, passed on November 8, 1994, by an overwhelming 59 to 41 percent margin, was crafted with the intent to challenge the Plyler v. Doe decision. The list of banned social services not only included public education but was extended to include child welfare and foster care benefits, family planning programs, and services targeting at-risk groups, including abused and parentless children, the elderly, blind, homeless, mentally impaired, and drug abusers (Muir, 1994). It should boggle the mind of every competent social worker to consider the innocence of the vast majority of the persons included in these client groups and the pervasive negative effects that would result from the denial of social services to these people.

Anti-Immigrant Sentiment

Social workers would be wise to remember that acceptance for the presence of immigrants in the country (both legal and illegal) tends to wax and wane. Variables that correlate most strongly with changes in the acceptance level are the vitality of the economy and anxieties about cultural diversity. It is not surprising that the current wave of anti-immigrant sentiment follows a period, 1989 to 1992, within which the U.S. economy was not robust and employment opportunities did not expand (Passel & Fix, 1994). Current anti-immigrant sentiment crystallized most recently in California, where the dream of economic and social prominence has been diverted.

Anti-immigrant sentiment is strongest in the states where immigrants (both legal and illegal) tend to cluster: California, Arizona, Texas, New York, New Jersey, Florida, and Illinois (Passel & Fix, 1994; Spiro, 1994). Although cultural diversity tends to be highly regarded in each of these states, the continued increase in the proportion and absolute number of foreign-born persons has resulted in increased anxieties about cultural diversity. This cultural diversity anxiety has been accompanied by an increase in anti-immigrant sentiment.

A powerful ingredient in the current increase in anti-immigrant sentiment is a lack of understanding among the general public, and embarrassingly, also in the social work community, of: (1) the different immigration statuses by which persons enter the United States, (2) the number of immigrants (legal and illegal) in the country, and (3) the linkage of each status to eligibility for public assistance (Drachman, 1995).

U.S. immigration policy is not one but really three fundamentally different sets of rules: those that govern legal immigration (mainly sponsored admission for family and work); those that govern humanitarian admissions (refugees and those granted asylum); and those that control illegal entry. A blurring of the lines between these three strands of rules and the resultant lack of understanding of how persons actually enter the country only exacerbates concerns within any single area, such as illegal entries (Passel & Fix, 1994).

The vast majority of immigrants in the United States are here with the country's express consent. Of the nearly 20 million immigrants counted in the 1990 census, only about 15 percent were here illegally. Although the number of foreign-born persons in the United States is at an all-time high, the share of the population that is foreign born, 8 percent in 1990, is much lower than it was throughout the 1870 to 1920 period, when close to 15 percent of the total population was foreign born. Approximately 1.1 million immigrants arrive in the United States each year. Approximately 700,000 are legal permanent residents, with family-based admissions accounting for almost three-quarters of the total. Refugees and other humanitarian admissions add another 100,000 to 150,000 each year. The amount of illegal immigration is invariably overstated. The number describing illegal immigrants that is most meaningful is not the 1 million apprehended at the Mexico–United States border. These people are largely temporary labor migrants who are often apprehended multiple times, make multiple trips to the United States, and often leave the country uncounted and largely unnoticed. The number that is much more meaningful is the 200,000 to 300,000 illegal immigrants who enter the country and stay, less than 30 percent of the immigration flow (Passel & Fix, 1994).

What is important for the general public to find out and for social workers to remember is that federal and state laws already bar illegal immigrants from receiving the benefits of social insurance programs, such as social security and unemployment insurance. Illegal immigrants are already ineligible for public assistance programs, such as Aid to Families with Dependent Children (AFDC) and food stamps (Muir, 1994). The participation of illegal immigrants in public assistance programs is almost undetectable (Passel & Fix, 1994).

Alternative Strategies

Strategies to address the problems related to the presence of illegal immigrants in the country tend to fall into two broad categories. The first category includes strategies that legally disadvantage illegal immigrants and their children in terms of social services, employment, and other opportunities (Spiro, 1994). These strategies generally contain faulty reasoning and should be discounted by social workers.

Consider, for example, the implicit causal assumption in the strategy of identifying illegal immigrants and then denying them social services. The assumption is that the denial of social services will cause illegal immigrants and their children to either leave the United States or deter illegal immigrants from ever entering in the first place. The problem is that there is no empirical foundation for such a deterrent strategy. Most illegal immigrants are not drawn to the

United States by the availability of social services but by the availability of work. Why not make it harder for employers to hire illegal immigrants, and make it more punitive for employers who habitually hire illegal immigrants?

The second broad category includes strategies that seek directly to enhance enforcement of federal immigration controls: those that sanction activities relating to violation of federal immigration laws (Spiro, 1994). For example, the Immigration Reform and Control Act (IRCA) of 1986 set standards by which employers could be sanctioned who knowingly hire, recruit, or continue to employ illegal immigrants. Also, employers who have engaged in a pattern of violating employer sanctions are subject to a criminal penalty of *not more* than $3,000 for each unauthorized worker or imprisonment of *not more* than six months (Muzaffar, 1995). Why are the fine and imprisonment limits so low? Why not shift the burden from illegal immigrants seeking work to the employers providing work illegally? Social workers should advocate for stricter compliance with the employer sanction elements of IRCA and a raising of the criminal fines and imprisonment levels for employers who knowingly violate the law.

In relationship to the provision of social services, the fact that illegal immigrants cluster in a small number of states and cities is a problem. This concentration of illegal immigrants in a small number of states and in already-stressed urban areas raises questions about institutional capacity and fiscal fairness. Although the states and cities are stuck with the direct and indirect costs of providing social services, any tax revenue generated by the illegal immigrants tends to flow to the federal government. Social workers should advocate for a strategy of intergovernmental fiscal equity, which includes greater rates of reimbursement by the federal government for state and local costs associated with social service provision to illegal immigrants. Specialized funding, such as an immigrant block grant, for states and cities where illegal immigrants cluster makes sense (Passel & Fix, 1994).

Conclusion

If illegal immigrants are ineligible for social insurance and public assistance programs, why all the hue and cry about social services? Operationalization of processes that lead to the denial of social services on the basis of citizenship are at best mean-spirited and at worst a replication of the anti-immigrant sentiment of previous eras. Social workers would do well to remember that one of the heroines of our profession, Jane Addams, did much of her work with immigrants, not all of whom were in the country legally. She and her colleagues created the Settlement House Movement in a historical era characterized by anti-immigrant sentiment (Trattner, 1994).

As well, social workers need to remember the admonishment of a federal judge in Plyler *v.* Doe. Strategies designed to disadvantage illegal immigrants in terms of receipt of social services will harm innocent people, and the negative effects will be pervasive and long-lasting.

References

Drachman, D. (1995). Immigration statuses and their influence on service provision, access, and use. *Social Work, 40,* 188–197.

Hull, E. (1981). Undocumented aliens and the equal protection clause: An analysis of Doe v. Plyler. *Brooklyn Law Review, 48,* 43–74.

Muir, F. W. (1994, November 10). Inside Proposition 187. *Los Angeles Times, A28:* 3.

Muzaffar, C. (1995). Immigration law: Its application in the workplace. *Human Rights, 22,* 18–21.

Passel, J., & Fix, M. (1994). Myths about immigrants. *Foreign Policy, 95,* 151–160.

Spiro, P. J. (1994). The states and immigration in an era of demi-sovereignties. *Virginia Law Review, 35,* 121–178.

Trattner, W. (1994). *From poor law to welfare state: A history of social welfare in America* (5th ed.). New York: Free Press.

Rejoinder to Dr. Nackerud
ALICIA R. ISAAC

There is no doubt that the problem of illegal aliens (undocumented persons) is a complicated one. And, based on my colleague's perspective, how can any *real* social worker turn his or her back on persons in need of services? How can any "ethics-abiding" advocate of the poor have a hand in the deportation of people back to economic and politically oppressed countries? My colleague makes a good point, and I understand it, but asking social workers not to participate in legislatively authorized eligibility determination tasks is like asking us to ignore the speed limit.

Spiro (1994) does cite a number of instances in which the Supreme Court has intervened in state cases regarding the provision of services and citizenship. The issue in one of the most famous of those cases, Plyler *v.* Doe, is not representative of the problem in toto, but is a specialized case. The reasoning of the justices in this case was based on the innocence of children and the detrimental effects of illiteracy on this country. Though I personally agree with the reasoning and the decision, the decision does present some problems for equal application, a major concern raised in my initial treatise. The reasoning may be tangentially applied to other cases involving children, but should it be applied in all cases involving children? Taken a step further, how easily can the reasoning be applied to illegal immigrants across the board? What happens when children begin to be used as pawns for adults to enter and remain in this country illegally? Until we have clear federal laws guiding the process for entering this country and receiving services, we cannot pick and choose which policies we will follow, and which we will not. It is unfortunate that the Supreme Court often rules on individual cases without there being the proper linkages in place for uniform implementation across the states.

Let us face it, the American public can appear fickle at times. There is no denying that. Just as there have always been the "deserving poor," there are immigrants in this country to whom many people are willing to turn "a deaf ear and a blind eye." However, these are not the illegal immigrants on which most of our discussions center. Current anti-immigrant sentiment clearly comes to rest at the feet of those from Mexico, the Caribbean, and other third-world countries, who tend to be poorly educated and unskilled except for menial labor by this country's standards. My colleague and I both agree that the American public is ill informed at best about the policies and laws that govern immigration into this country. But, if there is one thing that the American public has not been fickle about in the past ten years, it has been the vehement reaction to those who appear to take resources away from American workers and families in the face of scarce resources. As much as we would like to believe that bureaucracies are not influenced by public opinion, and therefore social workers are left to make choices free of bias and prejudice, we know that this is not the truth of the matter. It places a tremendous burden on individual social workers to determine the "deserving" from the "undeserving" illegal immigrant.

On a note closer to the realities of everyday living, I venture to say that, though it is not highly publicized, a large majority of illegal immigrants *do* already receive services through a number of different means. They receive them from ethnically sensitive private agencies, churches, neighborhood and family networks, and through many of the gaps in the workings of the bureaucracy. The depiction of thousands of illegal aliens wandering the streets dying before our very eyes is a bit extreme. I admit that my colleague did not exactly say this, and I might be embellishing his position just a bit, but my point is that illegal immigrants are receiving services. The services may not be ideal, and the processes for receiving them may not be the best promoters of self-esteem, but they do provide the minimum standard of care. This may be the best that we can offer until we change public policy. This is a harsh reality, but maybe this country will finally learn that effective social services programs cannot supersede or survive without good policy.

Current policies and programs to address the problems related to illegal immigrants are inadequate. There is much that needs to be done. Let us face it head-on and make the system work. Not participating in eligibility determination activities that may expose illegal aliens only prolongs the problem and jeopardizes the advances that could be made in the fight for global and national social justice.

References

Spiro, P. J. (1994). The states and immigration in an era of demi-sovereignties. *Virginia Law Review, 35,* 121–178.

Should Social Workers Rely on Genograms and Ecomaps?

Mark A. Mattaini, D.S.W., is an Associate Professor with the Columbia University School of Social Work, and is Chair and General Manager of the Walden Fellowship, Inc., in New York City. His research focuses on the use of behavioral methods in direct and community practice, particularly in the areas of violence prevention and substance abuse intervention.

James G. Daley, Ph.D., was Chief of Behavioral Sciences, Office of the Command Surgeon for Air Mobility Command at Scott Air Force Base in Illinois. Dr. Daley received his Ph.D. in social work at Florida State University in 1986, and his primary area of interest is in family assessment and intervention. He is now an Assistant Professor of social work at Southwest Missouri State University.

YES

MARK A. MATTAINI

Graphic tools such as ecomaps and genograms have proved not only helpful, but even essential in many fields dealing with complicated transactional phenomena, from applied fields such as meteorology to abstract theoretical physics (Mundie, 1989; Tufte, 1990). Social work, with its defining focus on the person in the environment, deals with similar complexity, and graphic tools can help to capture and organize case data contextually in ways that nothing else currently available can (Mattaini, 1993, 1995).

Ecomaps and genograms are the most commonly used visual tools in social work practice, and experience suggests that, if used appropriately, they have much to offer. At the same time, there are genuine issues that need to be addressed, and sophisticated differential use is important. I discuss each tool separately here, because I believe ecomaps, if constructed in ways that are likely to be valid and reliable, have wide potential for routine use; genograms, despite their ubiquity in practice, may be most appropriate only for a narrower range of practice situations.

Ecomaps

Ecomaps are indigenous to social work and were first discussed by Carol H. Meyer (Meyer, 1976, 1993a) and Ann Hartman (Hartman, 1978, Hartman & Laird, 1983). The core notion underlying these conceptual maps is the development of an icon of the case that identifies crucial exchanges between the client or client household and the environment. In some forms of ecomaps, intrafamilial exchanges are also depicted. Meyer's ecomap is designed primarily to "draw a boundary around the case"; to clarify the interacting systems and persons that may be most relevant to the work. Hartman's more detailed ecomaps also reflect an effort to capture the direction and quality of energy flows among actors in the case, permitting the worker to depict connections that are strong, tenuous, or missing (essentially a three-point scale) as well as to discriminate those that are stressful from those that are not.

Ecomaps can be prepared collaboratively with the client, or they can be completed entirely by the client, or entirely by the worker. They may be used strictly as clinical thinking tools, or they may become instruments that focus the clinical work itself. Practitioners who have used ecomaps report that workers and clients find them helpful in understanding what is happening in the case, and for communicating a worker's interest in understanding the contextual factors that contribute to the client's difficulties, thus perhaps reducing the tendency to blame the client. They are valuable for preventing an overemphasis on psychopathology as opposed to environmental determinants and contributors to the case situation. Ecomaps can be used for transactional phenomena involved in individual consultation, family work, as well as those relevant to community and organizational practice (Mattaini, 1993).

Problems experienced by client systems of whatever size and type are usually multidetermined. This is where the particular power of graphic tools lies, because they increase the bandwidth of perception, so multiple transactional variables can be seen "all at once," in a holistic way. A child's school problem may involve not only academic struggles but also peer problems or violence in the home; a neighborhood in transition may be experiencing high rates of violence because of drug trafficking, as well as substantial interethnic struggles and few employment opportunities—all of these issues can be portrayed together on various forms of ecomaps.

The data suggest that this matters, because social workers have a perhaps surprising tendency to ignore environmental factors that may be essential to the case. Rosen and Livne (1992) found that workers tend to attribute problems to intrapersonal factors and to deemphasize environment problems even if the client calls attention to them; Nurius and Gibson (1994) found that workers need to be explicitly prompted to include environmental issues in their case formulations or they tend not to notice them (cited in Kemp, 1995). In a small study with thirty-eight M.S.W. students (Mattaini, 1993, pp. 250–251), I found that preparing a simple ecomap significantly increased attention to transactional as opposed to intrapersonal issues. In follow-up single case studies, I found that, for some students, preparing an ecomap led to significant increases in transactional problem formulation, whereas others noted the issues on the map, but did not consistently translate this into their verbal case formulations. These students required a further level of prompting to do so.

Perhaps the most important value of ecomaps is that the vision they provide of the case often clarifies points for potential intervention. If high levels of aversive exchanges with one or more other systems emerge from the image, ways of reducing those should be explored. If a client has little or no emotional support from anywhere, building such sources needs to be an interventive priority. And even when an appropriate balance of positives and manageable aversives is present, they may be supporting undesirable behaviors (such as violence among gang members). Collaborative, rational clinical decision making grounded in the client's complex realities can therefore be facilitated when working from the image. If the underlying measures are valid, sequential ecomaps depicting the case at multiple points can also—as commonly noted by authors writing about ecomaps—be useful as multivariate tools for monitoring practice.

Despite their clear utility, there are important issues related to the use of ecomaps. Should an ecomap be used in every case? Clearly the answer is no; some clients come to social workers with very focused issues, and the time taken to inquire in detail about multiple dimensions of the client's life may not always be well spent. There also are situations in which a client may be so isolated that seeing the depth of his or her isolation could be disheartening (in these cases, however, it is crucial that *the worker* think contextually, and an ecomap can be helpful for those purposes). Other scenarios in which an ecomap may not be indicated also can be imagined.

More complicated issues relate to the underlying theoretical base of the instrument, and to issues of reliability and validity. Any graphic representation reflects not only "reality" but also the designer's abstraction of what is important. This is true for all maps (Wood, 1992) and even more so for a visual representation at a high level of abstraction such as an ecomap. For example, strength of connection and presence or absence of stressors are clearly central theoretical concepts in Hartman's ecomaps. The practitioner's underlying theoretical perspective will determine whether these are seen as the crucial constructs in case transactions.

I have suggested elsewhere that from a behavioral perspective, for example, the extent of positive and aversive exchanges among actors in the case may be the core variable for contextual understanding, and these can be captured in ecomaps (Mattaini, 1990). Note that these are quantitative issues; not just presence or absence of aversive events or conditions, for example, but their frequency and strength, may be important. Another issue with the standard ecomap is that the worker and client must classify a relationship as either stressful or not. This dichotomous distinction precludes portraying the concurrent positive and negative exchanges that often characterize relationships. The available data suggest that relationships typically involve positive and negative exchanges, that these tend to be relatively independent of and uncorrelated with each other (Bornstein et al., 1981; Bornstein, Hickey, Schulein, Fox, & Scollati, 1983; Mattaini, Grellong, & Abramovitz, 1992), and that each contributes substantially to quality of the relationship. It is important, therefore, that an ecomap be able to depict these orthogonal dimensions.

No data on the reliability or validity of standard ecomaps have been presented, complicating judgments regarding their adequacy as clinical tools. If the worker and client (multiple observers with different perspectives) agree that the image captures what is happening in the case well, there certainly is a degree of face validity present, but it would be good to know more. A valuable study might examine the extent of interrater reliability between client and worker. For purposes of enhancing reliability and validity, there are particular advantages to quantified ecomaps, on which the extent of positive and negative exchanges is determined using self-anchored rating scales. Such scales have demonstrated solid psychometric properties (Nugent, 1992). The specific scales used in developing quantified ecomaps like that shown in Figure 17.1 demonstrated average test–retest reliabilities of .83 in a study conducted by the author and colleagues, and other data from that study lend preliminary support to the construct validity of the scales as well (Mattaini, Grellong & Abramovitz, 1992). Families living in inadequate housing in crime-ridden neighborhoods were rated by clinicians as experiencing elevated ratings on aversive exchanges with neighborhood systems, for example, whereas those experiencing circumscribed family issues typically did not.

Figure 17.1 is a quantified ecomap representing the life situation of a client currently being seen by the author. This figure has been constructed from reliable rating scales and captures both positive and negative exchanges within her life situation in an integrated and comprehensive way.

Although questions remain, if ecomaps are grounded in tested theory and constructed using psychometrically adequate scales, their potential for ensuring that practitioners notice and attend to the environmental determinants of client issues is high. Routine use of such ecomaps is not only consistent with high-quality

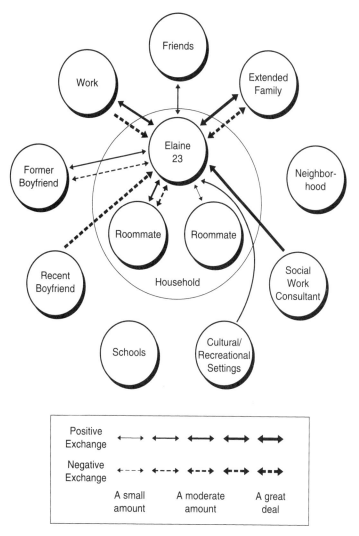

FIGURE 17.1 *An ecomap portraying the situation of a relatively isolated 23-year-old client.*

social work practice, but may significantly enhance such practice. Although these maps take time to prepare, they can be a relatively efficient way of gathering and organizing case data if the worker works from blank templates or a computerized system. Other professions take the time required to understand cases adequately, and social workers ought not to be willing to compromise quality of services by neglecting important issues too readily.

Genograms

A genogram is a form of graphic family tree, depicting at a minimum multiple generations within a family network, and often including substantial narrative overlays as well. Genograms are widely used in family therapy, family medicine, and social work. Many social work authors advocate their routine use (e.g., Hartman, 1978; McGoldrick & Gerson, 1985), particularly in family-centered practice (Hartman & Laird, 1983). A good deal of anecdotal evidence suggests that both workers and clients tend to like genograms. Given the time required to prepare them and their potential for diverting the focus of the work from the here-and-now to an overemphasis on the past, I argue here that they should be used routinely only in settings, or for clients, in which the information they produce is highly relevant to intervention.

There are practice settings in which routine use of genograms is indicated. In adoption work, for example, every detail included may be treasured by the adoptee in later years, and the medical history often collected as a part of the process of preparing the genogram can sometimes be lifesaving. Similarly, in case management, family medicine, and managed care settings, simply clarifying who fits where in the family structure (as well, again, as including important medical history) can ultimately be a time saver, ensuring that each staff member does not have to begin over again to understand who fits where in complex or blended families. If not too much time is spent developing the genogram, an argument can be made for their use in couples work for helping clients to see how they may currently be imitating behavior learned in their families of origin. This can sometimes increase motivation for change.

In many other settings, the routine use of genograms is probably not consistent with state-of-the-art practice. Obviously, this is a controversial stance. Some practice approaches, for example, those rooted in Bowenian thinking, suggest that surfacing and intervening in intergenerational patterns is the core of clinical work. Practitioners operating out of this frame would be likely to place heavy emphasis on tools such as the genogram. However, there is limited empirical evidence for the utility of these approaches; they are most applicable to persons with strong verbal repertoires, and they commonly require more time than is generally available in social work settings. There is little doubt that a person's learning history, heavily rooted in the family context, shapes much of human behavior, but focusing on changing current patterns, rather than hypothesizing about their origins from incomplete and perhaps unreliable data, is usually the preferable clinical course.

This raises a further issue with genograms, the quality of data included (again, a question of reliability and validity). Information to which the client has relatively direct access (e.g., names and number of siblings, occupations, medical history) is likely to be fairly accurate. The less direct experience the client has with what is included, and the more interpretation required, the more likely that distortions may be introduced, because no one—particularly not a close relative—is an unbiased observer. Little or nothing is known about the psychometric properties of genograms, so considerable clinical caution is indicated here.

Graphic Tools for Practice

In summary, I believe ecomaps have broad applicability for social work practice, and when modified as suggested here, can be psychometrically solid as well. Genograms are excellent tools, but I believe their applicability is much more limited than is commonly suggested. Other graphic tools can contribute in substantial ways to practice as well. Particularly important are contingency diagrams that enable the client and worker to understand and make plans to change the antecedents and consequences associated with behaviors (of the client, family members, or systems actors) identified as clinically or programmatically important (Mattaini, 1995). Visualization provides comprehensive and comprehensible access to complex systems in ways that words cannot, and can often breach language, cultural, and professional barriers (Meyer, 1993b). Yes, such instruments should be applied routinely in social work practice, so long as they do not become ends in themselves, but rather serve as tools that can assist clients to reach their goals.

REFERENCES

Bornstein, P. H., Anton, B., Harowski, K. J., Weltzien, R. T., McIntyre, T. J., & Hocker, J. (1981). Behavioral communications treatment of marital discord: Positive behaviors. *Behavioral Counseling Quarterly, 1,* 189–201.
Bornstein, P. H., Hickey, J. S., Schulein, M. J., Fox, S. G., & Scollati, M. J. (1983). Behavioral communications treatment of marital interaction: Negative behaviors. *British Journal of Clinical Psychology, 22,* 41–48.
Hartman, A. (1978). Diagrammatic assessment of family relationships. *Social Casework, 59,* 465–476.
Hartman, A., & Laird, J. (1983). *Family-centered social work practice.* New York: Free Press.
Kemp, S. P. (1995). Practice with communities. In C. H. Meyer & M. A. Mattaini (Eds.), *The foundations of social work practice: A graduate text* (pp. 176–204). Washington, DC: NASW Press.
Mattaini, M. A. (1990). Contextual behavior analysis in the assessment process. *Families in Society, 71,* 236–245.
Mattaini, M. A. (1993). *More than a thousand words: Graphics for clinical practice.* Washington, DC: NASW Press.
Mattaini, M. A. (1995). Visualizing social work practice with children and families. *Early Child Development and Care, 106,* 59–74.
Mattaini, M. A., Grellong, B. A., & Abramovitz, R. (1992). The clientele of a child and family mental health agency: Empirically-derived household clusters and implications for practice. *Research on Social Work Practice, 2,* 380–404.

McGoldrick, M., & Gerson, R. (1985). *Genograms in family assessment.* New York: Norton.

Meyer, C. H. (1976). *Social work practice: The changing landscape* (2nd ed.). New York: Free Press.

Meyer, C. H. (1993a). *Assessment in social work practice.* New York: Columbia University Press.

Meyer, C. H. (1993b). The impact of visualization on practice. In M. A. Mattaini, *More than a thousand words: Graphics for clinical practice* (pp. 261–270). Washington, DC: NASW Press.

Mundie, C. (1989). Interacting with the tiny and the immense. *BYTE, 14,* 279–288.

Nugent, W. R. (1992). Psychometric characteristics of self-anchored scales in clinical application. *Journal of Social Service Research, 15*(3/4), 137–152.

Nurius, P. S., & Gibson, J. W. (1994). *Practitioners' perspectives on sound reasoning: Adding a worker-in-context component.* Unpublished manuscript.

Rosen, A., & Livne, S. (1992). Personal versus environmental emphases in formulation of client problems. *Social Work Research & Abstracts, 29*(4), 12–17.

Tufte, E. R. (1990). *Envisioning Information.* Cheshire, CT: Graphics Press.

Wood, D. (1992). *The power of maps.* New York: Guilford.

Rejoinder to Dr. Mattaini

James G. Daley

Apparently Dr. Mattaini and I agree on several points. First, we agree that high praise should be given for techniques created by social workers, an event sadly infrequent. Second, his own review reflected that the ecomap has "no data" on reliability and validity and the genogram has "limited empirical evidence." Third, we concur that visual and graphic representation of the contextual world of the client is an invaluable assessment approach for a social worker to use and that such an assessment can result in a more accurate targeting of our intervention focus on contextual issues rather than psychopathology. However, we disagree on the conclusions from these issues. Dr. Mattaini then praises the ecomap and genogram as useful; my argument discards them until groundwork to prove their utility occurs.

I think we should use instruments for our assessment that are based on proven scientific utility rather than on lauded potential or anecdotal boasting. If we want to spotlight social work creations as techniques for our clinical use, then the social work authors must be held to the same rigorous scientific standards as any non–social work author of a measurement tool.

Other social workers have done the rigorous groundwork and would be better role models for how social workers can contribute to our repertoire of assessment tools. For example, let's contrast Hudson's Multiproblem Screening Questionnaire (MPSQ) (Hudson, 1982, Nurius & Hudson, 1993) with the ecomap or genogram. In Hudson's self-report measure, the client answers sixty-five questions and the answers allow a graphic display of the level of perceived functioning in such areas as marital relationships, peer relationships, job satisfaction, depression, and more. The assessment allows a rapid overview of many key contextual issues and provides a measurement that can be (and should be) repeated every few sessions to verify client progress.

The crucial difference between Hudson versus Meyers or Hartman is that Hudson has done the hard scientific work to demonstrate the measure's reliability ($r = .90+$) and validity (content, construct, criterion, factorial) before advocating its use in clinical practice. Furthermore, each perceived functioning area in the MPSQ is linked to a brief scale (usually twenty-five items) with proven reliability and validity, which can be used for assessing that area. For example, a client takes the MPSQ, and the only area flagged as problematic is family relations. The clinician can use the Index of Family Relations (a twenty-five item scale) in follow-up sessions to gauge progress. Every six sessions, the patient could retake the MPSQ to ensure that deterioration has not occurred in other aspects of their life.

Social work measures such as the MPSQ allow a contextual assessment without jeopardizing our commitment to scientific rigor. I wish researchers would do the same groundwork on the genogram or ecomap so that we can have confidence in its utility.

REFERENCES

Hudson, W. W. (1982). *The clinical measurement package.* Homewood, IL: Dorsey Press.

Nurius, P. S., & Hudson, W. W. (1993). *Human services practice, evaluation, and computers: A practical guide for today and beyond.* Pacific Grove, CA: Brooks/Cole Publishing Company.

NO

JAMES G. DALEY

Should social workers rely on genograms and ecomaps? Absolutely not! The utility of these "formal" assessment methods is unconfirmed by research, they allude to a formal interview schedule without having done the foundation work to justify their value, and the techniques distract from the clinical encounter.

Utility of Genograms and Ecomaps

Today clinicians are inundated with reportedly "invaluable" assessment strategies. Social workers must protect their clients and their own credibility by only choosing assessment tools that have proven utility. Utility is based on carefully designed research demonstrating that a tool has reliability and validity. How much research has been done on genograms and ecomaps to prove their utility?

Ten years ago, McGoldrick and Gerson (1985) published the only book to date on genograms. They acknowledged that the reliability, validity, and clinical utility of the genogram had not been shown and recommended that a wide range of basic scientific work be done on the technique. In sum, they had a popular tool but agreed that research needed to confirm its usefulness. There has not been a book published on ecomaps to date.

To confirm what progress has been made in the last ten years, I did a computer literature search. *Medline* (1966–1995) indicated thirty-eight articles on the genogram and two articles on the ecomap; a computer search of *Social Work Abstracts* (1977–1994) indicated five articles on genograms and one article on ecomaps. The vast majority of articles were educational/descriptive, primarily extolling the utility of the genogram. Some articles gave case studies as anecdotal evidence of the value of the genogram as a tool. Only four articles on genograms and none of the articles on ecomaps were studies researching the utility of these tools. Rogers and Rohrbaugh (1991) assessed five physicians seeing 189 patients randomly using one of three assessment methods: a patient-completed genogram, a physician-completed genogram, or no genogram. The authors then asked the physicians how the method impacted their thinking about and dealing with clinical problems. Concurrently, the authors asked the patients how the assessment method effected their view of the encounter. The findings were that genograms had "no impact" (p. 319).

Rogers, Rohrbaugh, and McGoldrick (1992) had six physicians evaluate the family history of twenty patient cases using genograms, patient demographics, or patient records and then try to predict the patient's health risk in the following three months. The authors of the study concluded that "genograms may be no more accurate than standard clinical chart review" (p. 209).

The other two articles looked at the time to gather information (Jolly, Froom, & Rosen, 1980) and the use of genograms by medical students (Shore, Wilkie, & Croughan-Minihane, 1994) but had no comparison groups for alternatives to the genogram. The studies lauded the usefulness of genograms as time efficient and teachable to physicians. However, both articles could be easily critiqued because an alternative technique (i.e., routine interview style) was not compared with the genogram.

In sum, the basic research to justify using the genogram has not occurred. The scant studies completed either have methodological flaws or did not support its utility.

Ironically, my literature search indicated that the genogram, though poorly researched, is popular. The genogram is now computerized, has color-coding added (Lewis, 1989), is lauded as "the root of it all" (Herth, 1989), and one author claims that the genogram can be found in nearly every family medicine textbook (Rogers, 1994). In contrast, the ecomap appears untested and virtually unmentioned in the literature.

Social workers should evaluate clinical tools not on popularity but on credible evidence of scientific merit. The ecomap has no proven merit; the genogram has evidence challenging its value.

Have Genograms and Ecomaps Proved Themselves as Formal Assessment Tools?

Ecomaps have not been used enough to even warrant discussion about their value as formal assessment schedules. In contrast, social workers are presented genograms as elaborate techniques with specific symbols, extensive discussion of what information should be gathered, in what sequence, and how that information should be interpreted. Case examples are presented to justify the genogram as producing a tangible diagnostic result: a rapid, clear picture of the patient and a systemic view of the family with all pertinent factors (both demographic and interactive) represented.

The problem is that every clinician seems to do the genogram differently. They modify the technique at will and interpret the data without clear guidelines on what the data mean. Clinicians confuse formality with formal assessment protocols, the genogram's squares and circles with a reliable assessment technique. Let us contrast, for a moment, the genogram with the Diagnostic Interview Schedule for Children (DISC), a formal assessment tool that is being subjected to credible evaluative research.

The creators of the DISC plan to have an interview protocol that can be used consistently to determine DSM IV diagnoses with children, just as the genogram creators planned to have an interview protocol that could consistently determine the impact of family factors on clients. The contrast is that the DISC creators are doing the groundwork to prove that assessors can produce reliable results (Jensen et al., 1995) and are comparing clinical interviews with results from DISC interviews to ensure validity of their interview schedule. They are carefully looking for flaws in the design or interviewing process before releasing this tool to the field. The proponents of the genogram have done no such work, even though it was released to the field more than ten years ago.

Social workers should be reticent to accept unproven techniques. The genogram and ecomap advocates should conduct the requisite scientific work first to ensure that these methods are reliable and valid tools with clear guidelines and distinct parameters for their use. Once such preliminary work is completed and these assessment methods have documented reliability, validity, and treatment utility, social workers could then begin using these tools as empirical clinical practitioners, not practitioners of folklore.

Genograms and Ecomaps Distract from the Clinical Interview

Besides unproven utility and inadequate groundwork, the genogram and ecomap are frankly distracting from the assessment process. Certainly clinicians can incorporate the technique into an interview as we can any distraction. But the interview process should flow as the client opens up. Avenues of exploration should be timed by client readiness and pursued when they emerge. Clinicians whom I have observed using the genogram or ecomap struggle between trying to put the information into the boxes and trying to go where the client's discussion is leading them. Certainly clinicians can work to involve the clients in the drawing of the genogram; Herth (1989), for example, uses a large flipchart with her elderly clients and has them add comments and information onto the page. However, the process of completing a genogram or ecomap remains awkward and, without proven value, is not necessary.

Summary

Historically social workers were reticent about and even fearful of using formal assessment techniques. However, contemporary social workers are being trained to be a discriminating consumer of a vast market of "popular" assessment and interventive methods. Genograms and ecomaps fall into the category of well-known but unproven, cumbersome, and not necessary to provide effective clinical service. There is a growing pool of well-researched methods of assessing our clients. Let us choose our techniques based on science, not name recognition.

REFERENCES

Herth, K. A. (1989). The root of it all: Genograms as nursing assessment tool. *Journal of Gerontological Nursing, 15*(12), 32–37.

Jensen, P., Roper, M., Fisher, P., Piacentini, J., Canino, G., Richters, J., Rubio-Stipec, M., Dulcan, M., Goodman, S., Davies, M., Rae, D., Shaffer, D., Bird, H., Lahey, B., & Schwab-Stone, M. (1995). Test-retest reliability of the Diagnostic Interview Schedule for Children (DISC 2.1). *Archives of General Psychi*atry, 52, 61–71.

Jolly, W., Froom, J., & Rosen, M. G. (1980). The genogram. *The Journal of Family Practice, 10,* 251–255.

Lewis, K. G. (1989). The use of color-coded genograms in family therapy. *Journal of Marital and Family Therapy, 15,* 169–176.

McGoldrick, M., & Gerson, R. (1985). *Genograms in family assessment.* New York: W. W. Norton & Company.

Rogers, J. C., & Rohrbaugh, M. (1991). The SAGE-PAGE trial: Do family geno-grams make a difference? *Journal of American Board of Family Practice, 4,* 319–326.

Rogers, J. C., Rohrbaugh, M., & McGoldrick, M. (1992). Can experts predict health risk from family genograms? *Family Medicine, 24,* 209–215.

Rogers, J. C. (1994). Can physicians use family genogram information to identify patients at risk of anxiety or depression? *Archives of Family Medicine, 3,* 1093–1098.

Shore, W. B., Wilkie, H. A., & Croughan-Minihane, M. (1994). Family of origin genograms: Evaluation of a teaching program for medical students. *Family Medicine, 26,* 238–243.

Rejoinder to Dr. Daley

MARK A. MATTAINI

I am pleased to discover that Dr. Daley and I agree in most areas, except with regard to his somewhat absolutist conclusions ("Absolutely not")! I believe he is correct about the need for additional study of the reliability and validity of these tools, as I discussed at some length in my original statement. I will focus here, however, on several areas in which I believe Daley and I interpret the available data quite differently.

First, and rather surprisingly, Daley makes several quite strong assertions that I believe to be unsupported by data, and probably incorrect. The first is that graphic tools "distract from the clinical interview," an accusation that has also been made about the use of Rapid Assessment Instruments and structured interview protocols such as the DISC (both of which I interpret Daley as generally approving). Although it is unfortunate that the poorly trained "clinicians whom [Daley has] observed . . . struggle" to use visual tools, every reference in the literature (see Meyer, 1993; Mattaini, 1995 for examples and further references), and yes, my own equally anecdotal data, suggest the opposite. Another clearly inaccurate assertion is that ecomaps are "virtually unmentioned in the literature." I am not surprised to find little attention to ecomaps in MEDLINE; they are not medical tools. I would suggest, however, that readers refer to the core social work literature, including many basic and foundation practice texts (e.g., Meyer & Mattaini, 1995; Sheafor, Horejsi, & Horejsi, 1994; Zastrow, 1995) and the work of major social work practice theoreticians (e.g., Hartman, 1978/1995; Hartman & Laird, 1983; Meyer, 1993) to test Daley's assertions.

I share Daley's concerns regarding reliability and validity, but believe that these issues need to be examined with regard to the alternatives proposed as well. Given his emphasis on psychometrics, Daley's apparent faith in the unstructured clinical interview is particularly startling; it is unlikely that, barring some guiding structure, independent clinicians gather identical data in such interviews, much less interpret it in the same way. For this reason, nearly every agency uses some form of structured intake or psychosocial outline; many even use standard forms. Although I believe that rapid assessment instruments are of considerable value, and often use them in my practice, even the best continue to have only weakly demonstrated psychometric properties for the populations most commonly seen by social workers. For example, in looking for ways to measure the effects of a youth violence prevention program, we tested several common measures of peer problems, on some of which a score above a certain level is supposed to indicate a potential for violence. Unfortunately, none of our demonstrably violent youth scored anywhere near the expected level. These were relatively "socialized aggressive" kids, who apparently saw themselves as socially effective in their deviant peer groups. Good instruments, wrong client group.

Worse yet, Daley indicates that the DISC "can be used consistently to determine DSM IV diagnoses" for children. The problem, of course, is that the reliability—not to mention the clinical utility—of DSM diagnoses themselves, particularly for children, is a serious issue (Kirk & Kutchins, 1993; Mattaini & Kirk, 1991). Of course we should use the best validated techniques we have available. However, Daley goes far beyond this; he asserts that social workers should, "only [choose] assessment tools with proven utility" (He also seems to indicate that utility should be defined by established reliability and validity.) I do not think Daley really believes this. His criterion would clearly eliminate the clinical interview, DSM diagnoses, and most other tools available for most clients. How, for example, should we assess clients of a program with which I am associated that works with often illiterate crack-addicted homeless persons?—surely not with instruments validated on college students. Urinalysis alone would provide a very thin database for practice, and no structured interview that captures all of the crucial information has been validated with this population. There are also no adequately sensitive and specific instruments for making reliable assessments of the risk of child maltreatment for all cases (although some can help), much less of factors that must be taken into account to intervene in such cases. Nevertheless, assess we must.

The core problem, as these examples suggest, is that social work cases are often complex and always unique. Assessment is not a simple quantitative process; it is a conceptual ordering of multiple data items, including quantitative information (Meyer, 1993). Clinicians need ways to order the complicated transactional data that constitute client lives. The primary utility of visual tools may in fact be to generate systemic hypotheses grounded in the case that can then be tested through the practice process. Social workers often do not see important case data (refer to my original statement above) as a result of idiosyncratic ways of looking. My preliminary research indicates that ecomaps can help with this. Workers find graphic tools valuable (surely there is a reason why "nearly every family medicine textbook" includes the genogram—perhaps someone finds it useful!). Our challenge, as I am sure Dr. Daley would agree, is to develop, test, and improve the tools we need to help clients through their struggles. And he is right; we have a long way to go.

REFERENCES

Hartman, A. (1978/1995). Diagrammatic assessment of family relationships. *Families in Society, 76,* 111–122.

Hartman, A., & Laird, J. (1983). *Family-centered social work practice.* New York: Free Press.

Kirk, S. A., & Kutchins, H. (1992). *The selling of DSM: The rhetoric of science in psychiatry.* New York: Aldine de Gruyter.

Mattaini, M. A. (1995). Visualizing social work practice with children and families. *Early Child Development and Care, 106,* 59–74.

Mattaini, M. A., & Kirk, S. A. (1991). Assessing assessment in social work. *Social Work, 36,* 260–266.

Meyer, C. H. (1993). *Assessment in social work practice.* New York: Columbia University Press.

Meyer, C. H., & Mattaini, M. A. (Eds.). (1995). *The foundations of social work practice: A graduate text.* Washington, DC: NASW Press.

Sheafor, B. W., Horejsi, C. R., & Horejsi, G. A. (1994). *Techniques and guidelines for social work practice* (3rd ed.). Boston, MA: Allyn and Bacon.

Zastrow, C. (1995). *The practice of social work* (5th ed.). Pacific Grove, CA: Brooks/Cole.

Should Medical Social Workers Take Clients' "Folk Beliefs" into Account in Practice?

EDITOR'S NOTE: The 10 December 1995 edition of *The New York Times* (page Y11) contains an article titled "Female genital mutilation by immigrants is becoming cause for concern in the U.S." Among the horrific statements were the following: "A couple of years ago, Meserak Ramsey dropped in on a birthday party in California and saw a little girl huddled in a corner. Ms. Ramsey, an immigrant from Ethiopia and a nurse, wondered what was wrong. She was stunned when the girl's Ethiopian-American mother said that her daughter, barely 18 months old, was recovering from the removal of clitoris and that the painful procedure had been done in Washington D.C."

Letha (Lee) A. See, Ph.D., is an Associate Professor of Social Work at the University of Georgia. Her book *Tensions and Tangles Between African Americans and Southeast Asian Refugees* has received favorable reviews in the academic community.

David Klein, M.S.W., received his M.S.W. degree from the University of Toronto in 1990. He is presently enrolled as a Ph.D. student in the Ecole de Psychologie, Laval University, in Quebec City.

YES

LETHA (LEE) A. SEE

The question of whether medical social workers should take patients' folk beliefs into account is gaining widespread attention worldwide. The escalation of this debate could be interpreted to mean that in the past insufficient attention has been devoted to folk beliefs, and they were discounted by practitioners. Or it could mean that medical social workers are realizing that there is sufficient merit in these beliefs to include them in their repertoire of practice tools.

It is my view that taking folk beliefs into account in practice is necessary because a large influx of foreign-born persons are entering North America with world views quite different from our own. A fundamental question then emerges: should medical social workers take into account the priorities, perspectives, and folk beliefs of these new aliens and other oppressed patient groups? Or should they continue pledging allegiance to the narrow model of medical service delivery embraced by the social systems in the Western world?

The literature shows that medical social workers concede that faith in folk beliefs can no longer be dismissed as trivial, because these beliefs intrude so forcibly in determining the strategies needed to combat disease. Most social workers also admit that there rarely has been an effort to explore folk beliefs. Furthermore, social worker have little training in investigating spiritual therapies, engaging in scientific research on these alternative therapies, or in making systemic attempts to collect data on various belief systems in the world community.

Thorp (1991) has observed that some health care professionals have begun using the *Index Medicus* database on "Alternate Medicine" to enhance their knowledge of homeopathic medicine and other alternative healing systems (e.g., voodoo, witchcraft, sorcery, shamanism, loss of soul, breach of taboos, intrusion of pathogenic foreign entities into the body, evil spirits, folk beliefs, etc.). Hopefully, greater knowledge of these indigenous helping systems will provide guidance in taking advantage of these approaches to service delivery.

When asked, therefore, if medical social workers should take into account a client's folk beliefs, my answer is—yes, they should. Three arguments form the core of my position: (1) the clash between Eastern and Western views of healing and belief systems, (2) the implication of mind over matter in medical social work practice, and (3) the use of folk beliefs when a society is financially strapped.

The Clash between Eastern and Western Views of Healing

At one time it would have been heresy for a Western academic to take the position that folk beliefs should be factored into healing strategies, especially because such beliefs fall outside traditional scientific views. Even now, for those who believe that all phenomena in the universe can be explained by European-dominated science, a debate on folk beliefs can be perceived as unscientific, and their advocates may be mercilessly pounced on and silenced. Such arrogance occurs because European–American scholars view western history, culture, philosophy, values, and health care systems as the center of the universe. This type of thinking has altered the metaphysical presuppositions that drive folk beliefs and has therefore suppressed the imaginative content and creativity of many scholars.

For three decades, research has been undertaken by a cadre of African American social theorists on the structure of American society and its accompanying service systems and institutions (e.g., Akbar, 1984; Nobles, 1980). The conclusion reached by these theorists is that two conflictual, oppositional, and incompatible themes permeate the Eastern–Western landscape, and it is doubtful if ever the "twain shall meet." For example, in the Eastern view, the primary emphasis is on what Baldwin (1985) describes as the corporate whole, which entails the "things of nature," such as indigenous belief systems. The antithesis of this concept is the "things of men," "things" generally accumulated by interfering with nature, engaging in unnatural alterations of the universe, and reordering objects in nature such as natural healing and belief systems. This is not to suggest that the theoretical brilliance and wonders of science and technology are not genuine achievements, but this brilliance can thrive only at the cost of stamping out valued aspects of humanity such as folk belief systems that have sustained cultures and millions of people throughout the world for centuries.

Of late, however, there is the appearance of "an emerging science of wholeness." What is interesting is that the proponents of this new paradigm are not careless, lost, and borderline professionals, but are often prominent scientists who have been exhaustively trained in the conventional traditions of their fields and are respected by their colleagues for competence, precision, and past contributions (Briggs & Peat, 1984; Kleinman, 1984). What is sending the traditional scientific establishment into apoplectic fits is that the paradigm proposed by these scholars could change the way we think about the scientific method. The "paradigm of wholeness" has the capacity to subsume all existing paradigms, and thus makes room for metaphysics (the prevailing model of reasoning preferred by Aristotle), allow space for paranormal events and experiences, Eastern cosmology, and folk beliefs (See, 1991). It is clear therefore that if intelligent scholars have no difficulty taking folk beliefs into account despite the fact that they may not be completely validated, medical social workers should have no difficulty in similarly taking folk beliefs into account in their practice.

Mind over Matter?

Let us turn now to our second argument, which holds that folk beliefs are actually characterized by evoking healing states of mind (sometimes referred to as "mind over matter"). LeShan (1976) observes that medical intervention should be congruent with the sociocultural reality of the individual, and must take into consideration the potency of a client's beliefs. In other words, if it is the reality of a patient that he or she can be cured through prayer and meditation, some improvement may indeed be observed. During the 1960s, medical researchers contended that the healing effects of the arousal of hope in a patient (customarily referred to as a "placebo effect") can increase a patient's well-being without medical, surgical, and psychological treatments. Most certainly this is an example of the powerful effect of mind over matter, which embodies the very essence of folk beliefs that are now being taken seriously by helping professionals (Beecher, 1961).

Folk Beliefs: Attending Physicians for the Poor?

Since their election to power, the 104th Republican Congress is threatening to dismantle an array of social and community-based programs designed to help poor children, the aged, and other oppressed groups. Because of the potential for retrenchment of benefits, the poor, children, certain segments of the population (e.g., African American and Hispanic women, particularly if they are unmarried) and other vulnerable groups will be further ghettoized, brutalized, and victimized. Thus, their further movement into poverty will have a profound effect on their health provisions. Under such dire conditions, medical social workers, whose mission is to help relieve pain and suffering, will find that folk beliefs are a major source of comfort to their clients (Holoman, 1987). It is clear, therefore, that medical social workers should indeed have prior knowledge of folk beliefs that will most certainly be used by their client systems.

REFERENCES

Akbar, N. (1984). Africentric social sciences for human liberation. *Journal of Black Studies, 4,* 395–414.

Baldwin, J. A. (1985). Psychological aspects of European cosmology in American Society. *The Western Journal of Black Studies, 9,* 216–223.

Beecher, H. K. (1961). Surgery as placebo. *Journal of the American Medical Association, 176,* 1102–1107.

Briggs, J. P., & Peat, F. D. (1984). *Looking glass universe.* New York: Simon & Schuster.

Holoman, T. V. (1987). Referral by default: The medical community and unorthodox therapy. *Journal of the American Medical Association, 257,* 1641–1642.

Kleinman, A. J. (1984). Indigenous systems of healing: Questions for professional, popular, and folk care. In J. W. Salmon (Ed.), *Alternative medicines: Popular and policy perspectives* (pp. 138–164). New York: Tavestock.

LeShan, L. (1976). *Alternate realities.* New York: Evans.

Nobles, W. W. (1980). African philosophy: Foundations for Black psychology. In R. L. Jones (Ed.). *Black psychology.* New York: Harper and Row.

See, L. A. (1991). "Folk medicine and folk healing in the rural South." In A. Busby (Ed.). *Rural nursing.* Newbury Park, CA: Sage.

Thorp, J. P. (1991). Alternative practitioners. In A. Busby (Ed.). *Rural nursing* (pp. 79–89). Newbury Park, CA: Sage.

Rejoinder to Dr. See

DAVID KLEIN

Dr. See begins by exhorting us as health care providers to accommodate the needs of minorities or face the charge of narrowness. She gets no argument from me here, although I have argued in my own essay that this can get rather complicated when competing rights are factored into the equation.

Next, she points to evidence that professionals are learning about "... alternative healing systems (e.g., voodoo, witchcraft, sorcery, shamanism, loss of soul, breach of taboos, intrusion of pathogenic foreign entities into the body, evil spirits...)...." "Hopefully," she continues, "greater knowledge of these indigenous helping systems will provide guidance in taking advantage of these approaches in their services." But does this imply that professionals are or should be making these practices their own? The remainder of Dr. See's essay demonstrates that the latter is precisely what she envisions and advocates as the only possible way of "taking folk beliefs into account."

Now where, I wonder, does this leave the medical curriculum of the future, and how many ethnic healing systems would she expect a young physician to master? Might we not be wiser just to inform ourselves about and sensitize ourselves to folkways that our clients could be counted on to bring with them? Finally, should we even aspire to mimic traditional healing roles for an ethnically disparate clientele—and might this not become a futile exercise in cultural appropriation?

The balance of Dr. See's paper is organized around three arguments, the first of which she describes as "The Clash Between Eastern and Western Views of Healing." Here Dr. See paints her argument in broad strokes, drawing on such disparate fields as philosophy of science and anthropology. She appears to argue that Western science is currently undergoing a paradigm shift, which she describes as an "emerging science of wholeness," containing "room for metaphysics ... paranormal events and experiences, Eastern cosmology, and folk beliefs." Thus, she continues, "(i)t is clear... that if intelligent scholars have no difficulty taking folk beliefs into account despite the fact that they may not be completely validated, medical social workers should have no difficulty in similarly taking folk beliefs into account in their practice." Expressed as a syllogism, the foregoing yields: (1) this as a trend; (2) some folks smarter than us are involved; therefore (3) we ought to follow suit. Now with my admittedly narrow Eurocentric rationality, this sounds to me more like an appeal to faith than a reasoned argument.

Dr. See's second main argument follows this plan: (1) placebos are known to work; (2) this effect depends on clients' beliefs; therefore, (3) we should incorporate the latter in our practices. Once again we are denied the option of keeping a respectful distance from clients' folk beliefs. Wouldn't we in fact be doing a better job by offering the traditional Western healing arts that we do best, while encouraging the client to supplement these with more exotic practices when appropriate? And are we not already doing this with the innumerable "New Age" beliefs so prevalent in the majority culture today?

I am most troubled, though, by Dr. See's closing discussion, where she predicts a growing role for traditional folk medicine as governments continue their retreat from funding health services for the poor. "Under such dire conditions," she proclaims, "medical social workers...will find that folk beliefs are a major source of comfort to their clients."

Again, Dr. See clearly views ethnic folk practices as displacing Western procedures. And while a strong case might be made for traditional practices as cost-effective alternatives in the treatment of chronic, non–life-threatening conditions, I see little evidence of their potential usefulness in the acute medical setting, where the ethnic minority client will have greatest need of our services.

What really disturbs me here is the prospect of Dr. See's arguments being harnessed by socially irresponsible decision makers in both public and private sectors to deprive ethnic minority clients of equal access to scientifically based medical care. As a social worker, and as a Canadian, I find unacceptable Dr. See's prescription that we offer folk medicine as a palliative remedy, while accepting the inevitability of further reductions in services. I believe that our profession must continue to advocate for universal access to decent, Western-type health care while remaining open to traditional practices in a supplementary role and as a matter of individual choice.

NO

David Klein

The year is 1992 and you are a medical social worker at a Montreal hospital that serves a large group of recent refugees from a war-torn Muslim country in North Africa. Fatima, a twenty-eight-year-old married woman, appears in your office. She wants you to find a doctor who will perform the traditional procedure of "female circumcision" on the external sex organs of her eight-year-old daughter, Nur. Other family members include mother-in-law Sara and husband Mohamed. You have recently attended a staff training seminar in which you learned something of the history and culture of this nationality, and you are anxious to demonstrate your sensitivity to the needs of its members. In the course of your interview with Fatima, you learn the following:

1. Mother-in-law Sara was raised in the traditional rural society of the country of origin. She has never been to school and underwent the operation that is normal for girls at the appropriate age. When she was young, it was impossible for a girl to find a husband without having undergone the procedure. She wants the surgery to be performed without anesthesia by a traditional practitioner within the immigrant community, as it was for her. She remembers no ill effects.

2. Husband Mohamed is opposed to the surgery but would normally be expected to assent to it if both wife and mother favor the option, because this decision lies within what is traditionally defined as the feminine sphere. Mohamed is an engineer whose radical, secular views led to the family's forced flight from their country of origin.

3. Fatima also underwent the traditional procedure, but continues to experience gynecological complications as a result of a subsequent infection. She would prefer to have her daughter operated on under aseptic conditions by a competent physician. Although her feelings about having Nur undergo the procedure are mixed, she holds the balance of power and wants to mediate the family conflict by having it done in a more modern way.

4. As you will later learn, the emergency room resident who sent Fatima to see you hoped that you could talk her out of the idea. However, Fatima apparently thinks your job is to help her find a doctor who will do the procedure in his or her office. She reports having been unable to find such a practitioner through the telephone directory, which is why she came to the hospital in the first place.

5. As is the custom in the country of origin, the opinion of the child has not been consulted.

Promising to look into the matter and making an appointment for the next week, you usher Fatima out of your office. You need time to gather information and to think about the case. In the course of your investigations, the following comes to light:

1. From the chairman of the hospital's ethics committee, you learn that procedures of this kind are currently legal, although test prosecutions are underway to have surgery of this kind included under federal Criminal Code definitions of assault. The College of Physicians in the Province of Quebec currently has the matter under study but does not yet have any official policy on the matter (and in fact will not until 1994). No physician would be permitted to perform the procedure in the hospital, but one might legally do so in his office, although this would certainly provoke the disapproval of colleagues.

2. You consult a Muslim clergyman regarding the practice. He tells you that ritual genital mutilation is not actually a part of the Muslim faith itself, although it is common in Muslim North Africa.

3. You also contact a social scientist of North African origin at the local university. She tells you that the procedure is still performed in rural areas of the country in question, but that it is becoming rare in the cities and among more Westernized segments of the population. The government of the country is at least officially trying to eradicate the practice.

You are worried that the family will have the procedure performed by a traditional practitioner if you do not help Fatima find a doctor to do it in his or her office. You are repelled by the idea, but mindful of what you learned in recent staff training sessions on being sensitive to ethnic value differences. You think of notifying the child welfare authorities, but wonder if they will have a legal basis on which to intervene in this case, and whether this would be good for the family unit.

You decide to apply a framework you learned about at a bioethics conference (Baylis & Downie, 1994). In this approach you try to answer the following questions: (1) Is this a culture? (2) Who speaks for the culture? (3) What if the culture is divided? and (4) What if the practice is oppressive? But these questions just seem to leave you with more unanswered questions. If the family is divided, then what? Who decides if the practice is oppressive? Does it matter that not all people from the country of origin believe in the practice, and if so, is it the more traditional or the more Westernized representatives of the culture whose opinion matters most? Should Nur enjoy the same degree of choice as would any Canadian-born child?

Decisions, Decisions...

It should seem clear from this case example that even the most conscientiously pluralistic among medical social workers would not always be able to indulge a "folk belief." This becomes even clearer if we move the case forward from 1992 to 1994, when medical authorities in Quebec explicitly banned practices of the kind under discussion. The case now belongs among those in which ethnic custom must unambiguously be denied. These, I suggest, might include situations in which: (1) The law of the host culture would be broken by the folkway in question; (2) The folkway, although not breaking the law, would in the perception of the professional bring harm to other individuals or violate their rights; (3) The folkway requires that the professional violate his or her personal or corporate code of ethics; (4) The folkway is simply too difficult or costly to accommodate because of resource limitations, organization of the helping agency, and so forth; (5) Although capable of being viewed as an example of category (2) above, the case in which the exercise of tolerance would require that the practitioner join with clients in supporting intolerant attitudes and behavior is worthy of consideration in its own right (cf. Guttmann, 1994). In examples of this kind, we see that the very notion of unlimited tolerance is fatally flawed by its own implicit paradoxes.

Our case example should at least have made two things evident: first, that medical social workers will at times be forced to draw the line on accommodating folk beliefs, and second, that this can become horrendously complicated in practice.

The real-life problem thus becomes how to deal consistently with complex and ambiguous situations and on what basis practitioners can make and defend their decisions. In the following discussion, I make the case that the best basis for social work decision making lies in what Donnelly (1989) calls a human rights perspective, a stance that takes us somewhat toward the less permissive end of the spectrum.

Human Rights and Multiculturalism

As recent authors have been arguing, claims based on "multicultural" principles can reflect values and agendas not necessarily friendly to our own liberal pluralism (cf. Atherton & Bolland, 1994; Donnelly, 1989; Rockefeller, 1994), leading us into positions that can contradict our own core beliefs and leave us without moral direction. How, for instance, do we decide what rights eight-year-old Nur should enjoy and on what basis can we defend our choice?

The solution being offered here is that we embrace a frankly Western-centric, individual rights–based perspective (Donnelly, 1989; Gewirth, 1994). This provides what is in my opinion the only reliable secular framework by which the acceptability of alien cultural practices can be rationally assessed. Such a moral gold standard would, in practice, be based on international declarations of human rights (cf. Donnelly, 1989) as currently interpreted and implemented in democratic Western societies—allowing of course that such interpretations are both subject to a degree of geographical variation and constantly in the process of mutating.

With respect to our case example, we find *Article 11.1* of the United Nations' *Convention on the Rights of the Child* (United Nations, 1989), requiring that the opinion of a child who is capable of forming an opinion must be taken into account in any matter affecting him or her. Our duty is now clear; we must begin by asking the child. A number of other clauses of the *Convention* could also be invoked against the ritual practice itself, such as *Article 6.2* requiring signatory countries to ". . . ensure to the maximum extent possible the survival and development of the child," and *Article 19.1,* which calls for ". . . measures to protect the child from all forms of physical or mental violence, injury or abuse . . . while in the care of parent(s), legal guardian(s) or any other person who has the care of the child." Once again, our duty is clear.

Conclusion

As Taylor (1994) has shown, claims for the public recognition of ethnic differences can represent two fundamental philosophical camps, one having given rise historically to the other. These can be dichotomized along such axes as liberalism versus radicalism, individual versus group rights, Western-centric moral universalism versus cultural relativism, proceduralism versus solidarity, and so forth. In the liberal model, the recognition of ethnicity is viewed as an extension of individual rights that seeks to accommodate the uniqueness of individuals, whereas in the radical model, similar rights are extended to groups as such. The latter presents a critique of Western-style definitions of human rights as ethnocentric (Gewirth, 1994; Taylor, 1994), and posits in its place a "third-world" definition of human dignity in which individual rights are subordinated to the social unit. My argument here has been that our practice of tolerance derives clearly from the former model and that we must unambiguously reject the latter as pernicious and alien to our democratic traditions.

From a human rights perspective, we are both obligated to take clients' folk beliefs into account when we can and bound to reject them when they violate the rights of others.

References

Atherton, C. R., & Bolland, K. A. (1994). *The multiculturalism vs. traditionalism debate: Implications for social work education.* Unpublished manuscript. Tuscaloosa, AL: University of Alabama.

Baylis, F., & Downie, J. (1994). *Child abuse through the lens of gender and culture.* Paper presented at the Sixth Annual Conference of the Canadian Bioethics Society, Ottawa, Ontario.

Donnelly, J. (1989). *Universal human rights in theory and practice.* Ithaca, NY: Cornell University Press

Gewirth, A. (1994). Is cultural pluralism relevant to moral knowledge? In E. F. Paul, F. D. Miller, & J. Paul (Eds.), *Cultural pluralism and moral knowledge* (pp. 22–43). New York: Cambridge University Press.

Guttmann, A. (1994). Introduction. In A. Guttmann (Ed.), *Multiculturalism: Examining the politics of recognition* (pp. 1–2). Princeton NJ: Princeton University Press.

Rockefeller, S. C. (1994). Comment. In A. Guttmann (Ed.), *Multiculturalism: Examining the politics of recognition* (pp. 87–98). Princeton NJ: Princeton University Press.

Taylor, C. (1994). The politics of recognition. In A. Guttmann (Ed.), *Multiculturalism: Examining the politics of recognition* (pp. 3–74). Princeton NJ: Princeton University Press.

United Nations General Assembly. (1989). *Convention on the rights of the child.* Reprinted by the Human Rights Directorate, Department of Multiculturalism and Citizenship, Government of Canada, Ottawa, Ontario.

Rejoinder to Mr. Klein
Letha (Lee) A. See

Although Mr. Klein and I live in different countries, from the differences in our world views it seems as though we live on different planets! Let me restate the respective positions held in this debate. The question is: "Should Medical Social

Workers take clients' folk beliefs into account in practice"? Bear in mind that the proposition is not that social workers should *accept* those beliefs, but merely to take them into account. I say "Yes" and Klein says "No."

I respect Mr. Klein's view, as he is indeed entitled to maintain a flawed belief. However, I wonder how he would suggest that practitioners serve culturally diverse clients whose collective experiences and inner forces of healing are inextricably linked with folk beliefs, folk medicine, and folk healing?

Klein presents a case that involves the traditional Muslim practice of female circumcision. Unfortunately, the ritual of genital mutilation is too rare, too restrictive, and too narrowly focused to represent the depth, intensity, and essence of folk beliefs and folk healing that most social workers experience in everyday practice. I interviewed a Muslim professional, Mr. Ibrahim Khashan (personal communication, 1995), who lived in Saudi Arabia before establishing residence in Atlanta, Georgia. My purpose was to gain a deeper understanding of female circumcision as a folk belief and practice. Mr. Khashan explained to me that not all children are circumcised in Muslim countries and that the practice is not associated with the Islamic religion as much as it is with various countries or populations for whom it is a rite of passage. According to his account, female circumcision is seen as passé, although some persons still engage in the practice. He believes that there was a very small possibility that an American or a Canadian physician or social worker would be involved in female circumcision, in part because folk healers perform this function, and those desiring the practice rarely live in North America.

Mr. Klein bolsters a weak argument by citing the abhorrent practice of female circumcision, which elicits emotional outrage. He then shifts his argument that opposes folk beliefs in general to a level of conceptualization that resembles a legal inquisition (constitutional issues, legal protection provisions, etc.).

Next he shifts concerns to human rights, seemingly unaware that one person's human rights can be another person's imposition. Klein asserts that in Canada it is the right of the nation to dismiss folkways and mores "when these cultural matters are in conflict with prevailing laws"! Realistically, Mr. Klein, social workers and medical doctors cannot wait for politicians or the United Nations to clarify when social workers should accept or reject a client's belief systems.

Although all of the moral and ethical issues Klein raises are intellectually challenging and invite thought-provoking debate, I found myself waiting for him to simply tell us why he rejects taking clients folk beliefs into account in everyday practice. Fortunately, along the way Mr. Klein shaped up, and stated, "From a human rights perspective we are both obligated to take clients' folk beliefs into account when we can and bound to reject them when they violate the rights of others." In effect, he changed his argument from "No" to "Sometimes." Fortunately.